The Islamic Quest for Democracy, Pluralism, and Human Rights

Florida A&M University, Tallahassee
Florida Atlantic University, Boca Raton
Florida Gulf Coast University, Ft. Myers
Florida International University, Miami
Florida State University, Tallahassee
University of Central Florida, Orlando
University of Florida, Gainesville
University of North Florida, Jacksonville
University of South Florida, Tampa
University of West Florida, Pensacola

Also by Ahmad S. Moussalli, from the University Press of Florida

Moderate and Radical Islamic Fundamentalism: The Quest for Modernity, Legitimacy, and the Islamic State (1999)

The Islamic Quest for Democracy, Pluralism, and Human Rights

Ahmad S. Moussalli

University Press of Florida

Gainesville/Tallahassee/Tampa/Boca Raton

Pensacola/Orlando/Miami/Jacksonville/Ft. Myers

08 07 06 05 04 03 6 5 4 3 2 1

Library of Congress Cataloging-in-Publication Data
Mawşililī, Ahmad.
The Islamic quest for democracy, pluralism, and human rights /
Ahmad S. Moussalli.
p. cm.
Includes bibliographic references and index.
ISBN 0-8130-2096-4 (cloth, alk. paper)
ISBN 0-8130-2649-0 (pbk., alk.paper)
1. Democracy—Religious aspects—Islam. 2. Religious pluralism—
Islam. 3. Human rights—Islam. 4. Islam and social problems. I. Title.
BP190.5.D45 M37 2001
321.8'088'2971—dc21   2001027597

The University Press of Florida is the scholarly publishing agency
for the State University System of Florida, comprising Florida A&M
University, Florida Atlantic University, Florida Gulf Coast University,
Florida International University, Florida State University, University
of Central Florida, University of Florida, University of North Florida,
University of South Florida, and University of West Florida.

University Press of Florida
15 Northwest 15th Street
Gainesville, FL 32611-2079
http://www.upf.com

Contents

Acknowledgments

I gratefully acknowledge the substantial support of the Earhart Foundation, which enabled me to devote the time necessary to develop and complete this book. I would also like to thank the American University of Beirut, which provided me with initial support in the form of a faculty development grant to start my research on the project.

Introduction

The Islamic Quest for Democracy, Pluralism, and Human Rights deals with the substantive basic doctrines of government and politics that were developed during the history of classical and medieval Islam. It aims to elaborate and develop those basic doctrines that are not contradictory to, and include the seeds of, modern liberal Western democracy, pluralism, and human rights, although they have followed in the Islamic world different historical paths. These doctrines include the notions of political contract and consensus; tolerance of differences, pluralism, and opposition; and human rights and rights of minorities.

This book is a sequel to my earlier *Moderate and Radical Islamic Fundamentalism: The Quest for Modernity, Legitimacy, and the Islamic State*, also published by the University Press of Florida. There I showed the diversified and multiple discourses of Islamic fundamentalism, or Islamism, which range from advocating complete radical totalitarianism to inclusive pluralistic ideologies. Here I aim to highlight—and, when necessary, to construct—the important ideological and religious arguments on democracy, pluralism, and human rights that have been under development in modern Islamic political discourses.

This study is not historical and does not attempt to account for all historical periods, or even one. However, it extensively uses historically developed religious and political formations, especially those of the period of the governments of the Prophet and the rightly guided caliphate. This period is seen as formative and constitutive in the making of Islamic thought because of its distinctive religious and political impact on the minds of Muslims. All Muslim thinkers, philosophers, jurists, ideologists, and historians refer to it to justify one ideology and understanding or another. Because of the importance of that period in validating any Islamic notion or system or, more important, in making a notion or system Islamic, this study also uses examples from different historical periods under, for example, the Umayyads, the 'Abbasids, and the Fatimids to pinpoint and show how some basic changes and reinterpretations have overtaken many main Islamic doctrines of government and politics. These dynasties represent moments of historical practices and interpretations that moved closer to or further from the original ideals developed from the first model of the Prophet and the rightly guided caliphate. The book aims at providing the historical and ideological formations that made the period of the governments of the Prophet and the rightly guided caliphate the model that almost all Muslims refer to in order to sanction their ideological and political models.

First, I will show how basic views on major political doctrines relating to *shura, ikhtilaf,* human rights, and minorities originally developed and will shed light on the negative and positive changes effected on their perception under the Umayyads, the ʿAbbasids, and the Fatimids. Second, the Islamic system of government will be theoretically explained in the light of the major doctrines to be discussed in the first part of each chapter: *shura* (consultation) and democracy, along with *bayʿa* (the oath of allegiance), *ikhtiyar* (choice), and *ijmaʿ* (consensus) in chapter 1; *ikhtilaf* (difference) and pluralism in philosophy, theology, and jurisprudence as well as the ideological and religious justifications for opposition and revolution in chapter 2; and the Islamic categories and philosophy of legal rights along with general and public rights that include those of minorities or, traditionally, *ahl al-dhimma,* women, and family in chapter 3.

Further, this study introduces the framework and points of reference that modern Islamic thinkers and movements use to justify the adoption of democracy, pluralism, and human rights into the main body of modern Islamic thought. It is the argument of this book that the notions of democracy, pluralism, and human rights are not only in harmony with Islamic thought, but their seeds are embedded in many notions of government and politics found in Islamic religious thought. Building upon classical and medieval thought, the book will show that Islamic philosophy, jurisprudence, and theology are very rich with comparable notions that postulate and protect individual and communal rights, that legitimize political, social, economic, intellectual, and religious differences, and that view the people as the source of ultimate political sovereignty on earth.

The discussion of democracy, pluralism, and human rights is undertaken in the spirit of the Enlightenment as well as of classical liberalism as advocated in writings like John Locke's *Two Treatises on Government,* Jean Jacques Rousseau's *The Social Contract,* Alexis de Tocqueville's *Democracy in America,* and John Stuart Mill's *On Liberty.* While moderate Islamism indirectly employs its most important doctrines to reinterpret Islam, the Enlightenment grounded its doctrines in natural reason, whereas Islamism ultimately grounds these doctrines in a novel interpretation of the fundamental Islamic texts, the Qur'an and the Sunna. Thus the moderate Islamists adapt and adopt into Islam such Enlightenment principles as the distinction between state and society; the need for civil government; the necessity of a social contract that can be dissolved; the centrality of civil society, the general will, political representation, and a body of standing law or a constitution; the importance of limiting political power, rejecting arbitrary power, and the right of opposition to governments; the significant value of equality, liberty, and individual rights; and the inviolability of property.

By linking classical and medieval Islamic thought with present political and religious debates, this book argues that modern Islamic thought in general, and today's moderate Islamism in particular, has absorbed and "Islamized" the notions of democracy, pluralism, and human rights. At the religious and ideological level, Islamicly developed doctrines on democracy, pluralism, and human rights constitute a theology of liberation and an epistemological break with the past. At the political level, they widen the individual, social, political, and philosophical space in the Arab world. At the international level, they provide the Arab world with common ground with the West. At the cultural level, they serve as a general context and a political language of dialogue between different civilizations, religions, and political orders.

The basic argument of this book is thus both simple and grand. While the history of the highest Islamic political institution, the caliphate, is mostly a history of authoritarian governments, the economic, social, political, and intellectual history of Islam abounds with liberal doctrines and institutions. In classical and medieval Islamic political thought, there are comparable doctrines of equality, freedom, and justice, older and much more universal than those subsequently developed by traditional Islamic thought.

Because the book is planned for maximum topical usage, it is structured so that the relevant notions of classical and medieval Islamic government and politics are developed and analyzed in the first part of each chapter. Chapter 1, "The Classical and Medieval Dialectics of *Shura* and Its Modern Islamist Constructions As Democracy," examines the doctrines of *shura* based on the choice (*ikhtiyar*) of the people, the contract between the ruler and the ruled based on an oath of allegiance (*bay'a*), and consensus (*ijma'*) of the community, and shows that these are the theoretical methods that should govern in political rule. Chapter 2, "The Classical and Medieval Interpretations of *Ikhtilaf* and Its Modern Islamist Expressions As Pluralism," shows that Islamic thought was historically and theoretically based on the notion of tolerating differences (*ikhtilaf*), manifested in the adoption and tolerance of pluralistic exegeses, philosophies, theologies, jurisprudence, politics, and public opinions. Yet on a higher level, political opposition and revolution had theoretical and religious justifications that center on numerous religious and political doctrines. Chapter 3, "The Classical and Medieval Roots of *al-Huquq al-Shar'iyya* and Its Modern Islamist Conceptions As Human Rights," shows the categories and philosophy of Islamic human rights, which include general and public rights as well as the rights of women, families, and minorities (*ahl al-dhimma*).

The second part of each chapter shows how Islamists developed the topics discussed in the first part to become the substantive theoretical foundations of modern democracy, pluralism, and human rights. The moderate and pluralist discourses of modern Islamic movements and theoreticians are first structured and then compared and contrasted with the discourses of radical and rejectionist movements and theoreticians. Here I have selectively borrowed from my previous book, greatly developing some of the arguments and then grounding them in classical, medieval, and modern Islamic political thought, something that has not been done in any Islamic discipline of knowledge.[1]

What emerges from this study is a tentative classical and medieval development, and a preliminary theoretical taxonomy, of modern Islamism on the very important topics of democracy, pluralism, and human rights as well as relationships with other religions, specifically Judaism and Christianity. The concluding chapter provides a theoretical assessment of the prospects of the ongoing Islamic dialectics on democracy, pluralism, and human rights.

Views on Islam in the Modern World

In recent times, modernist Islamic thinkers and, now, moderate Islamist thinkers are making medieval doctrines comparable to modern Western notions of democracy, pluralism, and human rights. This assumption about comparability is neither defensive nor apologetic. I show that Islamic thought has long viewed itself as more equitable, less racial, and more humane than Western political thought. Equality, freedom, and justice, for example, are cardinal Islamic doctrines, which throughout history have received various formulations and suffered various abuses. The different chapters of this book show the development, the uses and abuses, the perfection and imperfection of these and similar doctrines, stretching from the Prophet Muhammad's era to modern times. While most political studies by Islamic scholars have focused their consideration on the rise and fall of Islamic dynasties and on the historical developments of "traditional" Islamic law (*shari'a*) in order to construct possible Islamic views on democracy, pluralism, and human rights, they miss the fact that neither the study of dynasties nor the authentication of "traditional" *shari'a* is more formative to Muslims than the ideological developments brought about by opposition movements or reformist attitudes. A "view from the edge,"[2] and not only from the traditional centers of power, is necessary in order to comprehend the true nature of the Islamic system of government and the doctrines of democracy, pluralism, and human rights. While Richard Bulliet argues correctly that "the story of Islam has always privileged the view from the center,"[3] I show that such a view is mostly a political construct and, consequently, can be politically deconstructed. I also show that other constructs that were more liberal have been disregarded either under pressure from governments, for political expediency, or in preference for the official discourses of religious and political institutions.

Ann Mayer, for example, argues in her *Islam and Human Rights: Traditions and Politics* that the different conservative interpretations of Islam that developed during the Middle Ages and are enshrined in authoritative books of jurisprudence are responsible for Muslims' dealings with human rights issues. While she is emphatic in not attributing repression to Islam and recognizes the multiplicity of ideas and trends within the Islamic world, she feels that Islam has not specified a proper scheme of human rights from an international viewpoint. However, had she looked at the original texts of the Qur'an and the Prophetic Traditions (Sunna) as well as the early experience of Muslims, she could have developed a scheme of rights and could have found, even in medieval Islamic literature, schemes of rights, though they might not be exactly what she would like to label schemes of human rights.[4]

Mayer builds her analysis on her belief in "the normative character of the human rights principles set forth in international law and in their universality." She has no hesitation in looking on these rights as universally valid. Other observers have seen that diverse cultures produce diverse rights, and that the nonconformity of a particular culture to Western models of rights does not necessarily preclude the existence of different schemes of rights. However, because Mayer looks in a nonhistorical manner at the international schemes of human rights, which were developed within the context of Western conflicts, she feels able to position them in an absolute manner.[5] She could have been more helpful had she looked at the categories of rights rather than specific rights. For instance, when dealing with the right of belief and while acknowledging that Islam provides that right, she nonetheless insists on the Western origin of that right. She rejects any allusion to any historical Islamic influence, though hundreds of books are today published in the West on the diverse impacts of Islam on Western civilization.

Thus, one of my objectives in writing this book is to show how certain doctrines have come into existence or have gone into suspension—or, to put it differently, how we can understand or read them in their respective contexts. For instance, the Islamic right of belief cannot be treated like the Western in all of its aspects. The main Islamic texts, the Qur'an and the Sunna, assert the people's freedom of belief. However, apostasy is distinguished from freedom of (un)belief, since it also implies treason against an Islamic state. The Prophet himself treated the hypocrites as Muslims insofar as they did not work against the state, while the first caliph treated a group of Muslims who refused to pay their financial dues as apostates and fought them. Thus, unbelief and apostasy are treated differently in an Islamic context where an Islamic state exists. However, in later periods, the two merged, giving rise to current confusion about the meaning of each doctrine.

This is why I attempt to make sharp distinctions between Islam as a divine belief system and the Islamic state as a humanly developed political system. Such a distinction between the human and the divine opens unlimited possibilities of interpretation and reinterpretation as well as deconstruction and construction. As a belief system, Islam should be compared to other religions, but not to modern Western states. The rise and fall of Islamic states should be historically compared to the rise and fall of Western states. Thus a specific Islamic law like that of apostasy should first be treated in the context of an Islamic state and then be compared to treason in Western states. This is not to deny that many Islamic states and societies have historically misused what Muslims consider even to be Qur'anic duties—the complete individuality of women, the rights of minorities, and similar issues that will be treated later.

Again, while Mayer acknowledges the existence of Islamic support for democratization and human rights, she does not review adequately the current Islamist literature of mainstream Islamist movements. Instead she adverts to state Islamization programs in Iran, Pakistan, and Sudan—which are controversial to Muslims and even to Islamists—in order to compare them with international human rights. Because she considers such state programs to be a "middle-ground position," she becomes pessimistic about the future of human rights schemes in the Islamic world and reflexively defensive of the record of Western states. She treats most critiques of the West as obstacles to any comparison. For instance, many scholars and politicians regard Western critiques of human rights in the Middle East as tainted by Western hypocrisy and double standards, given the West's history of colonialism, genocide, racism, and sexism. However, Mayer dismisses this argument as rhetoric employed by regimes like Iran to maintain their grip over their societies.

It is true that violations by Western regimes of their own philosophies do not negate the validity of human rights in principle; still, such violations deprive those regimes and their institutions of the right to judge the moral standing of other, non-Western regimes. The West reacted to modern Western moral and political problems by developing its philosophy of "universal" human rights against the background of Western genocide and world wars, not against the background of the West's relations with the colonized world. More important, it is not only the regimes but also the peoples of the Middle East, both Christians and Muslims, that accuse the West of double standards. While most Middle Eastern regimes misuse this feeling and oppress their people, Western hypocrisy is nonetheless a glaring fact for people who have just seen what happened to the Bosnians in Europe and the Palestinians in the Middle East.

On yet another level, modern Islamist political thought postulates human rights, pluralism, and democracy as religious rights and, consequently, views their normative character as categorical. However, modern Islamic understanding of democracy, pluralism, and human rights depends on the possibility of modern interpretations of the sources of religion and major extensions of the meanings of some basic doctrines. These include consultation (*shura*), consensus (*ijma‘*), difference (*ikhtilaf*), minorities (*ahl al-dhimma*), enjoining the good and forbidding evil (*hisba*), and similar doctrines that are elaborated later. However, one finds that some scholars and thinkers attempt to show that the historical *shari‘a* is not capable of coping with doctrines like human rights, pluralism, and democracy.

For instance, Abullahi An-Na‘im argues in his *Toward an Islamic Reformation: Civil Liberties, Human Rights, and International Law* that it is not possible to expand the meaning of the historical *shari‘a*'s major doctrines like *shura* and *ijma‘* to modernize major concepts like freedom and equality. Instead he opts for a minor concept, abrogation (*al-naskh*) of certain verses of the Qur'an, and transforms it into a methodology of change. While he gives himself the right to abrogate and reactivate

Qur'anic verses as needed to accompany modernity, he denies to other Muslims, whether traditionalists, modernists, or Islamists, the right to expand the already existing major methodology of change, whether interpretation, reasoning (*ijtihad*), *shura*, or *ijma'*. He justifies that on the grounds that the historical *shari'a* is not capable of change.[6] In fact, as will be shown in chapter 1, the historical *shari'a*, the compendium of medieval Islamic literature, is capable of development if the Islamic centers of learning so decide. At times, they did, as was the case under the grand mufti of Egypt Muhammad 'Abdu (1849–1905) and, later, Shaykh al-Azhar Mahmud Shaltut (1893–1963).[7]

When Shaykh Shaltut, for instance, deals with the status of women as regards female testimony, he argues that the socioeconomic conditions of earlier Islam made two female witnesses equivalent to one male witness because women were not accustomed to financial transactions. However, women are now routinely involved in such transactions and their testimony should be equal to that of men. Thus, he rejects the argument based on female emotional volatility or male superior intellect. Again, Shaltut equates the rights and duties of minorities with those of the majority and maintains that the testimony of non-Muslims is valid in a *shari'a* court.[8] The point of this discussion is that if the authoritative and traditional centers of Islamic learning wish to effect modern changes in "traditional" and long-standing doctrines, they have the means and the *shari'a* provides the flexibility to do so. The traditional *shari'a* in itself is capable of internal modern development. But so far this development has not occurred.

Another example of the possibility of change from within the traditional centers of learning is the thought of Ayatollah Muhammad Mahdi Shams al-Din. Through a revisionist view of the role of the Islamic government, he brings into Shi'ite thought, in opposition to Ayatollah al-Khumayni's rule of the jurist, the necessity of democratic rule. Shams al-Din, the head of the Supreme Shi'ite Council in Lebanon, argues that the government's legitimacy is not derived from a Qur'anic text but depends on human interactions. There is no divine rule or representation on earth today. Reason calls on people to set up a political rule. Legislation is made to organize human interactions and socialization, and the state should be a natural outcome of society. Therefore, a Muslim society produces an Islamic state, and not vice versa. However, the nation as a whole is addressed in the Qur'an, and the basis of an Islamic government should be *shura* rather than the rule of the jurist. Thus, as opposed to the historical apathy of the Shi'ites toward governments and political involvement or the current dependence of the individual on the imam, Shams al-Din views the rule of the nation over itself as the appropriate modern Islamic doctrine of government. In *shura* the nation unifies its decisions and outlooks.[9]

Here I do not, then, aim to provide a defense of or apologia for Islamic political thought, for I recognize the negative aspects of classical, medieval, and modern Islamic political thought. I do attempt to show that Islamic political thought has initiated and developed throughout the ages doctrines compatible with Western doctrines of human rights, pluralism, and democracy. Their uses or abuses, while related to intellectual and philosophical understanding, are also tightly webbed into various socioeconomic and political contexts. Their proper application today not only requires their intellectual development, which is moving nowadays at a great speed especially by moderate Islamism, but requires, above all, liberal socioeconomic contexts that are mostly lacking in the Islamic world.

In contrast to Johannes Jansen's *The Dual Nature of Islamic Fundamentalism*, which first misleads the reader on modern Islamic thought and then obliterates differences between fundamentalism and reformism, I aim to clarify the differences. Jansen willfully associates both trends with violence and tries to prove the common platitude "Islamic fundamentalism is both politics and religion."[10] He assumes that—for Muslims alone—politics cannot exist without violence. Hence, "Islamic fundamentalism fuses politics, religion, and violence."[11] Jansen attempts to show that violence does not arise solely from the contemporary contexts of Islamic movements but has roots that go back to reformers like Jamal al-Din al-Afghani (1838–1897), Muhammad 'Abdu (1849–1905), and Muhammad Rashid Rida (1865–1935) and further back to Ibn Taymiyya—that is, to the essence of Islam.

More important, Jansen's logic is reductionist. For instance, he argues that "power in the perception of Islamic fundamentalism is not something that can be divided or shared with other groups, persons, or institutions."[12] He can make this argument only because his portrayal of fundamentalist views on political participation and government as well as political life is based on a few radical ideologists, who are condemned by the majority of the fundamentalists, and on a twisting of the writings of major fundamentalists like Hasan al-Banna. One might ask, is the Muslim Brotherhood's demand for "an Islamic form of the nation-state" a call for not sharing power—or, as Jansen puts it, indivisibility of power?[13] What then of the Muslim Brotherhood's long history, in Egypt and elsewhere, of attempts to share power by participating in elections? Examples of excluding the fundamentalists from participating and of their attempts to be included in political life abound in Egypt, Tunisia, Libya, Algeria, and Turkey.

Another reductionist point in Jansen's logic is his claim that to understand fundamentalism we need "a theologian's outlook" and that Islamic fundamentalism "even wants to enforce the advent of the Kingdom of God itself. In such a Kingdom the literal truth of the revealed book will be a minor self-evident detail." Thus, Islamic fundamentalism is "the creation of an Islamic religious imagination." My argument goes squarely against his. While it is true that fundamentalism aims at establishing the Islamic state, to identify the Islamic state with the Kingdom of God is the result of the author's confusion of Islam with Judaism or Christianity. Islam started as a polity, and Muslims, including the Prophet, never thought that they were setting up God's kingdom on earth. Muslims' belief in the afterlife—including heaven and hell—made them view this world as transitional and ephemeral, not a permanent abode. Also, while imagination is involved in all forms and types of thinking, the harsh contexts and realities that Muslims have found themselves thrust into, whether because of colonialism, imperialism, or the modern nation-states, have had a major impact on the politicization of religious thought.

Jansen does not stop at imposing the doctrine of God's Kingdom. He also, and more dangerously, imputes to all Muslims another unheard-of belief: according to him, Islamic fundamentalism "classifies individuals as human or subhuman as Islam does."[14] Now, we all know that, like most other religions, Islam classifies people as believers or nonbelievers and saved or condemned—but never as human or subhuman. As an example of this classification, Jansen mentions the recent history of Algeria and Egypt—but never mentions the colonialist, imperialist, and Israeli human and subhuman treatment of the Third World's peoples. As another example, Jansen characterizes the command to "enjoin the good and forbid evil" as an Islamic justification to use violence—a conclusion he reaches by twisting Fahmi al-Huwaidi's views on the subject. I argue in this book that, while a few radical groups and thinkers use the command to justify violence, Jansen has no idea that major fundamentalist theoreticians like Hasan al-Turabi, Rashid al-Ghannushi, Hasan al-Banna, and even al-Huwaidi himself use the command to justify political participation, elections, pluralism, public opinion, and even democracy.

Nor is the fact-twisting restricted to contemporary issues. Jansen argues that the history of Islamic fundamentalism started in the nineteenth century with Jamal al-Din al-Afghani. Against all accumulated and well-documented and -researched studies—or even a simple analytical reading—Jansen makes al-Afghani, Muhammad ʿAbdu, and Muhammad Rashid Rida "the founding fathers of Islamic fundamentalism." He denies the possibility that these thinkers were reformist, modernist, or liberal. Jansen's rejection of the existence of a modernizing liberal trend in Islam is due to his intellectual poverty, for instance, in defining and distinguishing between fundamentalism, modernism, and reformism, or in confusing the *shariʿa* with *hudud* (deterrents). Deterrents are only a small fraction of the *shariʿa*, which is a way of life that covers all aspects of life. Fundamentalism is the outcome of believing that Islam should be not only the center of politics but also the means for developing philosophy, morality, ethics, sciences, and technology. This is why I argue that the fundamentalists try to Islamize all aspects of Western civilization in order to bring them into conformity with Islamic texts. For fundamentalism, the Qurʾanic text is the highest authority of interpretation, understanding, and action.

I show below that the modernists, including al-Afghani and ʿAbdu, tried to interpret the text in terms of Western science, rationality, and modernity. In fact, they subjected long-standing Islamic traditions and texts to the discoveries of Western science. Thus, for instance, *shura* became equivalent to constitutional rule. They reinterpreted Islam to suit the modern age—at least, from their perspective. They made science the highest authority of interpretation, understanding, and action; they made Islam a force for civilization and morality. However, Jansen seems to suggest that to be reformist, modernist, or liberal amounts to rejecting Islam and its political understanding.

Here I briefly analyze comparatively the general political principles that have been developed by both Islamism and Islamic modernism, in order to provide the general background on political and intellectual issues and Muslims' interests during the last two centuries. I outline the various political views that help in understanding the newly developed Islamic discourses on democracy, pluralism, and human rights.

The latter part of the nineteenth century and the first half of the twentieth century witnessed the birth of two intellectual and political responses aimed at reforming both the Ottoman Empire and the Qajjar Empire. The first response, liberal and secular, called for an epistemological and political break with the Islamic past and a rejection of all forms of sultanic rule as well as the wholesale adoption of Westernization. Thinkers like ʿAbbas Mahmud al-ʿAqqad, Taha Husayn, Muhammad Husayn Haykal, and Lutfi al-Zayyat represented that response. The second response, Islamic modernism, called for the absorption of Western civilization into the Islamic heritage. Some reformers like al-Afghani called for revolutions, others like Rida called for establishment of a constitutional state, yet others like 'Abdu believed that the necessary prelude to political reform was the reformation of educational systems and social institutions.[15]

World War II constituted a turning point in the history of the imperial powers that sought domination of worldwide markets and cheap raw materials. Oppression by the imperial powers led to nationalist and socialist tendencies that weakened the liberal Islamic response and strengthened the secular but authoritarian response. Egypt, which was under the British mandate, is a good example to use here because of its political and intellectual influence all over the Arab world. During that period, Egyptians were focusing on liberating their country from British colonialism and were advocating democracy, both secular and religious. However, the rise of Arab nationalism under Jamal 'Abd al-Nasir brought about secular and socialist authoritarian nationalism. The secular response was adopted but democracy was rejected.[16] And while 'Abd al-Nasir accepted Islam as one of the three pillars of Egyptian foreign policy, in reality it did not amount to more than rhetoric. In this fashion, both the secular democratic response and the modernist Islamic response were aborted.

In recent decades, numerous movements that call for a return to the fundamentals of religion have flourished throughout the Muslim world. They pushed further for and developed a new Islamic response. Leaders of such movements believe that a modern development of Islamic spirituality, morality, and politics will definitely condemn moral corruption, glorify idealism, and lead to true representative governments. Such a development will mobilize Muslims to establish a modern Islamic civilization that reconstructs Muslim identity and consolidates Islamic power.

The genesis of Islamism, as of any other intellectual and political product, must be sought within a complex web of educational, political, economic, and intellectual crises and reactions. The mixing of the religious and the political is not new and was upheld even by the Seceders (al-Khawarij) at the beginning of Islam in the seventh century. They were the first to postulate the doctrine of divine rule or hukm and the ultimate authority of the Qur'an as the sole point of reference for Muslims. They denied as well the legitimacy of human judgment unless supported by religious texts. Because of this, they did not submit to the community, but instead removed themselves from social life and fought those who did not adhere to Qur'anic textual rulings. Moreover, they thought they had acquired the right to judge others' beliefs and behaviors, since every human action had a religious connotation. Such a view made them rigid in both principles and actions, so the general Muslim public viewed them as renegades to be fought.

In the eighteenth century, the Wahabiyya movement, following the well-known medieval thinker Ibn Taymiyya, called for the purification of Islam by a return to the fundamentals of religion, the Qur'an and the Sunna. It followed a strict line of thinking in its attempts to reconstruct society and government on the basis of divine oneness (*tawhid*) and the doctrine of good ancestors (*al-salaf al-salih*). However, the significance of the ancestors is their reluctance to engage in philosophical or intellectual argumentation and their adherence to the basic texts without any major attempt at reinterpreting or reworking the principles of Islam. They focused more on the spiritual and ethical aspects of Islam, while leaving political matters to politicians and traditional elites. Other important movements in modern times are al-Sanusiyya and al-Mahdiyya, which started basically as Sufi orders but were later transformed into political movements that struggled against Western intervention in Libya and the Sudan, respectively. The two movements were puritan, aiming at the restoration of genuine Islam through political activities. Again, fundamentals were entertained as the road to the Islamic community's salvation.

At a higher and more substantive level, Jamal al-Din al-Afghani has had a massive influence in drawing the modern political agenda that is still more or less the backbone of intellectual and political reform. He was ready to think over and adopt into Islamic thought any new intellectual, political, or scientific knowledge that might trigger the advancement of the Islamic people. On the political level, he was ready to adopt those institutions and systems that could serve the Islamic world and save it from its crises. His follower and colleague Muhammad 'Abdu and Rashid Rida, the inspirer of Hasan al-Banna (1906–1949), adopted different aspects of al-Afghani's intellectual and political thought. While 'Abdu tended more toward the modernist European aspect of al-Afghani's thought, Rida picked up the necessity of returning to the fundamentals of religion. Rida wanted to induce an intellectual revival and to develop new Islamic institutions for the establishment of an Islamic state, thus facilitating the renaissance of the *umma* (community) and guaranteeing the ethical foundations of society.

Muhammad Iqbal (1875–1938), the modernist, and Abu al-A'la al-Mawdudi (1903–1979), the Islamist, manifested similar differences. Both tried to reargue Islamic traditions dealing with knowledge and politics through attempts to reconceptualize *ijtihad*. But al-Mawdudi, the founder of al-Jama'a al-Islamiyya in Pakistan, was puritanical in his call for the reestablishment of Islam. He aimed at setting the Islamic state on purified Islamic roots and focused his efforts on establishing such a state, which would shoulder the implementation of Islam as both a comprehensive way of life and a complete system. Iqbal, on the other hand, showed liberal tendencies in reworking the Islamic traditions within Western modernity in order to renew Islamic systems of knowledge and politics. In his view an Islamic state was of only secondary importance when measured against the fundamental intellectual task that Muslims must first confront. The development of just and modern ideologies must precede just and modern politics.

Very much along al-Mawdudi's line of thinking, the Egyptian Muslim Brothers, also greatly affected by Rida and al-Afghani, centered their thought and actions on the political aspect of Islam to promote a modern renaissance. Thus, the Brotherhood urgently advocated the importance of establishing an Islamic state as the first step in implementing the *shari'a*. While focusing its intellectual reinterpretation on returning to Islamic fundamentals, the Brotherhood selectively filtered into modern Islamic thought a few major Western political doctrines like constitutional rule and democracy. These doctrines were seen as necessary tools for modernizing the Islamic concept of the state. Meanwhile, the Brotherhood's antagonistic dealings with the Egyptian government led some of its members to splinter off under the leadership of Sayyid Qutb. Qutb continued to uphold the need for establishing an Islamic state while rejecting any dealings or intellectual openness with the West. For him, the Islamic state was not a tool but a fundamental principle of creed. It signaled the community's submission to God on the basis of the *shari'a* and represented political and ideological obedience to God. Without such submission and obedience, he held, any constitution is illegitimate, and the state loses any shred of legitimacy and enters into paganism, or *jahiliyya*. Ayatollah al-Khumayni limited further the confines of a legitimate Islamic government: While the *shari'a* theoretically legitimizes a government, only the rule of the jurist actualizes its legitimacy. Within the Islamic world today, the demands of the mainstream Islamist movements in Algeria, Tunisia, Jordan, and Egypt are derived from al-Banna's discourse on the Islamic state, constitutional rule, and multiparty politics; radical Sunni movements follow the discourse of Sayyid Qutb, while Shi'ite political movements follow that of al-Khumayni.

The Islamists employ the doctrine of *tawhid* as the thread that stitches together all disciplines of knowledge and walks of life. Without this doctrine the pursuit of politics, economics, ethics, theology, and all other aspects of life is defective. God, as the fountain of every material and spiritual thing, is the ultimate authority and requires people's theoretical, theological, economic, and political submission. Complete submission is due only to God. Most Islamists thereby go beyond the traditional theological submission as understood in the classical, medieval, and modern history of Islam. They imbue *tawhid* with ultimate political and social significance. This subordinating of political life to the highest level of religious legitimacy has led many Islamists to equate, first, religiosity with proper political behavior and, second, the Islamic state with political legitimacy.

It should be noted, however, that denying the legitimacy of modernist and secularist endeavors does not turn Islamist thought into traditional thinking. In reality, the Islamists level their attacks on traditional religious and political establishments and ways of conducting religious and political affairs. For instance, Qutb argued that traditional religious scholars (*'ulama'*) do not understand the true spirit of Islam. Instead, they imitate an obsolete jurisprudence that throws Islamic thought into the realm of irrelevance, and they comply with any ruling political power that throws Islam into the realm of alienation. Islamists also criticize secular elites for their marginalization of Islam from the administration of the affairs of society and state. Rejecting both secular and religious elites forces the Islamists to develop a new Islamic model that harmoniously takes into account religion and modernity. Thus, even when emphasizing the fragility of Islamic civilization, Islamist thinkers insist that an untraditional Islamic revival is the only instrument for political and social mobilization. To recapture scientific and political supremacy, Muslims must develop new ideologies, sciences, and philosophies from within Islam.[17]

Islamist political projects are based, then, at both the theoretical and the practical levels, on renewing old doctrines and ideas and on authenticating new doctrines and ideas. Viewing themselves as synthesizers between traditional Islamic thought and modern Western thought, the modernists adopted Western political theories and ideologies and introduced Western political doctrines like democracy and republicanism into traditional Islamic thinking. Lacking a coherent theory, their political thought was oriented toward the survival of traditional thought and institutions and for immediate political goals. They tried to reinterpret and upgrade traditional doctrines and concepts to enable them to support Western notions of government and politics. They wanted to harmonize religion and science to keep the former alive and to bring together, scientifically and religiously, the West and the East. The modernists thus pioneered in Islamizing central notions like democracy and pluralism and in believing in a possible congruence between Islam and the West.

Modernists' interpretations did not invalidate the normative status of Islamic theological and jurisprudential schools. 'Abdu's rejection of man's complete understanding of divine things is theoretically and practically traditional. His argument is an unsophisticated reinterpretation of medieval theological doctrines and concepts without elaborate developments or explanations. Modernist arguments on the congruence of science with religion and on the negative and positive divine attributes are mainly adopted and reworded from al-Ghazali's numerous writings. These modernists were following in the footsteps of philosophers like al-Kindi, Ibn Sina (Avicenna), and Ibn Rushd (Averroës) in ushering sciences into intellectual circles and in encouraging the closed intellectual circles to rethink traditional interpretations of philosophical, political, social, economic, and religious doctrines and concepts.[18]

In opposition to the modernists, the Islamist rejection of both Islamic and Western past and present is total. The Islamists view philosophy, science, jurisprudence, and theology as historical constructs without universal values. They ground these disciplines in their historical social and political contexts and deny any universal validity for classical, medieval, and modern interpretations. Because these interpretations are only tentative readings of the religious text and the truth, the argument goes, they lack the power of the religious text. The Author, or God, can only entertain a final interpretation of the text. Humans can only read within a complex set of conditions that superimpose meaning on the text or the truth. The divergence of theological, jurisprudential, philosophical, and political interpretations indicates the variety of ways of living. Hence, the logic of a reading as well as its formal truth is derived from its utility to the reader. Most Islamists convert their rejection of historical readings into adopting new legitimate readings that are relevant to them here and now. However, this discourse on the reading and meaning of texts has given rise to multiple readings that call for religious, intellectual, ideological, political, social, and economic transformation. Both the discourse and the transformation manifest themselves in moderate and radical ideologies and behaviors.

Democracy, pluralism, and human rights, the basic ideological doctrines in the ever more globalized world, are not only fundamental doctrines of modern Western political philosophy but are now emerging as primary concerns of modern Islamic political thought. While the process of blending modern Islamic thought with democracy, pluralism, and human rights appears to astonish many politicians, intellectuals, and ordinary people, it is currently under way and is one of the main occupations of intellectuals and political parties in the Islamic world. Furthermore, the awareness of the need for democracy goes beyond the theoretical to become a demand of Muslims themselves, especially vis-à-vis their governments. Numerous political and intellectual conferences have been held to investigate ways and means to begin or enhance the process of political democratization and intellectual, social, and economic liberalization of the Islamic world. A majority view in Islamic intellectual circles, including even major Islamist theoreticians, with various expressions that adopt emergent Islamic doctrines on democracy, pluralism, and human rights, is now becoming vocal and central in Islamic studies.[19] All justifications for tyrannical thought and authoritarian politics are collapsing, since they are now perceived to have been major historical impediments to the development and freedom of Muslim communities as well as good religious life.

The disintegration of the Soviet Union has hastened the focus on the political legitimacy of democracy, the social necessity of human rights, and the intellectual suitability of pluralism to both the Middle East and the Islamic world. Secular and religious thinkers alike attribute the miserable conditions of economic, social, and political life to the absence of democracy and pluralism in the Arab world. A new political process that stresses the importance of political democratization and liberalization is on the rise and is entertained within a whole range of political and social strata, including the media and academia. For instance, the widely read London-based Arabic newspaper *Al-Hayat* ran an extensive series for many days on the issues of civil society, pluralism, and democracy in Egypt and the Arab world. A few meetings, like "The Democratic Experience in the Arab World" in Morocco, "The Crisis of Democracy in the Arab World" in Cyprus, and "Political Pluralism and Democracy in the Arab World" in Amman, show clearly the emerging interest in democracy and pluralism. The Beirut Center for Arab Unity Studies also convened a conference, in Cairo, to discuss democracy in the Arab world.[20]

However, the West at large has focused on Islamic threats to Western interests and orders while according no real attention or sympathy to the oppression of the peoples of the Islamic world or to the dialogues and debates that have been going on among diverse groups over political theories and rights of people. Scare titles in magazines and newspapers, such as "One Man, One Vote, One Time," "The Challenge of Radical Islam," "Will Democracy Survive in Egypt?" "The Arab World Where Troubles for the U.S. Never End," and "The Clash of Civilizations," have further pushed the West away from the East.[21] While quite a few Western academics concerned with the Middle East deal with people's real concerns, the West in general regards these concerns as negligible because their impact is localized and does not affect Western interests.

Current circumstances in the Arab world, especially in Algeria, Egypt, Lebanon, Sudan, and Tunisia, have led to ideological, political, and religious inquiries and debates on the compatibility of Islamic discourses, especially the doctrines of an Islamic state, with democracy, pluralism, and human rights, and indeed with Western ideas in general. However, a majority of Western media and scholars along with a majority of their Middle Eastern counterparts have directly viewed Islamist political thought, and indirectly Islam, as unfit for democracy because it is exclusivist by its nature and definition. There is no doubt that there are a few religious groups that are truly exclusivist and believe in the necessity of radical ideological, religious, and political transformation. They believe that only through radical coups and education can they achieve any meaningful victory. However, most popular and influential Islamic political groups adhere to new interpretations of inclusion that embrace pluralism and democracy. Ideological, religious, and political radicalism is not based on the main Islamic doctrines on the world, religions, knowledge, and salvation. More important, radicalism is a worldwide manifestation and is not restricted to a few Islamic groups. To make radicalism an essential part of Islamic doctrines or modern Islamic thought is only to miss the point on the need for inclusivist liberal contexts.

However, Professor Bassam Tibi's analysis of Islamic fundamentalism, which is close to Jansen's perspective, misses all distinctions between ideologies and behaviors of moderate and radical Islamists. One might start discussing his analysis by asking whether it is true that "the study of fundamentalism thus becomes an inquiry into the obstacles confronting the search for peace among civilizations and their religions"! And are Islam, Christianity, and Judaism the obstacles to achieving a world peace? It is well known that most, if not all, of the twentieth century's major wars as well as most civil wars were not conducted under the banner of or for the benefit of religions or fundamentalisms. The two world wars, and the wars of liberation that spread all over the Third World, stemmed from the naked self-interest of secular nation-states and empires—England, France, Germany, Russia, the U.S., and others—and not from any fundamentalist empire that fought secular states. Such unfounded remarks permeate and drive Tibi's theses, analyses, and conclusions.

Tibi starts well by not identifying Islam with terrorism or extremism. "Islam as a religion is definitely not a threat, but Islamic fundamentalism is and is replacing communism as a global enemy."[22] However, after an initial attempt to dissociate Islam from Islamic fundamentalism, and then Islamic fundamentalism from terrorism, his book ends up identifying Muslims with Islamic fundamentalists and then Islamic fundamentalists with terrorists. Most of his analysis is spent associating Islamic fundamentalism with terrorism or extremism. Tibi never stops to ask why religion is on the rise all over the world and why Muslims in particular are so frustrated.

Furthermore, Tibi's theoretical weakness leads him to define fundamentalism as a "political phenomenon [that] is an aggressive politicization of religion undertaken in the pursuit of non-religion."[23] In this statement, "political phenomenon" distorts fundamentalism and restricts it to politics. I argue here that while fundamentalism is much associated with politics, it goes beyond that to become a new interpretation of religion. Where Tibi takes the case of Professor Nasr Hamid Abu-Zaid, for instance, as evidence of the politicization of Islam, the fact of the matter is that the Egyptian (secular) government tried and convicted Abu-Zaid.

Moreover, all scholars of the Middle East know that it is not true that Islamic fundamentalists refer to their movement as *usuliyya* (fundamentalism).[24] In fact, they reject that term and instead use *Islamiyya* (Islamism). More important, Tibi's representation of Islamic fundamentalism is, like Jansen's, reductionist. For instance, most fundamentalists do not believe that democracy is unbelief (*kufr*); 'Ali bil Haj's dismissal of democracy as *kufr* cannot be generalized as the fundamentalist view on this issue,[25] and Hasan al-Turabi's reinterpretation of democracy is completely glossed over. Tibi's views on Islamic fundamentalism are built basically around the most radical fundamentalist thinkers, who have been attacked by moderate fundamentalists. Why did he not choose Rashid al-Ghannushi, or Tariq al-Bishri? Even when he uses the ideas of moderate fundamentalists like Muhammad Salim al-'Awwa, Tibi seems intent on distorting their views.

I will show that God's governance (*hakimiyyat Allah*), which Tibi wrongly translates as Allah's rule (*hukm Allah*), need not necessarily lead to totalitarian rule. Governance is not political rule or a system of government but is a doctrine used to empower people through divine texts to counter the naked force, despotism, and totalitarianism of rulers. It is an empowering doctrine that can be understood only in its context. However, Tibi seems to force fundamentalist arguments to fit his dichotomy between Islam and the West. For instance, Sayyid Qutb's Islamic system (*al-nizam al-Islami*) and paganism (*jahiliyya*) are made responsible for the Gulf War that engaged Islam to a degree unprecedented in modern history. The linkage between Qutb and the Gulf War is strange, given the fact that Qutb was executed in 1966 in Egypt. Again, *shura,* which for Tibi reflects the tribal tradition of pre-Islamic history that was adopted into Islamic thought during its formative years, cannot be turned into democracy. It is either *shura* or democracy. He declares this while most fundamentalist theoreticians interpret *shura* in terms of democracy.

This is why Tibi takes issue with John Esposito, who finds valid possibilities of reinterpretation of Islam in terms of democracy and who sees no inherent contradiction between Islamism and democracy. While Esposito correctly bases his argument on historical grounds and studies in comparative religion and sees no global threat coming from the Islamic world and makes a distinction between moderates and radicals, Tibi generalizes his observation on Algeria, whose failure to democratize is blamed on the fundamentalists.

On yet another level, I argue that it is true that Islamic fundamentalism presents "a worldview that seeks to establish its own order" but I dispute Tibi's assertion that it seeks "to separate the peoples of Islamic civilization from the rest of humanity."[26] Tibi believes that if the fundamentalists cannot impose their order on the world, they "can create disorder, on a vast scale."[27] He believes that Islamic fundamentalism has become a world challenge to current standards of politics, though he acknowledges that Islamic fundamentalism is not the cause of the current crisis of our world, but both an expression of and a response to it.[28] Islamic fundamentalism is not an intra-Islamic affair, but rather one of the pillars of an emerging new world *disorder*. Thus, there is a world *order* that is dominated and structured by the West and a world *disorder* that is dominated and structured by Islam.

Tibi innocently describes the existing world order as a process of "peaceful international interaction among sovereign states," then twists the logic of conflicts in the world, reducing war to "irregular wars in the Balkans, the Caucasus, Central Asia, and Somalia, in all of which Islam is involved" and pronouncing them "more an indication of unfolding disorder [read, fundamentalist world order] than of any new world order."[29] He views the activities of Hamas and Islamic Jihad in the Palestinian Zones as directed at obstructing the peace process through "terrorist activities justified as Jihad."[30] There is no criticism of the activities of Israel or the Palestinian Authority or the major world powers. While the West, in Tibi's opinion, did not aim to enlighten Muslims but to subject them to Western rule, this is not enough to explain the tension between contemporary Islam and Western cultural modernity. For him, the world is going through a clash between the divine (Islamic) and the rational (Western) views.[31] Even at a theoretical level, he avoids criticizing offensive Western doctrines and policies: it is not Samuel Huntington, for instance, but the Islamic fundamentalists who draw these fault lines of conflict between civilizations.[32] Western powers and intellectuals are exonerated en masse, while Islam stands firm on the ground that contradicts other options for a world order—other options being multicultural world orders.[33]

For Tibi, Western and Islamic civilizations must learn to live with each other on a footing of equality, refraining from their explicit or implicit claims to moral superiority and universality.[34] However, he soon rescinds his evenhandedness by pronouncing that Islamic fundamentalism must forgo its religious views and opt for an alternative international cross-cultural morality made up of human rights and secular democracy. Maybe this reflects Tibi's view that fundamentalism does not address religious belief but is "rather a sociopolitical worldview"[35] and expresses a practical preference.

Tibi acknowledges the existence of a basic division within the Islamic fundamentalist camp, but does not see that division as spelling differences over interpretation, or moderation versus radicalism. He is mainly happy that the disorganization will forestall control of the world. Thus, structural globalization is countered by national and international cultural fragmentation.[36] However, fundamentalism is a challenge to the nation-state. "Islam has become the West's leading challenger for one simple reason[:] Islamic perspectives are not restricted to national or regional boundaries. In this respect, Islam resembles Western civilization. The fundamentalists revolt against Western hegemony and compete with Western universalism. Fundamentalism is an ideology contributing to the war of civilizations."[37] But who is leading it? The strange answer Tibi gives is Islamic universalism, which might be capable of taking over the West. What makes the clash of civilizations sharper is the migration of Muslims to the West. Tibi talks repeatedly about globalization and compares it to Islamic universalism, although globalization, for him, is basically technological and economic, and universalism is religious and moral. If Islamic fundamentalists are universalists in their attitude, and if, as Tibi says, globalization is rampant in economics, politics, communication, transportation, and technology but is lacking in culture or civilization,[38] the fundamentalists may be able to employ globalization to the advantage of universalism. Tibi thinks that the fundamentalist revolt against the nation-state is a revolt against imported solutions, because the nation-states have failed in bringing about economic development and political participation.[39]

Unlike Tibi, I do not argue that the only way for Islam to become part of the new emerging global system is to be secularized. I argue that an international morality of democracy and human rights could be based on religions as well as secular thought.[40] Although the origins of human rights and democracy in the West are to be found in the making of Protestantism and its breaking away from Catholicism, and although Islamic thought is undergoing a similar process, Tibi denies Muslims the right to reinterpret Islam in the light of modernity and democracy. For him the condition for democratization is secularization, and the "goal is, rather, how to get us Muslims to speak the language of secular human rights in our own tongues."[41] But could not the Muslims be Muslims and find the necessary common ground with other civilizations and religions to build a universal framework for human rights and democracy based on their strong divine beliefs? Tibi's final surrender comes out in this West-bound ingratiating statement: "Despite my being a Muslim, my understanding of human rights is inexorably linked to the basic rights promulgated by the French and American revolutions."[42] Is this the choice for Muslims all over the globe whose understanding of human rights is not linked to the French and American revolutions but emerges from colonialist and imperialist experiences with the secular West and the tyranny and exploitation of their nation-states!

Tibi takes his stand against fundamentalism on Islamic grounds: the Sufi love of God, and the Islamic rationalism of Ibn Rushd and *Al-Madina al-Fadila* of al-Farabi.[43] He forgets that the Sufis and the rationalists in medieval Islam, especially al-Farabi and Ibn Rushd, were not democratic but elitist and against popular sentiments. Tibi's sad story is that while he claims to push forward Islamic liberalism as an alternative to Islamic fundamentalism, what one is left with is his urgent need to destroy any Islamic trend that is an ideology, a philosophy, or even a way of life. For him, Islam should be replaced wholesale with a globalized Western civilization.

Unlike Tibi's book, Emad Shahin's *Political Ascent: Contemporary Islamic Movements in North Africa* places Islamic resurgence in North Africa in its historical and cultural context. Shahin compares and contrasts the organizations, contexts, and developments of Islamic movements within both pre- and post-independence experiences. Furthermore, he provides essential information on Islamic movements, thinkers, and leaders as well as their ideas and discourses. He places emphasis on major

Islamic movements in the Arab West: al-Nahda, the Progressive Islamic Tendency movement, and the Islamic Liberation Party in Tunisia; the Islamic Salvation Front, Hamas, and al-Nahda Party in Algeria; and the Association of Justice and Benevolence and the Movement of Reform and Renewal in Morocco. His study of these movements based on extensive field research situates them within local conditions and follows their emergence as social movements that adopt Islam as a political alternative to Western models and as an instrument of social protest. The three countries, Tunisia, Algeria, and Morocco, share many characteristics. For instance, the states' control of the institutions of official Islam is used to affirm the political elites' legitimacy, while they are in fact committed to foreign models. Thus, the political elites expropriated Islamic institutions to cultivate bases of support for their modernization campaigns and to maintain the legitimacy and stability of their regimes.

Shahin argues that a few factors complicate the development of an objective and comprehensive theory of Islamic renewal: (1) the revival is still in a transitional phase, in flux; (2) Islamic movements operate in diverse environments and conditions; (3) they are still developing ideologically; (4) the revival is too often seen as only political in nature; (5) the secular framework of analysis leads to the marginalization of religion; and (6) Western intellectual and political responses to these movements reveal a confusion of political interests with ideological orientations. On reexamining the role of Islam and postindependence Islamic movements in Tunisia, Algeria, and Morocco, he concludes that the Islamic movements within these countries are forces for political change. Shahin tries to distinguish preindependence Islamic forces from and to juxtapose them with postcolonial movements, but while his main objective is to go beyond the conventional classification of these movements as being political, economic, or social, he himself falls victim to the same classification. He continuously refers to the Islamic movement as *political Islam*—never strongly as theological, intellectual, or economic.

On a higher theoretical level, while Shahin makes the argument that these movements are not new phenomena but are the expressions and continuation of a reform-protest trend that had appeared earlier, his main intellectual argument is that "contemporary political Islam is a widespread response to the determination of the post-independence state to relegate Islam to a subordinate political and social position and to the perceived inadequacy of the secular-oriented Western models of development in addressing the indigenous problems of society."[44] These movements are challenging the legitimacy of their rulers and seeking to reconstruct the religiopolitical base of society in response to the secular policies of the postcolonial incumbent elites.

While this argument does not make political Islam in North Africa any different from Islamic movements in the Arab East or the Gulf, Shahin insists that political Islam in the Arab West is unique, and is significant for the region as a whole, because political Islam in North Africa has shown a marked willingness to work within the system right from the beginning. This willingness has led to "some important contributions from various Maghribi thinkers about the relations between Islam and the state and Islam and democracy as well as the feasibility of non-violent struggle." Shahin then concludes incorrectly that in many ways "the Islamist intellectual center of gravity has moved away from the Mashriq to North Africa," a development he relates to the "particular role Islam has played and to its proximity to Europe and French culture." Furthermore, in North Africa, Islamic groups have actually at times been officially recognized and allowed to compete in elections.

In fact, there is nothing unique about North African "political Islam" that distinguishes it from other geographic areas of the Arab world. Shahin himself tells us, for instance, that the Islamic dimension of reform that asserted Islamic identity in Tunisia was advocated by Shaykh 'Abd al-'Aziz al-Tha'alibi, who was influenced by "the reformist ideas of Muhammad 'Abduh and the Salafiyya movement."[45] In Algeria too, Islamic reforms were "exposed to the ideas of the Salafiyya movement, either directly through its protagonists, such as Muhammad 'Abduh and Muhammad Rashid Rida, or while studying at religious institutions in the Arab East."[46] We are also told that even Shaykh 'Abd al-Hamid ben Badis, the great Algerian thinker and founder of the Association of Algerian Scholars, was "influenced by the teachings of Jamal al-Din al-Afghani and Muhammad 'Abdu and introduced Ben Badis to the reformist ideas of the *Salafiyya* movements."[47] Nor did Morocco escape the influence of the Arab East, for a major development by the end of the nineteenth century was, according to Shahin, "the emergence of an Islamic reform movement, the Salafiyya, influenced by the ideas of Islamic modernism propagated by Afghani, 'Abduh and the *Manar* group in Egypt."[48]

There is no value in denying the intellectual influence of the Arab East over the Arab West: even today, the ideological and political discourses of North Africa's major fundamentalist movements are still chiefly shaped by theoreticians from the Arab East such as Hasan al-Banna and Sayyid Qutb as well as Hasan al-Turabi. Also, the main fundamentalist movement in the Arab East, the Muslim Brotherhood, did not start as an underground movement but participated in public and political life, including parliamentary elections. This is likewise true of the Brotherhood's branches in Jordan, Kuwait, and other countries. Furthermore, the major work in constructing Islamic *shura* as democracy has been done by theoreticians from the Arab East such as Tawfiq al-Shawi, Muhammad Salim al-'Awwa, and Fahmi al-Huwaidi. Of course, every country of the Arab West has some distinguishing characteristics—a remark that can just as easily apply to the countries of the Arab East and elsewhere. These characteristics do not amount to any unique theoretical development that is unheard of or particularly North African.[49]

The general conclusion that the author makes is that while the nature of political Islam is complex, its connection to social change and development maintains its longevity. Its expansion is related to the marginalization of Islam in state and society and the importation of Western models that have failed to resolve socioeconomic and political problems. New intellectual elites are confronting Westernized elites as well as the elites of official Islam. While it is true that pluralism affects the level of cohesion and behavior of the Islamic opposition, Shahin makes no real efforts to differentiate between radical or revolutionary and moderate or tolerant movements. His main line of argument is that "when an Islamic movement is perceived as radical and dogmatic, the movement is likely to resort to a strategy of violence and dissent."[50] However, we all know that violence is not a *perception* but a reality—examples include the Armed Islamic Group and the Islamic Youth Association. I argue in this book that there are basic differences between moderate and radical Islamists that relate to philosophy, ideology, sociology, and politics.

In line with Bruce Lawrence's *Shattering the Myth: Islam beyond Violence,* I show that the deconstruction of the myth of Islamic violence requires a complex process of deconstructing stereotypes and constructing pluralistic images of Muslim lives. Lawrence's excellent analysis of Islam today brings together a great array of socioeconomic, historical, political, and religious elements and examines the resulting blend in a global context of transcapitalism and high technology. He provides insightful studies of the local, national, and international contexts of the rise of Islamic fundamentalism and the nation-states within the Islamic world. Looking not only at the theoretical and political discourses of Islamic fundamentalism but also at the larger economic and political orders, Lawrence argues that Islam cannot be understood except as a major and complex system shaped as much by its own metaphysical postulates and ethical demands as by the circumstances of Muslim polities in the modern world.

Addressing well-known stereotypes of Muslims, he shows that the longer view of Muslim societies offers hope rather than despair about Islam in the next century. He shatters the myth that Islam emanates from a hostile, "Arab" Middle East. Arab Islam is only one manifestation, which is itself diversified; there are other interpretations—Iranian, Bosnian, Malaysian. Equally important, he shows how the reality of Muslim women's active participation in their societies is glossed over and covered by a stereotype that projects the violence of male "Arab" Muslims everywhere: Muslim males hate the West and abuse their women. Against this background, Lawrence shows that women in India, Pakistan, and Bangladesh are forced to represent the cultural norms and that court cases involving women's legal rights not only reflect boundary markings between Muslims and other communities, they also heighten tensions about their maintenance, even as they complicate notions of what it is to be both Asian and Muslim at the start of the new millennium.

At another level, Lawrence gives due credit—or blame—for one of the defining events of the Islamic world in modern times: the imperialist intrusion of the West, which led to distortion of economic development and subordination to global—Western—economic interests. Even the rise of the local bureaucratic elites in the name of independence replicated the nationalist ideological superstructure of the colonizers. Counterelites returned to "authenticity" to contest the power and legitimacy of the nation-state. While Lawrence shows that Muslims have been subjected to structural violence, it is remarkable that they have not lost control over their destinies. The reason behind this is the diversity of the Muslim world. Although it uses similar symbols and values that influence conduct, its politics are reshaped by interacting with the world of the postcolonial or, generally, non-Muslim "others." It is structural violence that reduces the range of choice for European, African, and Asian Muslims. It is structural violence that restricts the options for Muslim nation-states in the post–Cold War world. Lawrence argues that it victimizes Muslim intellectuals by imposing limits on their discourses about Islam at the turn of the century.

While Muslims' politics may suggest uniformity of intent and practice, Lawrence shows—through analytical socioeconomic studies of Egypt, Iran, Saudi Arabia, Syria, and Tunisia as well as, later, of India, Pakistan, Bangladesh, and Malaysia—that the source of this uniformity is the manipulation of symbolic resources and the permeability of boundaries. And because authority in the Muslim world is fragmented, negotiations take the form of protest against the colonial and neocolonial power, the dominant state apparatus, the religious establishment, and the prevailing economic system.

However, Lawrence places protest in time and sequence when distinguishing different types of protest: thus, (1) revivalists are seen as a preindustrial response to European intervention, disruption to traditional trade, demographic shift, and agricultural decline, leading to reaffirmation of Islamic identity and values; (2) reformers are products of the colonial presence, who adapted to the nationalist and ideological legacies of the West and saw them as compatible with Islam; and (3) fundamentalists are a response to the imbalance with the West, who seek to empower themselves through control of "authenticity." All these responses have taken place within the context of structural realignments of global economic, political, and military powers.

To disconnect the equation of Islam with violence, or to shatter the myth, Lawrence draws attention to (1) blurring of the distinction between Islam as religion and as a political ideology that is competing with and dominated by nationalism, and (2) the colonialist European powers' use of religion to divide and control major segments of world population, from West Africa to Southeast Asia. According to Lawrence, not all fundamentalists employ direct confrontation with the nation-state that they see as a creature of the neoimperialist West. And there are other voices, like Malaysia and Bosnia, which are moving toward pluralism. Thus Islam's compatibility with democracy falls under the broader question of whether Islam is evolving and flexible or definitive and unyielding. Yet because of Muslim societies' underdevelopment and global marginalization resulting from advances in science and technology, the future seems to be centered upon economic dependence.

Some Muslims may choose jihad as a holy war to confront the hegemonic powers, but they risk further marginalization: in this case the narrative of jihad is not related to contemporary history and global politics or economics. Other Muslims, in Malaysia for instance, can reinterpret jihad as neocapitalist corporate culture—today's dominant world force—that leads to economic responsibility and social justice. Lawrence correctly argues that a reinterpretation of jihad within a modern global context, which takes into account the realities of economic and technical, structural changes, and whose terms of engagement shift to economic jihad, can lead to an Islamic religious discourse that is moderate, pluralistic, and democratic. This discourse creates an open public space that increases tolerance between Muslims and non-Muslims and among Muslims themselves. Along this line, I argue that Islam, like other religions, is shaped by its world context; Muslims are now victimized by the international power structure and economic disparity leading to despair and often violence where the have-nots drift to the margins of global exchange. Transcapitalism, high technology, and religion are shaping and are being reshaped by humankind.

1

The Classical and Medieval Dialectics of *Shura* and Its Modern Islamist Constructions As Democracy

The Dialectics of Classical and Medieval *Shura*

Muslim jurists during the classical and medieval periods of Islam were not oblivious to the role of political power in formulating political paradigms and in shaping general political behaviors. Abu Hamid al-Ghazali, the great and very influential jurist and theologian, considered power, in all its moral, economic, and physical manifestations, to be part and parcel of our understanding of the state and its role. While naked power for him was the ability to overcome, that ability should not be used to the detriment of the nation's higher ideals. In no way should power, especially its physical aspect, overcome the fundamental principles of justice, freedom, equality, social and political responsibility, and other public virtues. Briefly, man should not be subjected to arbitrary physical power. While power is essential for the internal and external well-being of the state and especially for its establishment, power alone does not carry within itself the justification for establishing the state. Al-Ghazali argued that the moral legitimacy of political power must be based on people's free choice and support, which is represented by a free public approval of Muslims.[1]

Another important theoretician, al-Mawardi, argued also that coercive power is needed to unite the nation, especially when the competition between groups and individuals is based on narrow interests, individual ambitions, and selfish struggles. In this case, it is the state's duty to secure the rights of the weaker parties and to apply comprehensive justice according to the stipulations of Islamic law.[2]

Shura, Ijmaʿ, and Political Authority

It is, then, theoretically true that state administration in Islam should be based on a correct system of *shura* or, in modern terminology, a democratic (consultative) government of the people. This form of government, based on *shura,* mainly postulates people's equality and individual rights and limits the state's function to serving people's interests and development. It also postulates the ruler's responsibility before God, the people, and the rule of law. Its main political principles are, therefore, freedom of, equality among, and justice for the people.

Muslims agree generally that the common political function of conducting people's affairs is the community's domain because the Qur'an addresses the community at large, not the ruler. Again, the Qur'anic concepts of human vicegerency (*khilafa*) and human empowerment (*tamkin*) produce the doctrines of general human sovereignty and responsibility. Both doctrines require that power be vested in the community (*al-jama'a*), because its vicegerency is mandated by the Qur'an, to fulfill the divine commandments, including the application of Islamic law, the development of morality, and enjoining the good and forbidding evil (*hisba*). However, because the community cannot act as one individual, it delegates its authority to one individual, the ruler, who is still theoretically subordinate to the community. The original right to rule is, however, that of the community; the ruler is its executive agent.[3]

The model that almost all jurists and most Muslims employ to justify their theories, the one they look to as the highest political model, is the state that Prophet Muhammad founded and ruled. His short rule of the first Islamic state and the formative political doctrines developed therein, such as shura, *ijma',* the contract, constitutional rule, freedom of religion, pluralism, and individuals' rights, became the highest political framework and point of reference for Islamic disciplines of knowledge. After his migration (*hijra*) to Yathrib (later Medina), Muhammad established himself as the leader, ruler, and judge of the community, in addition, of course, to his status as God's messenger. Muhammad achieved this by setting forth the first constitutional document in Islam, al-Sahifa, which established the first multireligious, pluralistic political entity for the Muslims at Medina. Al-Sahifa, the constitution, acknowledges the following points: Many religious and tribal communities form the city. While it is one political community headed by the Prophet, who has the prerogative to launch war or make peace, each religious community follows its own religion and rules accordingly. In case of conflicting interpretations of the constitution, God and Muhammad are its judges and interpreters. On the other hand, while tribal structures should be especially maintained for social and economic reasons, the individual and not the community is responsible for any transgression and bears the punishment incurred. Moreover, the Jewish community is part of the political structure and subject to it, for it fights along with the Muslims and participates in peacemaking. The *dhimma* (protection) of God and neighborly security are binding on all individuals and local communities. Therefore, every individual or community is safe in Medina, except the one who acts treacherously.[4]

The significance of this constitution is broad and deep for the development and reinterpretation of Islamic political thought. First of all, it was the basic formative political agreement sanctioning coexistence of many groups and recognizing collective identities with no attempt to convert non-Muslims to Islam. Second, instead of employing purely Qur'anic or Islamic justifications, general human principles of solidarity, mutual responsibility, and defense of the community against aggression became the frame of reference. Third, in that it accepted the Jews as believers and recognized their right to administer their own affairs and to use their religious and tribal laws to adjudicate their disputes, the constitution sanctioned multireligious communities. More important, the drawing up of this constitution and the mere adherence to it by non-Muslims signaled the Prophet's contractual legitimacy as the community's elder statesman and judge. By accepting the constitution, the Jews were not accepting Muhammad's religious leadership of their community. However, their political contract with the Prophet that recognized him as the chief political and legal administrator allowed him to take specific positions when their tribal structure failed to resolve conflicts arising within the newly developed society. The contractual agreement between the Muslim community, on the one hand, and the Jewish tribes, on the other, secured the Prophet's legitimacy and power as the political legislator. Thus, for instance, although he did not outlaw most tribal laws and customs, he issued a general public prohibition of infanticide practiced by Arabs and a special Muslim ban on wine drinking. What was revealed during his rule in Medina dealt mainly with the general Islamic views of the universe, life, and man, while most notions covering personal and criminal regulations were addressed after his rule of Mecca.[5]

While the direct interpretation of religion was the Prophet's prerogative, carrying out legal and religious laws and regulations was the community's responsibility. His contractual rule had almost the nature of arbitration rather than of forcible imposition of new political and economic orders. He did not, for instance, impose new taxes on trade, income, or inheritance. While a share of alms was given to the Prophet to distribute to the poor and the needy, it was again of noncompulsory nature. Thus, in terms of structural organization and political philosophy, the Prophet did develop a new form of government. The state then lacked ministries, administrative institutions, and police forces. Nonetheless, while the religious factor was present and the motivating force for Muhammad, the agreement was a compromise drawn from pre-Islamic concepts and in a nonreligious framework.[6]

The majority of Muslims agree that the Prophet did not specify a particular form of government but instead provided guidelines based on justice, freedom, *shura* in public affairs, and enjoining the good and forbidding evil. Fundamental guidelines include protecting religion, administering justice, defending the state, applying Islamic law and the laws of other groups, collecting and dispensing state revenues, appointing state administration, and following up on all matters of concern to the state and the community.[7]

The real and significant implications of this political contract appeared clearly after the Prophet's death. Instead of signaling the termination of the contract and its legitimacy, the manner of transferring political power to a caliph reinforced its validity in the eyes of the community at large—for the community acted to charge a new leader with the power to govern. Put differently, the contract to govern became the most fundamental characteristic of the newly established governing institution, the caliphate. In fact, the powers stipulated by the contract as well as those of political authority and interpretation of religious texts turned out to be the community's prerogative. In theory and in practice, the exercise of judicial authority, political rule, and religious interpretation became subject to *ijma'*, itself processed and ratified through *shura*.

The community's political power is justified by the Muslims' upholding of the doctrine of *ijma'*, or consensus. It was obvious after the Prophet's death that the idea of consensus had started taking shape in Muslims' minds; there was growing agreement that a Muslim should not go against his community's collective political will. While consensus at that time was not universal, it did include a large group of people or the majority of people, including the popularly acclaimed religious leaders and political notables. Muslims regarded the power of consensus as almost equal to the power of the text. Later, al-Ghazali would make consensus not only a political doctrine but also a principle of religion, for it extends the possibility of new legislation through the community's power and functions as a new text that guides the community in the absence of specific Qur'anic injunctions. Because the community was always in need of a guiding principle that dealt with the changing conditions of life, it viewed consensus as that principle.

On a higher level, the doctrine of consensus on religious matters helped the community to soften its coexistence, either through arriving at a consensual agreement that unified the community or through adopting pluralistic views—especially after the Prophet's death. The community's consensus became, at least theoretically, the highest binding authority, leading the community to accept, for instance, one sacred version of the Qur'an. A *shura* that sought the consensus of the community was the only legitimate basis for setting up a political authority and for legislating and developing new doctrines. Applying the outcomes of *ijma'* and *shura* meant that the community was empowered; the absence of *ijma'* and *shura* led to a vacuum that translated at times into political and social disunity and turmoil.[8]

In that sense, *ijma'* and *shura* have clearly been the cornerstones and roots for developing a free and representative form of Islamic government or democracy. While classical and medieval Islamic thought did not use the term "democracy," the theoretical power that was vested in the people and the community for the making of society and government as well as religious doctrine is of the highest order and comes very close to democracy. The legitimacy of any Islamic government is originally founded on the community's approval of the ruler's person and qualifications, and its continuation hinges on a continuing public approval. In this sense, the community's choice of its leader is not basically of a religious character but reflects the perception of the ruler's appropriateness to lead the community at a particular phase in history.

Abu Bakr, the first rightly guided caliph, said after his election as a ruler, "I was made a ruler though I was not the best among you. If I commit any wrongdoing, correct me. Obey me insofar as I obey the Prophet. If I disobey God and His Prophet, do not obey me." Also the second rightly guided caliph, 'Umar ibn al-Khattab, said, "If you see in me any deviation, correct it." These examples show us that the first two caliphs sought people's oath of allegiance as an evidence of approval. No individual in the community, not even Abu Bakr, considered himself to have inherited the Prophet's powers, whether the religious or the political.

Questions about the nature of political authority and its relation to divine law immediately followed the Prophet's death. From the point of view of the majority Sunnites, the Prophet had not appointed a political successor, at least not publicly. Many, and at times contrary, arguments were made about the characteristics of the Prophet's successor. At the meeting place Saqifat bani Sa'ida, the migrants (*muhajirin*) and the supporters (*al-ansar*) discussed numerous options: one suggestion was that the two groups each choose a prince (*amir*) to rule jointly. However, Abu

Bakr from the migrants was finally nominated as the new caliph, and people swore allegiance to him.[9]

This did not prevent later controversies about the manner of a caliph's appointment and the nature of his representation, because the ruler's post became the highest position in the Islamic state. In particular, three strong opinions, which still have significance to Muslims today, were voiced. The first was that the ruler represented God on earth; the second was that the ruler represented the Prophet; the third was that he represented the previous ruler. However, all these opinions were rejected in favor of making the whole community carry the responsibility of representation or vicegerency. The ruler represented humankind, or at least the community that elected him. The community represented God. Thus the elected ruler was theoretically responsible before the community. With ultimate authority reserved to the community, the ruler's continuation in government hinged on its approval.[10]

The controversy over the nature of this political office even reached the point of challenging the notion that a government is a religious need. A few scholars argued that it was a religious duty to appoint a political ruler and that those Muslims who did not select a ruler committed a religious sin. A related view stated that, because of the need for an authority to apply the religious law, an executive selected by the community was required. This was the view of the majority of Sunnites, Mu'tazilites, and Zahirites. Another view, based on human choices, did not regard the rulership as a religious post but argued that it was a rational duty because it served the natural (rational) choices of the community. This was the view of some Mu'tazilites and Zaydi Shi'ites. Yet another view, that of the Imami and Isma'ili Shi'ites, revolved around the notion that having a ruler was a rational necessity that God ought to fulfill, and that He in His goodness would not leave the world without a divinely appointed leader, especially after the end of prophetic missions.[11]

In practical terms, the elite's consultation and the people's consensus became the justifying mechanisms of historical political and social processes to set up rulers and dynasties. The jurists developed the concept of the necessity of a free general election of the caliph, whose legitimacy was dependent on applying justice and divine law. This is why the two main methods for selecting the head of state—choice by the Muslim community, and nomination by the reigning ruler, to be ratified by the people's oath of allegiance—have been historically upheld. Al-Mawardi postulates three other qualifications for becoming a ruler: justice, knowledge, and wisdom.[12] Those who were qualified to elect the ruler and supervise the activities of the government, traditionally referred to as the people who bind and loosen (*ahl al-hal wa al-'aqd*), represented informally the powers of society. It was informal representation because the direct mechanisms employed today to select the representatives of society were not technically feasible or even thought of in the early and medieval Islamic empires. However, these informal representatives should also have the qualifications of justice, knowledge, and wisdom. Also, the requirement that the caliph be from the Prophet's tribe, Quraysh, or an Arab was invalidated.[13]

A revealing example of this process occurred during the overthrow of the third rightly guided caliph, 'Uthman. The revolutionaries, those who aimed at removing the caliph, wanted to nominate 'Ali ibn Abi Talib, but he turned their nomination down. He argued that any nomination should come instead from the council of *shura* that was set up during the Prophet's lifetime. It was that council that nominated the rightly guided caliphs, who then received the oath of allegiance from the public. It was the same council that later agitated the people against 'Uthman, by distributing in Muslim countries letters objecting to 'Uthman's caliphate and calling for its end. The gist of these letters was that Muslims should come to Mecca to reassert their rightful claims because 'Uthman had turned the caliphate into a kingdom.[14]

Patently, then, the general theoretical view was that the community was the source of political authority, and when it concluded a contract with the ruler or swore allegiance to the nominated ruler, it gave the ruler the power to act on its behalf and be its executive. The oath of allegiance was a proof that only upon the community's approval did a designated ruler become legitimate.[15] Because the majority of Muslims rejected the view that the ruler was God's representative or shadow on earth, they cited Qur'anic verses that made vicegerency a public affair concerning all of humankind, not only an individual or his descendants.[16] No one could represent God and act on His behalf; while terms like "God's caliph" and "the Prophet's caliph" were used historically, the majority of the Muslims, the Sunnis, did not accept the theoretical implications and connotations.

Such a view of political authority allowed quite a few Muslims even during the first century of Islam to challenge the caliphate in the name of the community. Thus 'Abd Allah al-Zubayr, for instance, revolted against Yazid ibn Mu'awiya and organized a protest of hundreds of Muslims around the Ka'ba in Mecca. While Yazid failed to suppress this revolt and died before he ended it, al-Zubayr sought the approval of the great Qurayshites and submitted himself to a general *bay'a* and not only of his group. This meant that people thought of *shura* as the Muslims' right to contract a ruler. However, the theoretical development of this idea took place in the second century of Islam when the theological school, the *murji'a*, at Kufa suggested that the doctrines of *al-jama'a* (the community), *shura*, and *ulu al-amr* (those who are in charge) meant the greater number of the community. This understanding was further developed in the third and fourth centuries. Scholars like al-Harith ibn Asad al-Muhasabi and Imam Ahmad ibn Hanbal developed the argument that reason was a faculty common to all people. Therefore, there was no need for a special superior individual or a select group, since the collective reason of the community could administer its affairs, including the religious, political, social, and economic.[17]

Jurists differed even on the number of individuals needed for electing the ruler and made a distinction between nominating a ruler and his actual election. The most acceptable view specified no number to nominate a ruler, but required for his election the approval of the majority of the informal communal representatives in every country or region.

Because a legitimate caliphate depended on a contract between the ruler and the people, his legitimacy had to be derived from a popular consensus. And since the legitimate method for selecting a ruler was a contract, al-Mawardi as well as Ibn Hazm postulated the people's right even to choose a person who was less qualified from among a group of more qualified candidates. Put differently, while certain qualities were needed for nomination, it was ultimately the people's choice that set up a rightful rule. Conversely, compulsion was not a valid basis for rightful rule because any binding rule arose out of a legitimate contract between the community and the ruler.[18]

Also, jurists like al-Mawardi and Ibn Hazm had theoretically given equal weight to and had not discriminated among the different regions of Islam in election matters. The place of election was not limited only to the capital. Of course, the people who lived in the capital had the practical priority of space and time, and while the electing bodies of all regions had equal powers, the people residing in the capital were normally the first to nominate or elect the caliph.[19]

Another method of electing the ruler, which was historically more practiced than the first, was nomination by the reigning ruler on condition that the successor obtain the oath of allegiance from the public after the death of the reigning ruler. The caliph Abu Bakr, after consulting many of the Prophet's Companions, nominated 'Umar ibn al-Khattab. 'Umar, in turn, sought and acquired the oath of allegiance from the public after Abu Bakr's death.[20] The voluntary nature of the caliphate is also obvious in the case of the 'Abbasid caliph al-Muntasir (ruled 862–66), who received from the army and the public the oath of allegiance. The oath included an emphasis on the caliphate's acceptance without compulsion or force. Al-Mu'taz (ruled 866–69) had a similar oath of allegiance that emphasized people's freedom and choice as well as Muslims' future well-being. When al-Mu'taz abdicated the caliphate, he signed a detailed letter specifying that, because he was weak and unfit to rule, he freed the Muslims from their oath of allegiance. The Muslims thereupon withdrew their oath and were free to choose a new caliph.[21]

The ruler's right to rule or to bequeath his political authority ended with his death: the contract could not be extended to his heirs. However, nomination of a ruler by the existing ruler was different, because it ultimately depended on the people's approval. The ruler also forfeited the right to rule when he could not exercise it because of physical or mental incapacity. While the caliph usually ruled for life, there was nothing that prevented the people from removing him from government or limiting his term to a few years. Because political rule was a contract between the people and the ruler, he could resign and rid himself of the contract without any justification, whereas the people could rid themselves of the ruler only if there were strong justification. Examples included the ruler's loss of knowledge, wisdom, courage, freedom, mind, justice, or Islam. Some scholars postulated the legitimacy of his removal if he rejected Islam or became impious, which discredited his moral justice. Also, he could be removed if he exercised his powers arbitrarily or extended them beyond the limits assigned by jurisprudence. He also lost his powers if he was under the control of or imprisoned by foreign powers.[22]

Divine Rule and Human Choice

Another formative event in the history of Islam, which occurred immediately after the Prophet's death and which shows the community's power in structuring its systems and its ideologies, was the beginning of the division of the community into what later became its main sects, Shi'ism and Sunnism. Although no one denies that some Muslims preferred 'Ali ibn Abi Talib over Abu Bakr, most of Muhammad's Companions accepted Abu Bakr's caliphate. In fact, 'Ali tolerated and even accepted the caliphates of Abu Bakr, 'Umar, and 'Uthman.[23] Although at the beginning he declined the caliphate, the fact that concerns us here is his ultimate acceptance of the majority's view and submission to their judgment.

Meanwhile, a lot of important Muslims questioned 'Ali's fitness for the caliphate from the Prophet's death until ʿAli's own. When ʿUthman was assassinated, two camps started forming, each claiming its right to the caliphate.[24] Three great Companions of the Prophet, his wife ʿAisha, Talha, and al-Zubayr, formed an army of six hundred men and fought ʿAli and his army in what later became known as the Battle of al-Jamal (the camel), where the first camp lost.[25] Muʿawiya, then the governor of Damascus and later the founder of Umayyad dynasty, also rose against ʿAli, using blood-revenge claims, since ʿUthman was his relative. ʿAli removed the governors that were appointed by ʿUthman. Accusing ʿAli of having plotted against ʿUthman and aided in his assassination, Muʿawiya prepared an army, and ʿAli moved to Kufa and prepared another one.

The two armies engaged in bloody fighting known as the Battle of Siffin. Some soldiers in Muʿawiya's camp, when they felt that their side was losing, held copies of the Qurʾan on top of their spearheads and called for arbitration.[26] Impassioned debates over the validity of human judgment took place in ʿAli's camp, since he was on the verge of winning the war. Finally it was decided that two judges, ʿAmr ibn al-ʿAs, representing Muʿawiya, and Abu Musa al-Ashʿari, representing ʿAli, should resolve the conflict through human judgment. Abu Musa spoke first and nullified the caliphates of both Muʿawiya and ʿAli, as he and ʿAmr Ibn al-ʿAs had agreed. But then ʿAmr renounced ʿAli's caliphate and affirmed Muʿawiya's—an act that violated the arbitral agreement to free all people from their previous *bayʿa* to both. A large group of people considered the arbitration completed and swore allegiance to Muʿawiya, but ʿAli's camp considered it a trick and rejected the outcome.[27]

A militant group in ʿAli's camp, later known as al-Khawarij (the Seceders), rejected the whole process of human adjudication. Contending that the Qurʾan clearly would support ʿAli's claim, since he was proclaimed by many groups as the caliph, they subsequently adopted the famous motto "No judgment but God's" and used a Qurʾanic verse to support their position.[28]

Believing that Muʿawiya had transgressed and should be fought, the Khawarij asked ʿAli and his army to repent and go back to God's judgment. What was right could not be negotiated, they said; people had no right to change God's judgment, but had to implement it. Muʿawiya and his army were unbelievers, and their territories were subsequently a land of war (*dar al-harb*).[29]

Al-Khawarij portrayed ʿAli as deviating from true religion: by accepting human judgment, he renounced his status as the legitimate caliph. He had to repent by giving up human judgment and by fighting Muʿawiya, since human judgment, in their opinion, negated the validity of the Qur'an.[30] 'Ali was originally elected because of his personal qualities and not because of his relationship to the Prophet. They rejected the idea of blind obedience to the ruler; in fact, they revolted against all tribal structures and favoritism and demanded the pure application of the Qur'an.[31] Portraying themselves as the true personification of the Qur'anic spirit, and even calling themselves The Muslims, they maintained that those who did not take the Qur'an literally were unbelievers, and they upheld the notions of repentance from arbitration, martyrdom, and assassination.[32] Al-Khawarij recognized only the caliphates of the first two rightly guided caliphs, Abu Bakr and 'Umar. As for 'Ali, they accepted his caliphate up to the time of *tahkim* (arbitration); Caliph 'Uthman was pictured as renegading on true religion, six years into his caliphate, by such breaches of religious law as collecting the Qur'an in only one codex and rejecting the validity of other codices and giving public money to his relatives. Furthermore, they branded as unbelievers all those who had fought in the Battles of al-Jamal and Siffin, the two judges, and Mu'awiya and all his army.

The majority of 'Ali's camp rejected the Kharijite claim. They argued that 'Ali was right in saying that the Khawarij had already accepted the doctrine of *tahkim*, whose validity stemmed from the Qur'an. And although the Qur'an was the highest judge, it did not readily speak for itself, but required a human interpreter. Since the Kharijite argument did not stand by itself and was self-contradictory, the judges spoke for the Qur'an.[33] However, 'Ali's acceptance of the principle of human judgment did not prevent his rejection of the outcome of that particular *tahkim*.

'Ali's supporters, who became known as the Shi'a, started developing out of this judgment the doctrine of the divine imamate. The imamate became embodied in 'Ali and his descendants through his wife Fatima; his imamate was thought of as being stipulated by Scripture and/or by designation of the previous imam, the Prophet. However, the fact of the matter is that when 'Uthman was assassinated, a group of the Prophet's Companions at Medina and other Muslims from many other Islamic cities chose 'Ali as the caliph.[34] 'Ali, as an imam, was portrayed as the rightful inheritor of both the religious and the secular authority of the Prophet—and therefore, like him, infallible and to be obeyed. Only textual authority, the Shi'ites argued, made the political leader the legitimate authority. 'Ali's acceptance of human judgment has been justified, by some Shi'ite thinkers, by the principle of *taqiyya* (concealment) or in the interests of the community's unity. If this is true, then 'Ali ibn Abi Talib put the existence of the state and public opinion before any claim of divine legitimacy. Later, his acceptance of the principle of human judgment was justified as a means of acquiring the necessary legitimacy from the community. The imam justified judgment as an acceptable method of resolving political conflicts that arose from divergent views within the community.[35]

When al-Khawarij faced ʿAli with their slogan "No judgment but God's," his answer was, "It is a true word, but ill-directed. Yes, there is no judgment but God's, but there is a need for a human [ruler] whether good or bad."[36] Any society required, then, human authority so it could organize its affairs and apply the divine law.

One of the most important functions of an Islamic government is to unify the community; ʿAli yielded to all decisions of the majority after the Prophet's death, especially when *shura* was conducted.[37] In one of ʿAli's speeches after the arbitration, he made it clear that his differences with Muʿawiya and his group were not religious but political in nature. While asking his troops to reject the outcome because it was only a trick, he nonetheless yielded to their demand to submit to human judgment.[38] Had his appointment been a divine order, he would not have compromised over it. Addressing al-Khawarij later on, ʿAli rejected their demand for repentance, and then fought and defeated and dispersed them. More important, ʿAli did not proclaim himself caliph, but only claimed that some Companions and the *shura* council in Medina swore allegiance to him after ʿUthman's death.[39]

Although believing himself to be the rightly chosen caliph at that time, ʿAli thought that yielding to human judgment through arbitration might lead to his acknowledgment as the legitimate caliph by the different Islamic factions and, consequently, derive public legitimacy. And although he tried to convince his troops that the call to judge the Qurʾan was a charade, he nonetheless accepted the principle of human judgment and later argued for it against the views of al-Khawarij. Not only did he submit to human judgment, he even appointed as judge Abu Musa al-Ashʿari, upon the unwelcome but forceful suggestion of his troops.[40] ʿAli considered the result of arbitration to be false, because of the trick played by Ibn al-ʿAs. When his supporters started being divided on whether to accept human arbitration, he resolutely fought al-Khawarij, who rejected it in principle and insisted on the literal interpretation of divine judgment. Ultimately ʿAli was assassinated by a Kharijite group that also tried but failed to assassinate Muʿawiya and ʿAmr ibn al-ʿAs.[41]

However, the majority of Muslims, later known as the Sunnites, accepted the principle of judgment as well as the outcome of ʿAli's and Muʿawiya's agreement. Although that agreement should have led to the discrediting of both as rulers, 'Amr ibn al-'As upheld Mu'awiya's claim, since the written agreement acknowledged Mu'awiya's right to avenge 'Uthman's death as well as his possession of other qualifications for the caliphate, such as his Companionship with the Prophet.[42] Mu'awiya and his supporters accepted the principle of human judgment as well as its result—the legitimization of Mu'awiya's positions. Writing to Abu Musa about his view of judgment, he declared: "Intention does not count in agreements; what is right is what has been recognized publicly. If the two judges ruled against 'Ali and in my favor, then 'Ali has lost his claim."[43]

For the most part, Muslim *fuqaha'* (jurists) accepted Mu'awiya's caliphate and his dynasty in their attempt, again, to solidify the community. The great jurists of Medina such as 'Abd Allah ibn Abbas, Muhammad ibn al-Hanafiyya, 'Abd Allah ibn 'Umar, and Sa'id ibn al-Musayyab swore allegiance to the Umayyads. So too did the jurists of Iraq and Syria. The jurists did not legitimize revolting against the Umayyads, even after the death of Mu'awiya and the institution of his son Yazid. After a few decades, however, the Umayyad dynasty became a target of the jurists because of its tyranny, injustice, breaking of Islamic laws, and even unbelief.[44] Thus the jurists supported the Umayyad caliphate insofar as it upheld divine law and united the community, but turned against it when it no longer served the precepts of divine law and the spirit of the community.

More important, Mu'awiya, the founder of the Umayyad dynasty, was considered to have transformed the caliphate into an absolute and hereditary government. While he has been praised for uniting the Muslim community by ending the wars that raged among the factions, he has been criticized as well by many thinkers for changing the foundations of political rule in Islam. Mu'awiya in fact started a new model of political rule that continued, more or less, through the centuries up to modern times. His victory over 'Ali represented the victory of the tribal structure over the religious foundation laid down by the Prophet and his first successors. As the head of his tribe, Mu'awiya maintained its privileges over religious orientations. Put differently, he derived his legitimacy not from *shura* and *ijma'* but from restructuring the tribal organization, which he ruled like a tribal chief. While his tribe became dominant in running state affairs and enjoyed state privileges, the people were generally marginalized in political terms. The leadership of the state was given to people the caliph trusted rather than to those with qualifications and religious stature.

Mu'awiya's thinking about political rule can best be glimpsed in a speech he delivered when entering Medina during the first year of his rule.

He said, "I know that my rule is not popular among you, but is forced on you by the sword. I wanted my rule to be like those of both Abu Bakr and ʿUmar, but you refused. And while I would even accept similar allegiance to that of ʿUthman, you again refused. If you do not find me the best among you, accept the good that comes from me. If I do not deliver all of your rights, accept the rights that I give you. I do not care about my criticism. However, I warn you against any unrest."[45]

The theological school, Al-Muʿtazila, on becoming an opposition movement, did not merely invoke divine rule to discredit Muʿawiya, it developed a whole religious ideology against the Umayyads' rule. First it rejected Muʿawiya's claim that he was elected by *shura*. Then al-Jahiz declared that Muʿawiya had usurped political authority by not consulting the Muslims and by forcing his rule on the community. Arguing that the Umayyads committed a sin in turning consultative rule into a kingly one, al-Jahiz even accused Muʿawiya of unbelief. Furthermore, al-Qadi ʿAbd al-Jabbar, one of the main leaders of the Muʿtazili movement, characterized Muʿawiya as an illegitimate leader because his rule was not popularly approved by an *ijmaʿ*. And while al-Muʿtazila called for equality, the Umayyads enslaved a large number of non-Arab Muslims and even branded the necks of the enslaved. Because of these and other actions, the Umayyads were delegitimized, a situation that aided in the spread of discontent and, ultimately, their downfall.[46]

On the other hand, while Muʿawiya broke with the previous model of political rule that depended on *shura* and *ijmaʿ* by justifying the rule of political expediency, he also provided a new discourse on the nature of political power. While he wanted the people of Medina to approve his rule, he de-emphasized the need for the community's participation in running state affairs and instead directed diverse social segments to look for the benefits that could be derived from being obedient to him. Thus he would, for instance, allow freedom of speech only if it did not lead to an uprising against the state. Put differently, while Muʿawiya allowed political dissent and pluralistic attitudes toward the state, he sternly cautioned and harshly reacted against any revolutionary manifestation. At the same time, he bought various groups by providing handsome amounts of money on condition that they not take arms against him. In effect he was resorting to pre-Islamic customs by dispensing money in order to give people, especially the opposition, a stake in the economy—or the booty.

Meanwhile, a religious ideology of opposition was developed. While the main opposition to Muʿawiya came from those who viewed themselves first and foremost as Arabs—ʿAli's supporters and al-Khawarij—

they looked to religion as the highest source of ideology. Thus, while the state became tribally structured and ruled, the opposition reverted to religious mottoes in order to justify its actions. Put differently, while the power of the state rested on domination, the opposition forces sought justification in the doctrines of popular consensus and communal consultation, not age-old tribal ties. Other groups, like the Qurra' (Qur'an readers), withdrew from the political scene. This ushered in a new civil structure, the *'ulama'* (scholars), who held themselves remote from the government, and marked the beginning of the process of differentiation between the political and the intellectual elite.[47]

At a more substantive level, Mu'awiya's political acts were paralleled by the production of religious doctrines. For instance, it was when Mu'awiya wanted theological sanction for his political rule that the doctrine of predestination, known later as *al-jabriyya,* was developed. Simplistically, it runs like this: If God did not want Mu'awiya's tribe to triumph, then it would not have done so. And as it was ruling the state, God had predestined it to rule also over the community. Put differently, Mu'awiya was not content to claim that he had assumed the caliphate by force and cunning; he needed to endow his actions with religious connotations. While the rise and fall of dynasties resulted in fact from political competition between tribes and subtribes and peoples, state legitimacy was justified by religious doctrines. Thus, by a realistic understanding of the nature of power, supplemented by a theological invention of divine assignment and predestination, Mu'awiya was capable of leading his tribe to political success. For example, in a speech to the people of Kufa in one of the battles, he says: "People of Kufa. Do you think I am fighting you because [you left off] praying, almsgiving, and pilgrimage? I know that you pray, give alms, and go on pilgrimage. I am fighting you only to rule you, and God has given me this [rule] though you dislike it."[48] On another occasion, when he forced the people to swear allegiance to his son Yazid, he said the caliphate "is a matter of predestination, and people have no choice."[49]

The term "God's caliph" seems to be an Umayyad political reference to the Prophet's successor. Mu'awiya not only used the term but acted as such. While the caliphate was originally seen as the post that ran the political and economic affairs of the community, the Umayyads took a view rather closer to the Western theory of the divine right of kings. No longer did government stem from free, real, and popular political participation. The exercise of the divine right of the caliphate preceded the theory that would be developed to justify the status quo, or the usurpation of the community's role. It was already in full evidence when Mu'awiya assembled the notables in order to obtain the oath of allegiance from the people to his son. Mu'awiya's man al-Mughira ibn Shu'ba pointed to Mu'awiya, saying that this was the prince of the believers. Next, pointing to Yazid, Ibn Shu'ba said that if Mu'awiya died, this Yazid was his successor. Then Ibn Shu'ba raised his sword, saying that the person who refused the *bay'a* would get this—meaning death by the sword.

Thus, while the Muslims theoretically still enjoyed the right to choose the caliph—or else Mu'awiya would not have assembled the notables to approve the nomination of Yazid—from then on it was forced by the political or military power of the time. Most of the Umayyad caliphs ruled like kings and kept only the appearance of religiosity and lip service to the *shari'a*. Ibn Khaldun wrote that the Umayyad caliphate was turned into pure kingship, similar to the empires of the Persians in the East. Changes in motives were obvious: the religious motives became tribally sectarian and imposed by force. The true meaning of the caliphate disappeared, and nothing of it was left except its name.[50]

Evidence was ample that the caliphate had degenerated into a naked exercise of power. When the community of Medina withdrew its oath of allegiance from Yazid ibn Mu'awiya, Yazid sent an army to fight the community and triumphed in the famous Battle of al-Harra'. Then he ordered his commanders to treat Medina for three days as they would treat a conquered foreign city. It is alleged that during the three-day period about 4,500 individuals were killed, and the rest of the people were enslaved and forced to reswear the oath of allegiance. Those who refused were put to death. This was Quraysh's tribal revenge for the triumph of the people of Medina over the Umayyads in Mecca during the Prophet's lifetime.

Further evidence was the view of 'Umar ibn 'Abd al-Aziz—considered the fifth rightly guided caliph but actually the eighth Umayyad caliph—that the injustice of al-Hajjaj ibn Yusuf al-Thaqafi, one of Caliph 'Abd al-Malik's aides, equaled all of the injustice committed by all nations. Indeed, when Sulayman ibn 'Abd al-Malak assumed the caliphate, 30,000 people were let out of jails.[51]

During the Umayyad and 'Abbasid periods, public opinion and referral to the people's judgment still played a role, but less important, since the state then tried to institutionalize doctrines of the *shari'a* like arbitration and justice in specific offices such as controller (*muhtasib*) and judge, respectively. The office of judge was politicized, taken away from the people and given to the ruler and his lieutenants with no new fixed rules. In addition, because many non-Arab races converted to Islam during the

Umayyad period, they brought along with them new traditions and doctrines on authority and law, such as Roman law in Damascus, Beirut, and Egypt. However, the jurists attempted to adopt new doctrines and institutions such as the appeals court (*wilayat al-mazalim*) and adapt them to existing Islamic doctrines and principles.

The Collapse of *Shura* and the Rise of Authoritarianism

Islamic jurisprudence has provided certain rules that regulate political life on behalf of the community, which has the right to supervise the actions of the ruler. While Muslims in general have traditionally accepted rule for life rather than a fixed number of years, there is no guarantee or religious stipulation that the ruler should stay in power until the end of his life or without the people's consent. The silence of law on this matter gives the people the right to decide. The ruler is, like any other Muslim, subject to law and court decisions. He has been seen theoretically not as above the law but as subordinate to it, although in practice he has shown an opposite tendency, manifested in many rulers' exploitation of the law to their own benefit. Still, at a conceptual level, the law was the supreme authority, the nation the supreme power, and the ruler the supreme executive. The ruler had, however, great leeway on matters that were not covered by the law—which in fact included a wide range of activities and important issues. For instance, the ruler could set forth new juridical rules at will, as there was no provision for legitimate opposition.[52] The jurists deemed that a basic function of the head of state was to issue legal pronouncements and enact the law.

Because the majority of jurists have agreed that a general contract is indispensible for legitimacy, the rule of any individual who forces himself on the Muslims is theoretically illegitimate and should be ended. Many jurists, however, have been reluctant to oppose such a ruler out of fear of civil strife and bloodshed. In the absence of such fear, it is the duty of Muslims to rid themselves of the ruler and install a legitimate one. Seizure of power is illegitimate, though tolerated at times for the supposed interest of the community.[53]

Islamic jurisprudence postulates terminating the contract with the ruler for many reasons. The most straightforward is when the ruler is incapacitated and is unable to perform his duties or, simply, does not want the post anymore. Here it is very easy to end the contract, since it depends on agreement between the ruler and the ruled. The people can nonetheless insist on continued rulership if its termination leads to social and political unrest. A more acute reason for terminating the contract is when the ruler renegades from Islam, for rulership entails the application of Islamic law, and a non-Muslim does not morally have to apply the Islamic law. Also, any injury that leads to the ruler's inability to perform his duties is sufficient grounds for dismissal. Likewise, if he becomes permanently mentally incapacitated or becomes a hostage with no hope of recovery, he should be removed. Thus the ruler's freedom is made a condition for the continuation of rulership. Furthermore, if the ruler becomes permanently impious, he should be removed. More important, if the ruler becomes unjust or indecisive, he should be given some time to change his conduct; if he does not, then he must be removed. Finally, and with the passage of time, some argued that a successful coup is sufficient grounds for the old ruler's losing legitimacy, especially if there is fear that opposing the new ruler might lead to unrest.[54]

There are three main legitimate methods that jurists have elaborated upon as means for removing the ruler. The first, favored by the Zaydis, the Mu'tazilites, and a few Sunnites, is armed revolt, especially when the ruler renounces Islam or rules arbitrarily. However, most Sunnites have rejected this method because it brings about more harm than good. Another method is his removal by *ahl al-hal wa al-'aqd,* who installed or nominated him in the first place, because they are more capable of judging the ruler's actions. Yet a better legal way could be found in *diwan al-mazalim* (Appeals Court), which could decide upon both the ruler's personal qualities and the application and violation of the law.[55]

There is nothing in the history or theories of Islam that precludes the development of a liberal democratic form of government. The totality of jurisprudence and, even, creed testifies to the elasticity of human thought and the possibility for change along free and democratic lines if the proper context is available. In fact, the decisions in seminal cases involving the treatment of those who stopped paying alms after the Prophet's death, the collection of the Qur'an, the division of war booty and rewards, issues of inheritance and marriage, and political legislation were reached in that fashion.[56]

The power of the community at large is also apparent when one studies the issues that arose over the collecting and interpreting of the divine text, the Qur'an. When the Prophet was alive, no one contested his religious authority in terms of interpreting the text. His death made the Muslims face the problems that were brought about by the existence of many authorized versions (codices) of the text. The Prophet originally settled such problems by asking the different parties to read their versions of the

Qur'an; he would then sanction or deny the validity of the readings. One day 'Umar ibn al-Khattab, who later became the second rightly guided caliph, disputed the reading of another Muslim, Hisham Hakim, and forced him to appear before the Prophet for judgment. The Prophet asked 'Umar and Hisham to read their versions, then sanctioned both, commenting, "This Qur'an has been revealed in seven readings, so read whichever is easier."[57]

When the community lost its ruler and started expanding its state over vast territories that included many non-Arab races that converted to Islam, the different regions read the Qur'an differently. This situation led to friction and disputes among Muslims, even including charges of unbelief and heresy. This was why most of the Prophet's Companions (al-Sahaba) agreed to prohibit reading in six of the seven readings that the Prophet himself had authorized. When the Companions differed on collecting and copying the Qur'an, the dialect of Quraysh was used as the standard reference, and the authorized readings became those that conform to the letter of that Qur'an. This was done during the caliphate of 'Uthman, and that version—the version used today—is called the 'Uthmani Codex (Mushaf 'Uthman). The Prophet's Companions, at the behest of Caliph 'Uthman, thus restricted the codices that can be used in reading the Qur'an, although the Prophet authorized seven codices.[58]

What this indicates is the *umma*'s empowerment to adjust, judge, or even restructure many of those things that the Prophet had settled. The argument that was used to authorize this change was that the community was about to split, and its unity was threatened, as different groups started claiming exclusive authenticity for their reading and accusing the others of absolute unbelief (*kufr*). This led the Prophet's Companions to initiate a process of consultation of the community in order to unify its religious and linguistic texts and, consequently, its political symbol. However, their decision became binding only after a consensus was supposedly reached. Thus the community in general acquired the power to judge and the power to put forth formative principles—the legitimate codex of the Qur'an, the legitimate exercise of *shura*, and the mandatory nature of *ijma*'.[59] However, all of this is based on the power that was thought to belong to the community, and not to the elite who started the process.

It was also under the Umayyads that the political and social distinction between Arabs and non-Arabs took place. The Umayyads based their rule on Arab tribes, especially their own, and made them the cornerstone of the administration. In disregard of Qur'anic precepts that exhorted the equal treatment of all races, the Umayyads favored the Arabs at all economic, political, and social levels. This favoritism extended to all regions and jobs; a time came when non-Arabs were wholly excluded from the posts of judge and imam of prayers.[60] For this reason many types of movements arose against the rule of the Umayyads, and there were many revolts against their rule.

Since the main grievances against the Umayyads' misrule were presented under the broad charge of neglecting and moving away from Islamic law, the 'Abbasids centered their claim for legitimacy on returning to the rule of Islamic law. In a speech to the community after receiving the oath of allegiance, the first 'Abbasid caliph, Abu al-'Abbas al-Saffah, assured them: "You have the *dhimma* of God, and His Prophet, and of the 'Abbasids. We will rule according to what God revealed and apply the Divine Book and follow privately and publicly the example of the Prophet. This rule is in us until we hand it to Jesus, son of Mary." Subsequently, however, al-Saffah—literally, the butcher—ruled according to his idiosyncrasies and his passion for revenge. The 'Abbasids dug up the graves of the Umayyad caliphs and pursued the Umayyads all over the empire. Some Umayyads fled to Spain and established the Umayyad caliphate there, and the 'Abbasids contacted the Franks in an effort to abolish it.

As is obvious from this speech and from their history, the 'Abbasids followed in the Umayyads' footsteps by treating their caliphate as predestined and by consolidating religious and political authority. The main difference was that the 'Abbasids did not depend on the Arabs, who were suspect in their loyalties, but replaced them with the Persians, who, along with the Turks later, became the center of power. Thus the caliphate was reduced to a symbol of state unity. Later the Tatars, who invaded the capital of the caliphate, ended the 'Abbasid rule. However, a new branch of the 'Abbasid caliphate was set up by the Mamluks in Cairo and lasted until the Ottomans occupied Egypt in 1517. Most of the 'Abbasid period witnessed revolutions of all types, including those of the Khawarij, the Zinj, and the Shi'a, against the 'Abbasid way of running the state.[61]

The Mu'tazila, for instance, objected to the 'Abbasid rule in many ways. First, they stood against racial discrimination and against the introduction of Persian political and philosophical elitist traditions. Also, they opposed the 'Abbasids' policies in suppressing all manifestations of freedom until the time of Caliph Harun al-Rashid who turned against the Persians in general and the Barmicides in particular. Many of the Mu'tazila were persecuted and imprisoned, and some even suffered because of their theological views.

A major issue was the legitimacy of a ruler when there was a more qualified person for the post. While the Mu'tazila themselves split into two camps over this issue, they theoretically maintained the illegitimacy of the 'Abbasid rule. Under Caliph al-Mutawakkil, they were denied such civil rights as being allowed to testify in courts. Their doctrines, like the justice of God and the free choice of man, were later officially outlawed, and the Mu'tazila were prohibited from private and public teaching.[62]

While the second 'Abbasid period witnessed some attempts to revive the caliphate, many minor states were ultimately set up within the Islamic empire, and the notion of popular sovereignty was further weakened. An added cause of the disintegration of the 'Abbasids was their interference in the administration of justice by forcing judges to yield to political and personal interests at the expense of the general public. This situation led many jurists to refuse official judiciary posts. Moreover, interest in reasoning or *ijtihad*, which was nongovernmental in nature, was fading away. Instead, specific books of the Prophetic Traditions, or *Hadith*, were circulated as the authoritative ones, while the main legal schools took solid positions that made jurists opt for following one legal school or another. All of this, in addition to political weakness and divisions and the beginning of the Crusades, would finally give the upper hand to authoritarianism and traditionalism and reduce the margins of free public space and weaken the original powers of society.[63]

Thus it was more under the 'Abbasids than the Umayyads that the notion of the caliph as God's *sultan* (power) and shadow on earth was philosophically and politically entertained. Another factor was the impact of Persian political thinking on the development of the caliphate and political rule. A new Persian elite spread a new genre of writing like Ibn al-Muqaffa''s *Al-Adab al-Kabir* that mirrored philosophically and politically what the caliph wanted. Now, in this sultanic literature, the sultan's power was derived from the Divine Will and was no longer subject to the community, not even nominally, as it had been under the Umayyads. The 'Abbasid caliph acted on God's behalf, whereas the Umayyad, while destined to be caliph, had still sought a nominal *bay'a*. Furthermore, the caliph was not a leader of the elite, the tribe, or the people anymore, he was above all. While the Umayyads depended on the tribes for their legitimacy and popular base, the 'Abbasids attempted to destroy the tribal structure and to replace it with military professionals who, of course, had neither the right to participate politically nor the will to question the wisdom of public policies. People had simply to obey. In this manner the 'Abbasid caliphs, especially in the latter period, gradually distanced themselves from their original bases of support and became dependent on a military that ultimately placed its own survival and profit ahead of the caliphate's needs. As for the people, it turned out that what was required of them was nothing less than total obedience to the ruler in all matters, except those that might constitute an obvious violation of well-established religious doctrines and rituals. Otherwise, the sultans and the military enjoyed a free hand in society, politics, the economy—indeed, in all arenas.[64]

In one of his sermons, the 'Abbasid caliph al-Mansur told the believers: "O people. I am God's authority on His earth; I lead you with His guidance, direction, and support. I am the guardian of His money, I spend it as He pleases and wills. I distribute it with His permission. God has made me a lock over His money." Compare this with a sermon given by the second rightly guided caliph, 'Umar. He says: "Study the Qur'an and work according to it. . . . No creature has a right to be obeyed in committing a sin against God. I have made myself a custodian of your money, [like] the custodian who runs the money of the orphan. If I have my own money, I will not touch [yours]. If I do not have money, I will take only what I need [to live]."[65]

Even great jurists yielded to political authority and went along with many of the new doctrines introduced into politics because they believed that the caliphate was a necessity in order to preserve the unity of the Muslims and to preempt civil wars within the community. Al-Mawardi in his *Al-Ahkam al-Sultaniyya* and al-Ghazali in his *Fada'ih al-Batiniyya* reflected the need for a new political jurisprudence (*al-fiqh al-siyasi*) either to adjust to the harsh realities of the time or to justify them. The lowest level of political thought was reached when any usurpation of power was accepted and justified by the need to maintain the unity of Muslims. By then, freedom and justice and knowledge as well as the *bay'a, ijma'*, and *shura*—the primary underpinnings of Islamic ideology—were dropped as the necessary conditions for legitimate Islamic rule. Simply, the new philosophy of right became dependent on might.[66]

Further weakening of the community's function occurred under the Fatimids, who contested the 'Abbasid caliphate and succeeded in establishing their rule in North Africa and Egypt. The Shi'ite Fatimid caliphate, like the Umayyad and the 'Abbasid, was based on hereditary rule, and oaths of allegiance were usually exacted after the accession of caliphs. The Fatimids went a step further and claimed divinity for their caliphs. Al-Hakim bi Amri Allah claimed that he was the embodiment of the Divine, and his followers used to kneel before him on the roads. The Fatimid period was full of unrest and upheaval. Like the 'Abbasids, the Fatimids fell under the sway of their non-Arab ministers and advisors as well as

Persian imperial customs. On the religious level, the Isma'ilis believed in the double meaning of the Qur'an, condemned the first three rightly guided caliphs and other Companions, and forced their Egyptian employees to adopt the Isma'ili Fatimid creed and their judges to rule only by the Isma'ili legal school. They even prevented the Sunnites from applying the rulings of their legal schools and prohibited some religious practices.[67] From the point of view of the majority of Muslims, the Isma'ilis went beyond any possible rational extension of the meanings of religious doctrines, and their counterforce was not any state but only the community, specifically the civil group of scholars, the *'ulama'*.

The imperial tradition was the more successful in imposing its views and conduct. Both the Umayyad and the 'Abbasid rulers called themselves the caliphs of God (God's successors) and continued to obtain the oath of allegiance for their sons by force. The situation further deteriorated when the caliphate became weak and the sultanate was invested with the real power. In this period, the Muslims looked to the caliphate as the symbol of Islam, while the sultan became the political leader. The sultan would appoint the caliph; the military forces and their leaders would appoint the sultan. Most of the time, the people had to swear the oath of allegiance without even knowing to whom they were swearing it. This sultanic tradition ruled over the Muslim world for many centuries. While the Muslims did not really legitimize it, they coexisted with this tradition because it provided the minimum requirements for a stable life: it allowed the flourishing of the institutions of civil society like *al-awqaf* (endowment), schools, professional groups, and Sufi orders as well as other organizations such as the merchants and the scholars, which mitigated the arbitrariness of the political power of the sultanic state.

The reasoning used by the sultanic state to justify its rule, whether under the Buwayhids, the Seljuks, or even the Ottomans, was the defense of the community against external enemies. During the rule of the sultanic state a major shift took place. Politics was separated from Islamic law, which moved practical politics wholly outside the domain of the law and into the domain of internal and external power struggles. Political power now became restricted to sheer force. In the last days of Buwayhid rule, a new kind of literature appeared that justified the seizure of power and dividing the community into distinct groups: the elite and the public, the military and the intellectual.[68]

Nonetheless, throughout the rules of successive dynasties, the historical legitimacy of the community's formative function was reserved by the *'ulama'*, the civil body of scholars that was supposed, in theory at least, to direct the action of the state. While Islamic thought does not generally sanction the existence of a formal clergy, one of the distinguished social groups that represented communal power was the *'ulama'*. Its main preoccupation was not the preservation of a particular government but upholding law and order to allow people to exercise their rights and duties as postulated by the *shari'a*. Since Prophet Muhammad had left his followers without any specific theory relating to politics and society, legislation was not then a state function, but was performed by the *'ulama'* in a civil capacity.

Again, generating legal opinions to resolve new or controversial issues was not a state function, but was the domain of scholarly circles of civil society that became organized into powerful and popular legal schools and doctrinal trends. And because their legitimacy was grounded in the community and not in formal state institutions, their influence was moral and, therefore, was usually beyond the coercive power of the state. Insofar as they expressed only scholarly opinions, they basically depended on the acceptance of other segments of the community, and not on state approval per se, although at times different governments adopted one legal school or another. Of course, the survival, influence, and power of any school of thought or jurisprudence depended on the number of people who would follow it. In principle, the state did not have any authority over the opinions that were expressed, but could debate unaccepted opinions within scholarly circles. Even when a ruler expressed his opinions on certain legal matters, he supposedly did so in his capacity as a scholar and not as the ruler. For instance, when Caliph al-Ma'mun attempted to force the opinions of the Mu'tazilites, specifically the notion of the createdness of the Qur'an, on other schools and the community, the majority of the scholars solidly opposed him. Muslim societies looked on themselves as theoretically free from the authority of the state and even at liberty to legislate for themselves within the boundaries of the *shari'a*, although governments had repeatedly succeeded in encroaching on the public and private space and in enforcing their political will and ideologies against the interests of the community.[69]

The resistance that was displayed by the founders of legal schools to ideological, political, and religious pressures emanating from the state and its circles may show how religious scholars dealt with political authorities. Abu Hanifa, the founder of the Hanafi school who lived through the last period of the Umayyads and the beginning of the 'Abbasids, refused to accept the judgeship of Kufa and consequently was punished with one hundred lashes and jailed. Malik bin Anas, the founder of the Maliki school, received similar treatment because he cast doubts on the 'Abbasids' legitimacy. And the founder of the Hanbali school, Ahmad ibn Hanbal, for refusing to yield to the state's view of the createdness of the Qur'an, was flogged and imprisoned as well.[70]

It is obvious that the intolerance of the state was linked to its weakness. The weaker the state became, the more oppressive it was. While *ijtihad* was theoretically a public and private affair, and not a state prerogative, it became practically restricted and almost frozen. The development of state-educated secretaries also threatened the independent role of the religious scholars. Nonetheless, the scholars were able to hold their own against the tyranny of the state, and they remained a force whose demands had to be taken into consideration. Even when the state developed its judicial systems, it could not make them equivalent to the community's civil institutes of scholars. While the administration of state judicial systems was subject to the directives of the rulers, unofficial religious institutes and circles mainly developed legal thought, including political thought.[71]

The Construction of Modern Democratic *Shura*

The problematic (*al-ishkaliyya*) of heritage (*al-turath*) and modernity (*al-hadatha*) occupies a central space in contemporary Arabic-Islamic discourse. Studies that treated this problematic started with Husayn Murwwa's project and continued with Tayyib Tizini, Hasan Hanafi, Muhammad 'Abid al-Jabiri, and Muhammad Arkoun.[72] In this respect, 'Id considers that the West has kicked out the Arabs from history because of what it was capable of doing during its colonialist and imperialist stages. The West considered that the Arab civilization had reached senility, living either outside history or on its margin. Thus, the West's formation of a global culture is not seen to be affected by the Arab heritage.[73]

'Abd al-Malak contends that the confrontation of the Egyptian national movement with the West had two phases. The first was the phase of struggling against European domination and the reconstruction of the Egyptian national state (1798–1882); the second was the phase of struggling against the British occupation to gain independence and democracy (1822–1939). Both phases focused on the necessity of establishing a democratic nationalist revolution. This is the military historical perspective.[74]

From the intellectual perspective, the shock of cultural confrontation was transmitted by the first mission that Muhammad 'Ali Pasha sent to

France and was expressed in Rifʿat al-Tahtawi's book *Talkhis al-Ibriz fi Talkhis Bariz*, published in 1834. In this book al-Tahtawi lays the foundations for combining (*tawlif*) the French Revolution principles of liberty, equality, fraternity, in addition to the doctrine of *watan* (homeland), with Islam and its traditions. Al-Tahtawi started an intellectual trend that offered the Arab world the bases of a liberal renaissance. He was followed by leaders and thinkers like Adib Ishaq, Farah Antoun, Shibli al-Shumayyil, ʿAbd al-Rahman al-Kawakibi, ʿAbd Allah al-Nadim, Mustapha Kamil, and Salama Musa.[75] Also, Muslim reformers such as Jamal al-Din al-Afghani and Muhammad ʿAbdu were influenced by his thinking and the French Revolution. Followers of ʿAbdu such as Ahmad Lutfi al-Sayyid, Qasim Amin, Ahmad Fathi Zaghlul, and Saʿad Zaghlul were linked to liberal thinking in the Arab world, as were the grand shaykh of al-Azhar, Mustafa ʿAbd al-Raziq, and his brother, ʿAli ʿAbd al-Raziq, as well as Ahmad Amin and Khalid Muhammad Khalid.[76]

Pan-Islamism was able to promote both Islamic unity and national unity. Jamal al-Din al-Afghani called for not differentiating between people on the basis of ethnic identity—Arab or non-Arab—because religion is based on belief and not on tribalism or nationalism. However, the feudal system of the Ottoman Empire was based on exploitation, which disabled nationalist aspirations. The coming to power of Muhammad ʿAli in Egypt and Syria challenged the bases of feudalism and promised the development of other economic systems. This is why his attempt at unifying Egypt and Syria was aborted by the Ottoman Empire with the help of European powers.[77]

At the turn of the twentieth century, the policies of the Young Turks sharply focused attention on Arab concerns, which led to a rupture of relations between the Arabs and the Young Turks. After the collapse of King Faysal's rule in Syria in 1920, Arab nationalism spread widely. This nationalism was fed by world political developments ranging from World War I to the collapse of the Ottoman Empire, and by rising secular philosophies calling for separating religion from politics and restoring the importance of cultural and linguistic factors. Najib Azoury, Butrous al-Bustani, and Satiʿ al-Husari represent such secular philosophies.

Earlier, the Ottoman Empire had witnessed in the eighteenth century a real threat to its existence from external factors, such as the scientific revolution that turned Europe into an economic and political force. Many intellectuals saw a need for imitating European models in state building. However, nationalism originated in the middle of the nineteenth century when Arab sensibilities were provoked. Sulayman Musa tells us that the first Arab attempts, by the Egyptians under the leadership of Ibrahim Pasha and by the Wahhabis, failed in establishing an Arab state or uniting Arab land. Musa pinpoints the middle of the nineteenth century as the starting point of nationalist thinking, with Arab intellectuals in Syria forming secret literary associations that called for reform. Thinkers of this period included ʿAbd al-Rahman al-Kawakibi and Najib Azoury. After World War I, Sharif Husayn declared the birth of revolution in 1916. His followers in the Hijaz decided in 1926 to set up an Arab state with Husayn as its king.[78]

The history of the Arab world between the two world wars is the history of the Arab nationalist movement. While aiming at independence, this movement saw the solution in religious and political reform developed along European lines. The best representatives of this movement were Taha Husayn, Mansur Fahmi, and ʿAli ʿAbd al-Raziq in addition to Shibli al-Shumayyil, Salama Musa, and Farah Antoun. However, most Muslim thinkers believed that the rise of civilization in the West was derived from progress in science.[79] Science should itself be a prime concern, they felt, whereas the nationalist movement opted for ideology or the ideologization of science, as it did with religion and other disciplines.

Other thinkers find the defining moments in (1) the French invasion of Egypt (1798–1801), which brought Egypt into contact with modern Western civilization and its political doctrines, administrative systems, science, printing, and journalism; (2) the scientific mission that Muhammad ʿAli Pasha brought to Egypt along with French experts and technicians starting in 1820; (3) the great waves of missionary schools in the nineteenth century, such as ʿAyntoura in 1834, al-Jamiʿiyya al-Suriyya in 1847, the Protestant Syrian College in 1866, and the Jesuits in 1874, which led to the active spread of translations and modernization of Arabic—and thereby influenced the idea of Arab renaissance; (4) printing, which led to the propagation of great historical works and the translation of European books; and (5) the press, which published the political campaign for Arab unity. In Syria there was a great campaign for translation that was mostly restricted to religious books. Muhammad ʿAli, however, favored translating European books as an instrument of state modernization. The Europeans also founded literary and scientific associations, such as Jamʿiyyat al-Adab wa al-ʿUlum, set up in 1847 with the help of American missionaries, al-Jamʿiyya al-ʿIslamiyya al-Suriyya (1852), and Jamʿiyyat Shams al-Bir (1869), a branch of the American YMCA. In Egypt the literary and scientific associations al-Maʿhad al-Masri (1859) and al-Jamʿiyya al-Jughrafiyya al-Khiduawiyya (1875) were set up by the French. In this Arab intel-

lectual climate pervaded by admiration of Western civilization and acceptance of Arab backwardness, calls for an Arab renaissance focused on
reviving the Arab spirit and imitating the advanced European peoples.[80]

First, however, Jamal al-Din al-Afghani (1838–1897) and Muhammad
'Abdu (1849–1905) thought it necessary to identify the components and
elements of the Western civilization that the Muslim should adopt and
those Islamic religious components and elements that should be maintained. Therefore, they tried to distinguish between Islam as a religion and
as a civilization and determined that it was politics, and not Islam as such,
that had played a major role in Muslims' backwardness.[81]

While al-Afghani paved the way for an intellectual Muslim modernist
and reformist trend of great potential, it was displaced by the rise of a
nationalist trend that was inspired generally by liberal secular Western
thinking and particularly by the doctrines the French Revolution. Al-
Afghani and 'Abdu educated a whole generation of intellectuals, including
Lutfi al-Sayyid, Muhammad Husayn Haykal, Taha Husayn, and Ahmad
Amin, but this generation opted to tie its thinking to Western thought
and to cut it off from Islamic thought. This is why the Arab renaissance
remained superficial and did not penetrate basic social fabrics. The Arab
renaissance blindly and unconditionally adopted Western thought and
generalized its suitability to the Arab and Islamic world. This view of
Western thought paralyzed the possibility of developing the Islamic civilization from within and linked liberation movements of that time to the
very doctrines used to exercise and justify Western domination. Therefore,
Western domination and powers were replaced by their distorted images,
that is, authoritarian Arab domination and powers that raised, like Western powers, the slogans of freedom, development, science, and secularism.

Some scholars explain this problem by arguing that the doctrine of
progress adopted by the renaissance intellectuals was not the result of any
direct experience with European Enlightenment and its intellectuals but
from an acute awareness of the gap between the West and the East, most
particularly the Arab and Islamic world. Arab intellectuals were conditioned, too, by their reading of Ibn Khaldun's problematic of progress
manifested as urbanization and civilization. That trend of urbanization
and civilization is represented by Rif'at al-Tahtawi and Khair al-Din al-
Tunusi, while the trend of Enlightenment progress is best represented by
'Abd al-Rahman al-Kawakibi and Qasim Amin. Tahtawi's doctrine of
progress is linked to Shaykh Hasan al-'Attar, who called for change and
development through reviving knowledge and sciences. It was al-'Attar

who instructed al-Tahtawi to log everything that he might see or hear in France, which materialized in al-Tahtawi's *Talkhis al-Ibriz fi Talkhis Bariz*. However, this does not mean that the doctrine of progress is al-'Attar's but that he was the catalyst for deriving knowledge from other civilizations.[82]

The personality of Amir Shakib Arsalan, who lived through the failures and victories and the weakness of the Ottoman Empire as well as the renaissance, represents the trend of renaissance that confronted Western challenges. He devoted his writings to proving Islam's capacity to stage a revival and Arabism's ability to confront political invasions. The challenge posed to Islam and Arabism by the West had characterized Arab renaissance, which developed with regional and social fragmentation. Thus, Islamic reformism turned into a movement that linked political bankruptcy to religious bankruptcy. Arsalan launched an anti-Western campaign revolving around the West's claims of civility and progress. His famous book *Limadha Ta'akhar al-Muslimun, wa limadha Taqaddam Ghayruhum* is an example of such a revolt against both the Islamic world and the West, which led the French to confiscate his writings.[83]

Arsalan decides that the central cause of Arab backwardness is the Muslims' deficiency in developing the sciences; in this Arsalan is in agreement with al-Afghani, al-Tahtawi, and al-Tunusi. Islam is civil in nature. Its call for deep belief in a divine creed as a source of unity among mankind to fight ignorance and injustice was the motive for the rise and expansion of the first Arab and Muslim state. The subsequent backwardness and decline of Muslims resulted from losing such belief and, therefore, lacking knowledge and power.[84]

This renaissance reading of the Islamic heritage (*turath*) was aimed at adjusting to the modern age in pursuit of an Arab revival. However, the reading led Muslims not only to acknowledge the supremacy of Western thought but also to make it central in their reading of Islamic cultural heritage. Thus the discourses of Arab enlightenment and renaissance turned into attempts to forge such doctrines (*talfiq*) as nationalism, democracy, and socialism into selective components of Islamic heritage.

The discourses of Arab renaissance took root in societies that were fragmented after the collapse of the Ottoman Empire, and these discourses turned into radical discourses for struggle and independence. Since the culture of the renaissance arose during the weakness of the Islamic nation, and its discourses were the result of the intersection of Western and Islamic culture at the moment of the collapse of universal Islamic empires, the relationship between the West and the Islamic world turned into a question about the factors that led to that collapse. In the ensuing inquiry into failure and success, both questions and answers were distorted.

The concept of heritage was one of the problematics of the renaissance and the pivot of intellectual debates, both religious and secular. The discourse of the renaissance on Islamic heritage was a reading of the confrontation and clash with the West, and consequently the intellectual was under the same conditions of reading the Islamic heritage. The different readings of heritage were discourses over past, present, and future. Tizini views the renaissance as hybrid (*hajin*), Hasan Hanafi as alienated, and Muhammad 'Abd al-Jabiri as removed from realities. All these adjectives indicate the state of confrontation with the West and the fracturing of reading *al-turath*.

The discourses of the renaissance tried to distinguish between two methods, one divine and the other human. This was an attempt to elevate the Qur'anic text outside modern epistemological, social, and political frameworks. The ideologues of the renaissance thought that the reading of Islamic heritage from a liberal perspective would lead to the rise of a democratic national revolution under the umbrella of Islam itself. Thus, Islam was turned into conceptual justifications for democracy, social justice, and modernization.[85] Muhammad 'Abdu argued, for instance, that real modernization is identical to Islam. Under the impression that it was absorbing the dominant Western concepts, the Islamic heritage instead fell under the epistemological and political domination of Western thought during a period of imperialist and capitalist expansion.

Muhammad Arkoun classifies Muslim intellectuals in two groups: modernists who are open to Western culture and scientific socialism, and traditionalists who adhere to Islamic values. The consciousness of the Muslim intellectual is linked basically to the Qur'an and lives in a state of interpretation and development of his most dynamic and productive historical period, that is, within the medieval Islamic epistemological space. Seeking to reconcile his lived heritage with modernization, the intellectual faces all manner of tensions generated by his rupture from his cultural fundamentals and his proximity to the modern West. This proximity to the West creates a resisting ideology that distorts his ability to criticize the lived heritage. The difficulties that the Muslim intellectual faces are: first, the narrowness of his intellectual horizons and his fragile discovery of bourgeois Western culture, which leads to an imbalance in his consciousness; second, internal social and political crises resulting from the political wars of liberation; and third, the struggle against internal backwardness among imported ideological dangers.[86] According to Arkoun, Islamic consciousness is predicated on the experience of the Prophet's city-state of Medina as the myth of the formative age, and revolves around the issue of the caliphate and the imamate as reflected in the ideas of Ibn Hajar al-'Askalani and his predecessors. Thus the Muslim intellectuals did not deal with the issue of heritage in an analytical framework and did not try to reexamine the root fundamentals of religion or reinvent those fundamentals.[87]

Burhan Ghalyun, in his examination of the crisis of Arab culture, sees a different balance between the traditionalism of Islamic heritage and the imitation of the West. Islamic heritage, he says, prevents the Muslim community from getting swept up by every new fad.[88] This heritage limits the elite's ability to manipulate the public, who lack a culture of resistance but use their heritage as an empowering authority.

'Id disagrees, and argues that the according of such sacredness to Islamic heritage prevents enlightened activity or advanced ideas from penetrating the fabric of the nation to bring it into the modern age. The Muslim world regards any modernist experiment as an elitist authoritarian action to rob the community of its authority. For this reason 'Id rejects Ghalyun's view that secularism has become an instrument of social and political repression used by the elites.[89]

Still, the past cannot be abolished, either as history or as consciousness. It should be studied, absorbed, and then transcended in a process similar to what the West did with its Greek heritage. The Islamic heritage represents the accumulation of the nation's consciousness of itself; its analysis leads to a study of the rise of Islamic and Arab consciousness and, then, to a move to deconstruct it and reconstruct it from a modern cultural perspective. The modernist who rejects this heritage is doing no less than smashing this consciousness and linking consciousness with a liberal or Marxist West that has a different heritage. Similarly, however, the traditional thinker who looks on his heritage as a sacred text is effectively nullifying the cumulative experience of consciousness. The works of al-Ash'ari, al-Ghazali, Ibn Sina, and Ibn Khaldun are only moments of these intellectuals' consciousness and views of their ages, views limited by a specific time and place, with no absoluteness. An absolute denial of the importance of heritage or an absolute affirmation of its sacredness is, to an equally extreme degree, an expression of misunderstanding of the role of heritage in the construction of nationhood and knowledge. Either the sanctification or the rejection of heritage prevents the possibility of learning through absorption and the accumulation of knowledge necessary for science, society, and politics.

Rejection of Democracy

The Islamists split over the validity of their heritage and its relation to modernity and over whether heritage and modernity can be read through reinterpretations of divine texts. Democracy stood out as a good case for such an interpretation.

Iran's Muhammad Husayn Tabataba'i (1903–1981) was one of the leading Shi'ite Qur'anic commentators and philosophers. He studied religious and philosophical sciences at Najaf in Iraq, then returned to Tabriz in 1934 and, after World War II, gained prominence through his opposition to communist domination of Azerbaijan. Tabataba'i devoted his life to writing and teaching at Qum.

According to Tabataba'i, an Islamic theory of government must be separated from modern socialist and democratic theories because within the fixed essence of Islam, the ideological and religious part, is the divine nature of legislation. The majority's role is, therefore, not the decisive element in the legitimacy of a particular law or decision, though *shura* is not to be disregarded and should be used in political administration. The fixed essence of Islam is subject not to whim and desires but to social interest. In a devoutly Muslim community, the believers' social interest would be in accord with the fixed essence of Islam.[90]

Along the same lines, the constitution of the Islamic Republic of Iran stipulates, in its Second Article, the bases of the political system. They are: belief in the one and only God as well as His *hakimiyya* and law, belief in divine revelation and its sole authority in elaborating the law, belief in the day of judgment, belief in divine justice relating to the Creation and law, belief in the imamate and its continuous leadership and role in the revolution of Islam, and belief in human dignity and freedom.[91] These strict constitutional bases of the republic exclude non-Muslims from an ideological commitment to the state, even if they want one. Indeed, the constitution excludes from total adherence not only non-Islamic minorities but also non-Shi'ite Muslims who do not believe in the necessity of the imamate. Both the *hakimiyya* and the imamate doctrines automatically reduce the number of full citizens, threaten pluralism, and affect the political rights of non-Muslims and non-Shi'ites.

The constitution further vests authority and the imamate of the community in the just jurist, who does not need the approval of the majority. *Shura*, referendum, and election of the president and members of the *shura* council are to be the procedures of managing political life.[92] The constitution still divides authority among the three well-known institutions of the executive, the legislature, and the judiciary, but the jurist imam, whose judgments take precedence over all others, whether institutions or individuals, supervises them all.

'Ali bil Haj (1955–) is the vice president of Algeria's Islamic Salvation Front. He pursued his education in religion and the Arabic language at al-Zaytuna Mosque, then taught both subjects in Algeria. Bil Haj was exposed to many readings by political Islamist writers like Hasan al-Banna, Sayyid Qutb, and 'Abd al-Qadir 'Awda. He became involved with the Armed Islamic Group and enrolled in the Islamic Mission Organization. He was arrested during 1982–83 because of his activities in the Algerian Islamist movement and his contact with al-Haraka al-Islamiyya li al-Jaza'ir of Mustapha Buya'li. Bil Haj was a founder of the Islamic Salvation Front and was chosen vice president under 'Abbasi Madani. In August 1991 both were arrested and then sentenced in military court to twelve years in prison. Bil Haj was released in 1997.

Bil Haj makes an elaborate argument to the effect that *shura* is a political duty that Islam imposed in order to eliminate tyranny and that, therefore, all governments not chosen by their peoples are illegitimate and can be forcibly overthrown.[93] Obedience to the ruler, then, hinges on his following Islamic law, and the contract between ruler and ruled is nullified if the ruler does not follow the law, becomes unjust, or takes non-Muslims as allies and lieutenants. For Muslims to help such a ruler constitutes unbelief. Furthermore, a ruler loses legitimacy when he usurps the divine *hakimiyya* by legislating and by adjudicating philosophically, judicially, religiously, and politically according to non-Islamic authorities or ideologies.[94]

More important at the ideological level is Sayyid Qutb, the founder of radicalism. He built a fundamentalist system of thought based on human paganism and divine governance in the Arab world. Qutb himself was a major victim of radicalism and violence and was transformed under 'Abd al-Nasir's regime from extreme liberalism to utmost radicalism. His imprisonment and ferocious torture are abstracted into a radical political theology of violence and isolation.[95]

At the end of his liberal experiment and the beginning of his Islamist one, Qutb's first book adopted Islamism along with a political agenda as a way of life. *Al-'Adala al-Ijtima'iyya fi al-Islam* (Social justice in Islam), which appeared while he was in the United States, was far removed from radicalism and closer to al-Banna's moderate discourse. Qutb's stay in the United States, from 1948 to 1951, made him review his Westernized attitudes. The materialism, racism, and pro-Zionist feelings that he personally encountered in the United States seem to have brought on his alienation from Western culture and his return to the culture he was born into. Upon his return to Egypt after the death of Hasan al-Banna and the first ordeal of the Brotherhood in 1948, he joined the Brotherhood and became very active in its intellectual and publishing activities and wrote numerous books on "Islam as the solution." Up to that point, no radicalism or violence was involved. His priority was to frame a modern understanding of Islam and the solutions that Islam provides to the basic political, economic, social, and individual problems of Egypt and the Arab and Islamic worlds.[96]

In 1953 Qutb was appointed editor-in-chief of the weekly *Al-Ikhwan al-Muslimin,* which was banned in 1954 at the time of the Brotherhood's dissolution after its falling-out with the Free Officers' regime. In fact, the Brotherhood in general and Qutb in particular had been instrumental in paving the way for the the Officers' revolution of 1952. However, the Brotherhood refused to accept the Officers' absolute power and called for a referendum on what kind of constitution the people wanted. Furthermore, it supported General Najib against Colonel 'Abd al-Nasir. After major disagreements with 'Abd al-Nasir, the Brotherhood was accused of cooperating with the communists to overthrow the government. The movement was dissolved in 1954 and many Muslim Brothers were jailed, including Qutb. He was released that year but arrested again after the Manshiyya incident, in which an attempt was made on 'Abd al-Nasir's life. Qutb and others were accused of being affiliated with the Brotherhood's secret military section and Qutb was sentenced to fifteen years in prison. In 1955 he and thousands of the Muslim Brothers and their supporters were subjected to severe torture leaving psychic wounds unhealed to this day. He shifted to radical Islamism and exclusionism. His most important books—the gospels of radicalism, *Fi Zilal al-Qur'an, Ma'alim fi al-Tariq, Hadha al-Din, Al-Mustaqbal li Hadha al-Din,* and others—were written because of, and despite, the torture that he and others underwent year after year. Qutb was released in 1965, then arrested on charges of plotting to overthrow the government. He was executed in 1966.

During his isolation from the outside world, under daily pressures such as witnessing the slaughter of dozens of the Muslim Brothers in a jail hospital, Qutb could not but blame others. He blamed those who were free outside the jail but would not defend the unjustly imprisoned and ferociously tortured; the free people became for him accomplices in the crimes of the regime and therefore, like the regime, infidels.[97]

Qutb transformed his discourse into a rejectionist discourse wherein it was not the state and society that were repressing him, but rather he, as the leader of the believing vanguard, who was excluding individuals, societies, and states from true salvation. The whole world became a target of his condemnation and isolation. The state's vengeful oppression and intolerance of any sort of popular opposition was counterbalanced by his desperate spiritual, moral, social, and political exclusion and intolerance. This is a clear contextual and historical example of how the parameters of radical Islamism developed. From then on, from his cell, he started developing his radicalism.

For Qutb, universal divine laws as handed down in the Qur'an must be viewed as the bases for freedom and relationships of all sorts. Put differently, all people, Muslims and non-Muslims alike, must link their views of life with the Islamic worldview, and Muslim countries and non-Muslim countries must finally submit to the divine laws without exception. The state and civil institutions as well as individuals may codify legal articles only should the need arise. The reason Qutb gives for this is that *hakimiyya* or divine governance, the essential political component of *tawhid,* must be upheld at all times—when forming a virtuous and just society, and when providing personal and social freedom, and under all conditions, within or outside the confines of the prison. Freedom is perceived in a negative way; the people are free insofar as their choice of social and political systems does not violate divine governance and does not hinder religious life. The state is perceived as the agent for creating and maintaining morality, both individually and collectively. Because legislation is divine, individuals and societies and states cannot legitimately develop normative rights and duties, whether related to political freedom, pluralism, political parties, or even personal and social freedom.[98]

While ultimate sovereignty is reserved to God, Qutb argues, its human application is a popular right. State authority is not based on any divine text, but must be popularly sought. Only free popular consent makes social, political, and intellectual institutions legitimate. Adherence to Islamic law must be from a popular viewpoint, not an official interpretation, for it is the people who represent the divine will.[99] Qutb's view of jurisprudence as a practical discipline severs it from its golden past on a pedestal of theory and links it to contemporary needs. People are freed to reconstitute modern Islamic political theories and institutions. His rejection of the historical normative compendium of Islamic disciplines leads him to uphold the people's freedom to restructure their systems and lives.[100] Though this perspective postulates communal precedence over state control, the legitimacy of both is linked to the application of divine prescriptions. Again, according to Qutb, obedience to government is neither limitless nor timeless, because any violation of Qur'anic prescriptions nullifies its legitimacy; people should disobey and even revolt when necessary.

However, a theocracy cannot be a sound Islamic state because no elite may claim divine representation. A proper Islamic state is both communal and constitutional. The judiciary and the legislature as well as the executive can rule only through delegated powers by means of *shura,* the theoretical and practical doctrine central to government and politics. Any social agreement that is not contradictory to *shari'a* is Islamicly sound and can be included, though elitism is excluded and rejected in principle.[101] Qutb denies, then, the unique legitimacy claims of any specific system or form of government; for instance, he would include any form, whether republican or not, with consensual agreement as its base.[102]

From Qutb's point of view, the basis of freedom, the command to enjoin the good and forbid evil, must be extended to general communal interests such as unity, and political, social, or personal interests such as elitism and monopoly must be subordinated to it. Personal freedom tuned to communal interests and united in broad unitary ideological orientations is the source of social peace. A religiously good society cannot rise on ideologically and religiously conflictual bases, but requires goodwill, solidarity, security, peace, and equality.[103] Qutb's discourse so far gives the impression that even radical Islamism respects communal choices. While this may be partially true, it still excludes pluralism, free civil society, and multiparty systems—or, simply, liberal democracy.

The Power of Democracy

While Bil Haj rejected democracy, 'Abbasi Madani, following the lead of the Muslim Brotherhood, produced a political program for Jabhat al-Inqadh in Algeria calling for adherence to *shura* in order to avoid tyranny and to eradicate all forms of monopoly, whether political, social, or economic. The program calls also for pluralism, elections, and other elements of democracy in politics and social life to secure the community's salvation.[104]

Contemporary movements have been able to put forward such a program because the ideological and political discourse of the Muslim Brotherhood's founder and first supreme guide in Egypt, Hasan al-Banna (1906–1949), laid down the bases of inclusionary views on the theological and political doctrine of God's governance. While this doctrine has been invoked at times, both historically and presently, to exclude whatever is considered to be un-Islamic and, for some, even non-Islamic, al-Banna transformed it into a source of both legitimacy and compromise—a position shared by the majority of moderate Islamist political movements. Given the circumstances of Egyptian society during the first half of the twentieth century, and the relative freedom of Egyptians therein, a forcible seizure of power was not on the Brotherhood's agenda. Though interested in the Islamization of government, state, and society, al-Banna aimed essentially to be included in the existing political order and to compete with other political parties.

Founded in 1928, the Brotherhood within a few years had spread to many regions of Egypt and attained great power. Its growth, however, was largely accomplished through concealment from the government. In 1933 al-Banna, a teacher, was transferred to Cairo. He saw this as an opportunity to expand and strengthen the movement. He created special magazines for it, which circulated widely. The organization went beyond Egypt's border, reaching Sudan, Syria, Lebanon, and North Africa. Still, the Muslim Brothers did not attract the attention of the government because their activities were well hidden behind the veil of religion. During the Second World War, the movement doubled its efforts and won support from university students.

The state ultimately became aware of the Brotherhood's far-reaching political capabilities. Both al-Banna and his secretary-general were arrested, then later released. Al-Banna ran for election, but Premier al-Nahhas asked him to withdraw and instead allowed him to circulate his magazines and printed material under government sanction. The peaceful involvement of the Muslim Brotherhood in Egypt's political life is well documented. It was involved in the struggle of the Azhar during the 1920s and 1930s and sided as well with the king against the government. By 1945 the Muslim Brothers were directing all their efforts and activities against the government, and their interests and demands would reach a far greater number of people. They set up commercial companies, which yielded profits and won support from the working classes. They also set up camps for military training. The Muslim Brothers devoted themselves to stirring up the consciousness of the people, calling for jihad and for the complete independence of the country.

The Brotherhood built its headquarters with voluntary donations, after which it built a mosque and schools for boys and girls. In 1946 the government provided financial aid, free books, and stationery to the Brotherhood schools, with the Ministry of Education paying all their educational and administrative expenses. Al-Banna established as well holding companies for schools, and this became a success since most of the Brotherhood's membership was composed of middle-class professionals and businessmen. Only a year after the establishment of the Brotherhood in Cairo, it had fifty branches all over Egypt. Worried about the spread of Christian missionary schools in Egypt, the Brotherhood called on King Faruq to subject this activity to governmental supervision. But after a meeting with a Christian preacher, al-Banna wrote on the necessity of men of religion uniting against atheism. That same year, the Brotherhood decided to set up a press and publish a weekly, *Al-Ikhwan al-Muslimin*. In 1946, during the rule of al-Naqrashi Pasha, the Muslim Brothers called for a nation-wide jihad and published articles criticizing the government for persecuting and oppressing the movement.

With the Palestine question, the Muslim Brothers' active involvement intensified tensions between the movement and the government. In 1948 the Muslim Brothers participated in the battle of the Arab armies for the liberation of Palestine, thereby arming themselves and gaining valuable combat training. The Egyptian government feared this newly found power and conducted a series of seizures and arrests against the organization and all its branches. The Muslim Brothers' position grew weaker with the assassination of al-Naqrashi and the government's blame of the group as the murderers. The association was officially dissolved in 1948, and a year later al-Banna was assassinated.

An enduring strength of the Brotherhood has been its ability to mobilize the Egyptian masses. Al-Banna, for instance, included boy scouts in his organization. The scouts' pledge was essentially of a moral tune, not political and revolutionary but rather centered on faith, virtue, work, and the family. The Brotherhood had an active membership of half a million, another half million supporters, and, at the time of its dissolution, one thousand branches in Egypt. By 1951 the Muslim Brothers were picking up the pieces and slowly rebuilding all that had been lost. In October 1951 they made their presence felt by participating in the liberation movement against the British. They regained some of their political voice only when the government saw that they did not violate any laws. During the ʿAbd al-

Nasir period, the Muslim Brothers suffered another severe blow when they confronted 'Abd al-Nasir and were accused of an attempt on his life. The government once more dissolved the organization and imprisoned its leaders. In 1965 the detainees were released and began drawing up a plan to topple the government. The members of the Brotherhood were again put on trials and in jails. In the seventies President Sadat granted the Brotherhood permission to publish a monthly, *Al-Da'wa*, edited by 'Umar al-Tilmisani and aimed at the student body. In 1977, the year of its launch, student elections produced an Islamist victory. Sadat used the Brotherhood to lend legitimacy to his government, though the Brothers were still not allowed to form their own political party. They broke with him over his trip to Jerusalem in 1977 and the Camp David agreement. Their protest led to the imprisonment of hundreds in the Brotherhood and other radical groups. But the Muslim Brothers have not officially sanctioned and used violence to achieve any political or religious objective. In October 1981 a radical Islamist group, Islamic Jihad, assassinated President Sadat. Since 1984 the Brotherhood in Egypt and elsewhere, and similar movements like the Islamic Renaissance Movement in Tunisia and the Islamic Salvation Front in Algeria, have sought to be included in the political process and have been involved in setting up civil institutions. Because in Jordan the Muslim Brotherhood has functioned since the 1950s as a political party, some of its members have become well placed in the government and the parliament.[105]

While Islam contains basic legal substance, its denotations and connotations cannot be restricted to or derived from past historical conditions only. Al-Banna argues that, in dealing with modernity, Islam must present itself as a worldview, not only as a law. Both the law and the worldview must deal with the real world, not in abstract terms, but essentially in practical terms, and therefore must take into account other interpretations, political ideologies, and philosophies. Because Islam is both religion and society, both a mosque and a state, it must deal effectively with religion and the world by the inclusion of diverse substantive and methodological pluralistic interpretations, while maintaining the basic doctrines of religion.[106]

In his quest for recognition and inclusion of the Brotherhood in the state's hierarchy and administration, al-Banna turns the doctrine of *hakimiyya* basically into an organizing principle of government and a symbol of political Islam, all the while allowing inclusionary and pluralistic interpretative policies. Al-Banna's emphasis on the proper grounding of political ideology does not exclude individual and collective reformulation of Islamic social and political doctrines in accordance with modern society's needs, aspirations, and beliefs.[107]

Al-Banna transforms constitutional rule into *shura* by a subtle reinterpretation in a modern light and yet in a spirit that is not contradictory to the Qur'an. *Shura,* as the basic principle of government and of the exercise of power by society, becomes inclusionary by definition and empowers the people to set the course of their political actions and ideology. If the ultimate source of *shura*'s legitimacy is the people, their representation cannot be restricted to one party, which may represent only a fraction of them. Continuous ratification by the community is required because governance is a contract between the ruled and the ruler. Because the *shari'a* is viewed as a social norm, al-Banna frees its application from past specific methods and links its good practice to the maintenance of freedom and popular authority over the government, and the delineation of the authority of the executive, the legislature, and the judiciary. Western constitutional forms of government do not contradict Islam when grounded in both constitutionality of Islamic law and objectivity.[108]

Al-Banna's theoretical acceptance of pluralistic, democratic, and inclusionary interpretations plants the seeds for further acceptance by the Muslim Brotherhood of political pluralism and democracy, notwithstanding its link to *tawhid* and its political counterpart, unity. This acceptance may even extend to the existence of many states. Party politics and political systems, for al-Banna, can accommodate substantial differences in ideologies, policies, and programs. However, an Islamic state does exclude parties that contradict the oneness of God.[109] The illegitimacy of atheistic parties is not in al-Banna's view an infringement on freedom of expression or freedom of association insofar as the religious majority and the religious minority accept religion as the truth. Such parties would be outside the society's consensus and therefore a threat to its unity. If Islam is chosen as the basis of government and society, then its opposition becomes a matter of anarchy and opposition to society, not freedom. Still, this is not a negation of pluralism in Islam, since foreign ideas and systems of thought can be incorporated.[110] The state must reflect social agreement and provide a framework for resolving conflicts peacefully.[111]

As a minimum requirement for the government's legitimacy, it should present the *shari'a* as a social law that reflects people's views.[112] The catch is that its presentation as a social law requires its implementation by a representative body.[113] In order to get around the problem of the priority of Islamic law over government or vice versa, al-Banna specifies no particular method for the implementation of law. What is important is its application whether by a secular or a religious government. Al-Banna sees no inconsistency with Western-style constitutional rule because, in common with Islam, it maintains personal freedom, upholds *shura*, postulates people's authority over government, specifies rulers' responsibilities and accountability before their people, and delineates the responsibilities of the executive, the legislature, and the judiciary. For al-Banna, constitutional rule is thus harmonious with the *shari'a* while Marxism, for instance, stands contrary to it.[114]

On the theoretical level, al-Banna grounds constitutional rule in *shura* and finds it the most approximate method of government to the nature of Islamic politics. More important, al-Banna finds textual justification for the adoption of constitutional rule as *shura* by grounding its necessity in a Qur'anic text: ". . . and consult them in affairs [of moment]. Then, when thou hast taken a decision, put thy trust in God" (III:159). Such a derivation is possible for al-Banna because this Qur'anic revelation is interpreted as "the basic principle of rule of government and exercise of authority." The Qur'anic power is employed by al-Banna to highlight the community's power in making and unmaking political systems, governments, forms of government, and political behavior. It provides the community with further power vis-à-vis the state, which must act in conformity with people's ambitions and needs.

For al-Banna the Islamic government represents the central organ of an Islamic political system. It derives its legitimacy to exercise power from the people and its responsibility is twofold: religious and political, before both God and the community. It is morally and politically responsible for the people's unity and therefore must be responsive and defer to their preferences and wishes. The ruler's power over and responsibility before his people derives from the fact that Islam views the setting up of government as a social contract between the ruler and the ruled so that the interests of the latter are taken care of. The ruler's reward and punishment must hinge on the people's view. The nation enjoys moral supremacy over the ruler in matters of general and particular concern. Therefore, a legitimate ruler or government must always refer to consultation with the community and yield to its will. Political forms and shapes may change from time to time and from one locality to another, but the basic rules of Islam must always be adhered to.[115]

While al-Banna upholds people's power over the government, his view is not based on the philosophy of natural rights. Rather, it is developed in the light of such a philosophy and from textual references to the people's consultation and to the illegitimacy of unlimited political power. However, the whole concept of people's choice is Qur'anicly justified by a rein-terpretation of texts to conform to the democratic notion of popular governments. While the role of reason is not denied in political matters, it is employed more at the theoretical level to derive political rights and duties. The equality of men is enunciated by the Qur'an; that this means equal political rights and duties is however the rational derivation of that. Again, this means that no individual or group can claim privileged positions, whether political or religious. Al-Banna does not refer this issue again to human reason, but refers to Qur'anic texts for proof of the necessity of people's rule, though within divine *hakimiyya*.[116]

For al-Banna, the ruler is accountable not only to God but to the *umma* as well. By believing that the exercise of authority requires the continuous ratification and approval of the *umma*, governance is transformed into a straightforward contract between the ruled and the ruler, and politics is democratized. Thus al-Banna's democratization of *shura* is related to his ability to distinguish divine *hakimiyya* from human *hakimiyya*. The first can never be properly represented; consequently no individual or group or institution can claim to possess a specific mandate or a divine right to rule. However, the legitimacy of representing human *hakimiyya* must be sought in the fulfillment of and adherence to Qur'anic instructions—or the Islamic constitution—and in observing the proper conditions for carrying out *shura*. This theoretical principle, the fulfillment of the Islamic constitution, defines to the *umma* at large the kind of *nizam* or system to be upheld; the practical principle, the fulfillment of the conditions of *shura*, makes the *umma* the sole legitimate authority, or *sulta*, for government. For al-Banna converts the doctrine of enjoining the good and forbidding evil from an ethical concept into a formulation of public, legal, and political right to watch over the government.[117]

Al-Banna's view of the need for the *umma* to control the government's exercise of power becomes for the Islamists a basic component in the making of righteous politics and the fulfillment of the divine *manhaj* (method). Only through such popular power could Islam be reinserted into politics and could a method of control be made effective and subject to change from time to time. However, any Islamic system must always be characterized by adopting Islamic rules of *shura* and equality and by striking a balance between the ruler and the ruled and between the text and the people. Without proper handling of political matters and without sound social consciousness, textual authorities may not lead to the Islamic revival that the community is seeking.[118]

Meanwhile al-Banna provides the executive power of state with almost presidential powers, whether of delegation or execution, in a manner similar to medieval Islamic political thought.[119] What is new is the limitation imposed by the *shari'a* as interpreted not by jurists but by the people. Two central doctrines are needed for legitimacy: justice and equality. These are the philosophical and religious guidelines that both the ruler and the ruled must adhere to and take into consideration while legislating or exercising power.[120] *Tawhid*, then, is manifested politically and morally in equality and justice.[121]

Tawfiq al-Shawi, a moderate Islamist thinker and member of the International Organization of the Muslim Brotherhood, argues in line with Hasan al-Banna that Muslims must rid themselves of tyrannical government and establish a just Islamic government. All privileges of special groups should be abolished and people treated equally. While the establishment of the Islamic state is essential, so too is its dependence on people's *shura*. The Islamic government must be not absolute but constitutional and must adhere to Islamic law. The Islamic government is the government of the law. The ruler must submit to the same law as the ruled and enjoy no specific privileges or precedence over the rest of the people.[122]

The Muslim Brotherhood, prohibited from undersigning its publication in Egypt, published in 1992 a manifesto in Islamabad condemning violence and terrorism. Condemning violence has always been the Brotherhood's proclaimed public policy, although neither a dialogue nor inclusion in a normal public and political life has developed, and under the current regime such a prospect seems increasingly remote. The most important articles of the manifesto condemn and call for an end to all forms of violence, including revenge and vendetta. Instead of bloodshed, people should use wisdom in the propagation of God's message. The Brotherhood also calls for the participation of popular forces in the political processes and the lifting of all restrictions on political activity, including the banning of party formation, in order to arrive at comprehensive social, economic, and political reforms. All political forces are asked to unite to break the vicious circle of violence and to seek real popular participation.[123]

Similarly, Taqiy al-Din al-Nabahani, the leader of the Hizb al-Tahrir movement in Jordan, views the institutions of the community at large as the legal source of authority, and the government as obligated to respect the community's wishes and enact its will. The people are free to give or to withdraw power, especially since a consultative council or *majlis al-shura* should be elected and not appointed. Al-Nabahani downplays the importance of the executive power and highlights the pivotal function of elected bodies, because of their representation of the people and the protection of their "natural rights," including the right to form parties.[124]

In fact, though, since the fifties Hizb al-Tahrir has been either unable or forbidden, on both the East and West Banks, to realize its program and play its imagined role. In 1976 the Jordanian government banned the party, especially because of its emphasis on the necessity of elections for the legitimacy of government. To escape persecution, al-Nabahani went to Damascus and then to Beirut; his party, which the Jordanian government viewed as aiming to end the monarchy, did not get a license.[125]

Along the same line of thinking, Munir Shafiq, previously linked to Hizb al-Tahrir, argues that the relationship between governments and society faces major obstacles, foremost among them the lack of social justice, human dignity, and *shura*. These issues transcend the Western ideas of human rights, the sovereignty of law, and democracy, and form the basis for a proper relationship between the ruler and the ruled. Shafiq does not accept any justification for the conditions that beset Muslim life, such as the absence of political freedom in the interest of the ruling elite and the existence of widespread economic injustice. Any modern resurgence must address these issues by spreading social justice, uplifting human dignity, maintaining man's basic rights and the sovereignty of law, and extending the meaning of *shura* and popular political participation through the development of representative institutions.[126]

Hasan al-Turabi, the head of al-Jabha al-Qawmiyya al-Islamiyya in Sudan, is the most prominent and powerful thinker of contemporary Islamic movements. Holder of graduate degrees in constitutional law from England and France, Dr. al-Turabi has been the Muslim Brotherhood's general guide, the leader of the Islamic and Nationalist Congress, the Sudanese parliament's speaker, and the supposed power broker of the al-Bashir regime until 2000. In launching his new interpretation of Islam and democracy, he imposes more Islamic limitations than al-Banna on the power of the state and makes them equal to those of liberalism and Marxism. He drops many conditions about the nature of institutions that may be allowed by an Islamic constitution and in an Islamic state.

While the state may set general rules enabling a society to organize its affairs, the *shari'a* limits the powers of the state and frees society. Al-Turabi grounds this idea in the religious command to enjoin the good and to forbid evil.[127] For him this command becomes the parallel of pluralism, because its performance is obviously of a communal nature. In order to exercise their prerogatives of *shura* and *ijma'*, the people require many opinions or *ijtihadat* from which to choose. This is more urgent today since Muslims are beset by dire conditions and unprecedented challenges. The situation demands a new understanding of religion—not a mere addition and subtraction of particulars here and there but new organizing principles appropriate for the modern era.[128]

Third World countries have failed in developing democratic institutions for four reasons, according to al-Turabi. First, societies are still traditional and not easily open to change. Second, poor economic conditions—exploitation as well as unequal distribution of wealth—do not encourage a transition to democracy. Third, military institutions are by nature undemocratic, and long-standing cultural, military, and political imperialism have not been conducive to the establishment of a democratic atmosphere. And fourth, as people become psychologically conditioned to tyranny, they lose an individual political awareness of the need for democracy.

All these factors together led to a deep-rooted conviction that, though democracy might be a good political ideal, real politics rested on actual power, itself dependent on the use of force, coercion, and the monopoly of authority. The exercise of democracy in the Third World became a charade used by political regimes to give an impression of popular legitimacy before the international audience, especially the West.[129] It was no more than hero-worship ceremonies imposed by the ruler on a people who were mobilized to serve his standing internally and externally. Such false democracy weakened real democracy, and instead of governments serving the people, we had people serving governments; freedom came to mean the freedom of governments to use all means and methods to coerce people into following unpopular views and systems. Yet such contemporary Eastern practices, as well as unedifying developments in the West, do not push al-Turabi to decry democracy. On the contrary, they indicate to him the possibility of remodeling democracy in a modern form that could do away with the historicity and misuse of the doctrine. He exhorts Muslims to adapt it after having redefined it in Islamic terms and after reformulating it within the conditions of contemporary Islamic life.

Mere imitation of Western democracy without proper consideration of the conditions of its new environment may lead to faulty situating, be it social, philosophical, political, or ethical. It also makes democracy an alien doctrine superimposed on an ancient culture, and consequently a sign of foreign hegemony. For al-Turabi, what is needed is the reacquisition of democracy and its Islamization so that it becomes self-induced, native, natural, and beneficial. The adaptation of democracy to the general conditions of Muslims and its proper grounding in an Islamicly developed new discourse seem to al-Turabi essential for both democracy and *shura*. While Islam for al-Turabi is open to foreign ideas and doctrines or even a non-Islamic view, it filters them through its own priorities.

Al-Turabi uses the pre-Islamic proverb "Support your brother whether he is the oppressor or the oppressed" to convey the openness of Islam to all possibilities of adoption and adaptation. While for al-Turabi this proverb has a general, literal, and absolute significance, Islam has made support for the oppressor a matter of advice and reorientation toward what is just and away from what is unjust. On a higher methodological level, al-Turabi reminds us that Muslims adopted Greek logic without hesitation and have used it extensively in all fields of knowledge. These two examples show, as al-Turabi explains, not only a liking or a dislike for a particular proverb or science but also the cultural and political relationship and a relation of power.[130] When the dominant discourse was the Islamic one, Muslims had no problem with introducing and Islamizing foreign or non-Islamic doctrines, sciences, and methods, and developing Islamic terms for them.

According to al-Turabi, while the caliphate literally means a human vicegerency for conducting the *umma*'s general affairs, it developed later to indicate a particular system of government. The experience of the rightly guided caliphate introduced into Islam the doctrine of a particular system of government. However, the nature of the relationship between the government and the people changed when seizure of power became the norm of governmental succession. Instead of signifying choice, which was the original meaning of the caliphate, government came to signify political force and coercion. Similarly, while the oath of allegiance indicated the free acceptance of a contract between equals, it was transformed later, because of rulers' arbitrary and coercive power, into no more than a formal act of submission, automatic delegation, and commitment to rulers. In this case, the very essence of political government, contractuality, was reduced to a ceremonial act, rendering *al-bay'a* more or less insignificant. The response of Islamic thought during that period was to overlook the real and original meaning of *al-bay'a* and adopt descriptive definitions based on realities, instead of adopting corrective prescriptions that would restore the original meaning.[131]

Islamic political thought has, therefore, been mostly derived from submitting unreflectively to the realities of the time and to the dominant political discourse of rulers, and more specifically to the relationships of power and its distribution. Jurists have yielded repeatedly to governing powers and developed their discourses accordingly. Political powers have always been capable of influencing religious discourse directly and indirectly, so religious discourse has never been purely abstract or innovative but rather imbued with ideas dominant among the political or military elite or, simply, the powerful. This is mirrored on the international level today. When the Islamic civilization confronted other civilizations and Muslims lost both geopolitically and scientifically, weakness crept into their discourses. The ascendance of the discourses of the victorious marginalized Islamic discourses and made them unattractive. Put differently, the dominance of a particular discourse is related to power.

Al-Turabi believes that Muslims are now on the rise and are attaining some power, and a new Muslim discourse—that is, the Islamist—is also on the rise. This makes al-Turabi confident that Muslims can again readopt and readapt foreign doctrines in order to deal with modern conditions of life. Muslims can in particular seize and reconceptualize significant and powerful terms such as revolution, democracy, and socialism in order to reorient and reinforce their liberation theology or discourse.[132]

For him, there is no doubt that political dominance produces dominant intellectual discourses. In turn, dominant discourses increase power and the spread of its civilization. When the Islamic civilization was dominant, its discourses were spread universally, directly and indirectly. When the West became dominant, its discourses became dominant universally. Muslims should borrow now from the dominant Western culture in order to strengthen their discourse and consequently their power, otherwise their discourse may become a mere appendage to the dominant Western discourse. But if Muslims adopt into their discourse what is valuable, they need not sacrifice either their discourse or culture and have them replaced with others. Selective borrowing from the dominant others is one of the sources that allow the rejuvenation of Islamic thinking and prevent its sinking into oblivion. Thus, al-Turabi poses the necessity of developing a new formative discourse using the modern and dominant language. This development can take place either through a process of original linguistic and historical interpretation or through Arabization, in order to spark a revival and strengthen the political conditions of Muslims.[133]

The Islamization of democracy as *shura* needs only its linkage to *tawhid*, which makes the doctrines of equality and freedom religious and universal instead of secular and human. *Shura* and its concomitant doctrines thereby become more compelling and concrete. Because democracy occupies a major role in al-Turabi's discourse, he argues that it epitomizes Islam's capability of adoption and adaptation of modern doctrines. This adoptive and adaptive process makes democracy and *shura* equivalent. Muslims cannot turn a blind eye anymore to the importance of democracy. Introduced irrevocably into Muslim areas by the dominant West and its discourses, it must now be reworked into modern Islamic thought, linked to Islamic political jurisprudence, and in particular identified with *shura*. While it is true that *shura* as democracy has not been actually practiced, al-Turabi nevertheless has tried to solidly conceptualize *shura* as a synonym for democracy and has seen no religious or cultural obstacle to doing so. Furthermore, he advocates linking it to the two fundamentals of Islam, the Qur'an and the Sunna. In fact, *shura* as a general method of government can be read from and into the texts, if they are read in a specific way, for the religious texts exhort the community to take responsibility for its own affairs, which would include issues of rule and organization.[134] *Shura* in Islam is a doctrine that is derived from the roots of religion and its general postulates, and not specifically from any particular text.

For al-Turabi *shura* must become the Muslim way of thinking about and behaving toward Islam. Because Qur'anic references to *shura* relate to one aspect of life or another, Islam has viewed the important issues of divinity, governance, and authority as being the domain of God. It has also viewed all members of mankind equally, and therefore held that vicegerency belongs to them generally. The crisis of applying the Islamic system of *shura* in Islamic countries cannot be resolved by just adding some sort of formal and cosmetic institutions to existing power structures. It must be addressed through the spirit of Islam where the entire community, not only an individual or a group of individuals, carries the responsibilities of government. *Shura* must be transformed into a system of living, not a limited political practice. A state that is not built on such a system does not lead its society to success but ends up being an instrument of social oppression and destruction. Modern national states of the Islamic world do not pay any regard to human rights or similar concerns because these states are founded not on freedom but on the sultanic conception of authority, which leaves no room for the community to express its views, much less to develop a representative system.[135]

Contemporary realities call on Muslims to feel ashamed of their situation and to create a discourse that reinstitutes the Islamic state and Muslim society. While rejecting a mere imitation of the West, Muslims must focus on the issues of freedom and democracy and must then direct all of this toward developing a dialogue with the West.[136] Part of this dialogue in the new system as called for by al-Turabi is the relationship between *shura* and democracy—or between the Muslim world and the West. He argues that the difference between Islamic democratic *shura* and Western democracy is not merely formal but also conceptual, since the former is based on and derived from the divine *hakimiyya* and thus from mankind's common vicegerency (*istikhlaf*), while the latter is based on concepts of human nature. In Islam, freedom is both metaphysical and doctrinal; that is, freedom is a religious doctrine whose violation goes beyond a mere civil or criminal infraction to constitute sin. Freedom in Western liberalism is, however, legal and political but never religious or divine. Thus Islamic discourse can and should address not only the interests of individuals or their fears of government but, in fact, strengthen their own consciousness so that it may serve as a guarantee against any violation of political rule or arrogation of powers properly reserved to the community.[137]

In this sense, *shura* becomes a liberating religious doctrine that cannot be usurped by any authority; all authority may rule only contractually and in the service of the social structure. Al-Turabi theoretically justifies such an interpretation by arguing that both the organizing principles and the specifics of religion, being historically developed, are subject to change in response to the community's needs. Their historical nature means that no normative standing inheres in them and that their replacement with new principles and specifics is not a violation of religion. While this replacement does involve the Qur'an and the Sunna, the new *usul* or organizing principles must be the outcome of a new *ijma'*, itself the consequence of a popular choice in the form of contemporary *shura*.[138]

However, al-Turabi cautions against breaking any fundamental principle of Islam that the Qur'an provides. For him, if *shura* and democracy are viewed outside their historical conditions, then they may be used synonymously to indicate the same idea. While it is true that ultimate sovereignty in Islam belongs to God, practical and political sovereignty belong to the people. *Shura*, therefore, includes communal freedom to select an appropriate course of action or set of rules or even representative bodies.[139] While Muslim societies are in dire need of change, al-Turabi does not perceive the West to be the model that leads to the softening of conflicts, as the West is suffering more than the Islamic world from all sorts of philosophical, economic, and, to a lesser extent, political problems.

However, the modern era witnessed the superimposition of the dialectical problems of modern Western living. While Islamic states should have adopted only what was good and relevant to the Islamic world, they took the West as a complete model along with its inherent troubles and tensions, displacing the model of the *shari'a* that Muslims could work with and develop from within. A new political life, characterized by sharp economic, political, and ideological tensions and conflicting claims between the individual, the state, and society, has become a main feature of Muslim societies. Briefly, what has occurred is the transportation from the West to the East of problems that did not exist initially in the East. Muslim societies lost their original powers without gaining the powers of their Western counterparts.

Put differently, they suffer doubly: first, by the negative aspects of their history, intellectual backwardness and traditionalism, and second, by the emergence of new and "modern" tyrannical states and comprehensive conflicts as well as the states' control of individual and social life. However, true liberation and freedom should be sought in the elimination of the root cause of unbelief. True belief eliminates the narrow problem of freedom and brings about true liberation for all: the individual, the society, and the state. Religious liberation leads to political liberation from the earth's lords and to the proper functioning of the Islamic state through the spread of free religious consciousness. The imposition of a state's political objectives on the believers without a proper Islamic philosophy of life leads the state into outright paganism and illegitimacy. Modern Muslim societies are therefore, in al-Turabi's opinion, in need of a major change of priorities, to turn upside down the social and political agenda by making Islamic liberation the immediate objective of change for the benefit of religion.[140]

Such liberation requires a force that will redraw the parameters of conflict from a reductive quest for mere personal freedom to the very essence of the problem, which is man's corruption of his original nature. The combination of religious unity and political freedom is, for al-Turabi, a proper religious liberation that functions as the ideological equilibrium between different and diverse claims for rights and duties. The *shari'a* is the source of that equilibrium, since it gives equal weight to the individual's rights versus those of society, the society's versus the state's, and the state's versus the individual's. Priority of rights is not a matter of human forces and their balance of power, but is religiously derived and defined. Religious consciousness, and not the material gains of the individual or society or the state, functions as the motivating force to settle the issues of rights. In this sense, sheer power could not be the source of rights, even of individuals; rights are of a more fundamental, religious nature. If proper consciousness is developed at all levels, then political rights interact with political and social realities and inform the individual life with a social dimension and the social life with an individual dimension. Only through proper consciousness can conflicts between claims be resolved. The individual's consciousness becomes representative of social consciousness, and social consciousness represents the people's will.[141]

While employing such an analysis to shed doubt on the legitimacy of modern Islamic governments that repress religious liberation and political freedom or consciousness, al-Turabi also contends that contemporary Islamic societies are in need of a process of transmuting the political and social into the metaphysical. The posing of today's problems in terms not of religious consciousness but solely of economic and political difficulties may lead to unsatisfactory solutions. Al-Turabi views today's Islamic societies as combinations of traditionalism and modernism—traditionalism because the traditional way of thinking is identified by the people with religion, and modernism because the people, if not developed, are still beset by the imported problems of the modern West. Ending traditionalism by renewing the roots and understanding of religion may resolve major problems. But Al-Turabi downplays the importance of acquiring the skills necessary for the creation of an advanced civilization, though mere religious consciousness alone cannot trigger a process of working toward the elimination of underdevelopment and the setting up of an efficient administration. Al-Turabi's assumption that the resolution of social and political problems comes with the fulfillment of religious liberation, the development of the *shari'a,* and the elimination of *jahiliyya* curtails the potential for reform and gives rise to uncalled-for hopes. On the other hand, it may encourage believers to forgo any concern about the development of this life, accept backwardness and miserable living conditions, and instead focus on the afterlife.

A view like this may not be conducive even to the program that al-Turabi is calling for. It is doubtful that a revival of Islam could be attained without highly developed technology and an economy that satisfied the people's needs and aspirations. Of course the contemporary crises might be blamed in great part on the regimes, but their abolition would not necessarily lead to a revival. Historically, implementation of the *shari'a* has not necessarily ended the ruler's oppression. Some medieval Muslim political thinkers such as al-Ghazali, al-Mawardi, Ibn Taymiyya, and Ibn Jama'a did not see any religious problem with oppression as long as the ruler adhered even nominally to the *shari'a.* While the *shari'a* could be cast as a source of freedom, other non-*shari'a* postulates must be added to any modern revival of Islamic thinking and religious awareness.

The doctrine that al-Turabi attempts to reinterpret, *shura,* has been seen in some ages of Islamic history as a nonobligatory principle and, in fact, secondary to the issue of political rule. Yet al-Turabi introduces *shura* as the central and legitimizing concept of political rule, and calls for the conditioning of *shari'a* in prevalent conditions of existence. While *shura* has been perceived as a supporting principle in political life, there is no text to limit its interpretation as such. The limitations are social and political, not textual. In modern times, it is edging closer to democracy. Not only this, but the whole question of *shari'a*, for al-Turabi, must be separated from its development and history and reworked in modern times through *shura*, itself in need of a modern interpretation. Put differently, a modern Islamic political discourse cannot flourish on the underpinnings of medieval discourse. The *shari'a*'s derivative interpretations were seen as absolutes back then, largely because medieval social and political practices conditioned such interpretations.

Indeed, *shura* and democracy are denotatively similar, both calling for public participation and representation in the making of political affairs, but they are connotatively quite different. Democracy grounds its ultimate reference in the people, who become the sovereign; in contrast, *shura* grounds its reference in God's revelation, making God the supreme sovereign. The advantage that *shura* has over democracy for al-Turabi is that while human thinking is fluid, a divine text that is always present unifies people's consciousness. Democracy has no text but that of human reason, which leads to the establishment of equal discourses that may be equally full of shortcomings. When *shura* tackles or arrives at, for instance, constitutional, legal, social, and economic principles, it always does so in the light of the *shari'a* and not only in the interest of this group or that. Even when a majority makes a particular claim, it could be negated by the *shari'a*.[142]

Therefore, the *shari'a* is important not only in substantive terms but as a regulative principle that fills the deficit of human reason which always acts within the boundaries of its social setting. *Shura* also differs from liberal democracy, where the enjoyment of political rights is mostly figurative and essentially controlled by economic structures. Without the grounding of human reason in what is beyond reason itself, it produces defective, sectional, and partial theories and doctrines. Such theories and doctrines include capitalism, which concentrates wealth in a few hands, and communism, which tries to disperse personal wealth but in fact places real authority with the few. This dialectical result stems from the conditionality of human theories that precludes the possibility of arriving at any social, economic, or political absolute.[143] All human theories and even religious interpretations are tentative and conditioned by time and place and, as such, can never claim finality.

However, an Islamic order whose discourse goes beyond the mere issue of formal sovereignty and centers around *tawhid* as the organizing principle may have a much more realistic possibility of arriving at perfection. When *shura* is systematically exercised, equality becomes genuine at all levels, for equality is a divine postulate and is not dependent on the development or needs of this society or that. As religious consciousness, it then infiltrates all aspects of life, at home, in academic life, even in religious circles. Because *shura* for al-Turabi is the principle that must govern relations between people, no individual may claim particular powers over others, for the text justifies none. Even religious scholars of renown cannot claim any special privileges or status; they are, because of *shura*, equal under the principles that must govern economic, social, political, and even religious life. Put differently, the opinion of a scholar or an academician is equal to that of an ordinary individual, with no right to impose itself on society and political life.[144]

For al-Turabi, no system may transcend its conditionality without being grounded in the all-comprehensive, unifying, and equalizing doctrine of *tawhid*. If *shura* in modern times is separated from *tawhid* it becomes equivalent, in its frailty and tentativeness, to democracy. Thus any discourse that disrupts the connection between *shura* and *tawhid* derails the objective of the divinely ordained discourse. This applies to other doctrines as well: unity without *shura* is tyranny, unity without freedom is likewise tyranny, and freedom without unity turns into licentiousness. Islamic liberation, grounded in *shura*, is the balance of both unity and freedom and is the instrument that frees the people from intellectual *jahiliyya*, religious *shirk* (polytheism), and political tyranny (*taghut*). Again, an Islamicly derived liberating *shura* becomes for al-Turabi the instrument of change and of searching for the true meaning of *tawhid* and constant transcendence of human intransigence. A new discourse based on the ideology of a liberating *shura* must be adopted and advocated in order to redirect the course both of religiosity and of political action. It should be treated as an essential part of a modern Islamic philosophy of transcendence, negation, and challenge. Such a philosophy of liberation can, then, produce a political ideology capable of ending ideologically conflicting discourses and of unifying Muslim actions.[145]

A philosophy like this could very well, for al-Turabi, become a motivating force for developing a political discourse based not on traditional historical discourses but rather on a newly found intellectual discourse that leads to progressive reinterpretations grounded in abstract underpinnings of his liberation philosophy. Without the development of a major new interpretative discourse the people have no chance of any real revival. According to al-Turabi, the West has penetrated the Muslim world ideologically because of the absence of such a discourse and because of the Muslim regimes' repression of people and their ideological imposition. However, the starting point of revival is adopting liberation discourses that can free the Islamic *umma* from the earth's tyrants (*tawaghit al-ard*) and spark a revolt against all externally imperialistic and internally suppressive forms and discourses. Such liberation discourses are capable of motivating people to reorganize their forces and reorient their powers toward unity. Again, this cannot be done by rehashing old ideological slogans, without first developing a new and authentic set of roots or *usul*. Only a discourse that is constructed on a basic process of innovative interpretation may lead to a theoretically and politically solid form that could make important issues such as freedom a totally religious and unifying fundamental. This might constitute the inception of a new liberation theology.[146]

To put this more concretely, al-Turabi sees that a liberation theology leads by necessity to political reconceptualization and to the formation of a new discourse on power and social, economic, and political relations. If *shura* is deconstructed or "liberated" from its historical constructions and practices, it might be reconstructed as democracy—or, conversely, democracy as *shura*. Thus a process of deconstruction and construction makes *shura* and democracy synonymous and even identical and, in fact, creates a unifying discourse. For example, al-Turabi argues, to the Greeks "democracy" originally indicated mobocracy and was only partially exercised. Later Europeans deconstructed and reconstructed it to mean direct government of the small and limited entities of Europe. But then Europe's extension of its political geography without the means of immediate communication transformed democracy into indirect representative governments and parliaments. By the end of the Middle Ages, European thought considered democracy to be the basis of government.[147] The Muslim world is, then, in need of a philosophy or discourse that takes into consideration and reformulates important issues like freedom, *shura*, and democracy.

However, such a reformulation of democracy and *shura*, al-Turabi continues, has some Islamic root, for democracy in the West developed under the indirect impact of Islamic political thought and, specifically, under the

Islamic doctrine of religious and political equality of Muslims. *Ijma'* in the history of Islam has been theoretically viewed by Muslim scholars as the source of political authority whose legitimate continuation depends on popular confirmation or what is referred to as the contract of allegiance (*'aqd al-bay'a*) between the people and the designated ruler. In fact, without external references and experience Western philosophy could not have developed the concept of equality of all and the need for a contract between the ruler and the ruled. The Western view of contract was not historically derived, but rather advocated as a means of reducing the absolute powers of rulers and increasing the limited power of the people. The doctrine of freedom was originally aimed at liberating the people economically and politically, but democracy developed to mean the free exchange of opinions and the interaction of free wills. Consequently, the theory of a social contract in liberal democracy became the source of compromise and interdependency between the government and the people. However, the uneven distribution of power and wealth led to another breed of democracy, the socialist, which attempted to deconcentrate the capital held by the few and to reintroduce the essence of democracy, political equality.[148]

2

The Classical and Medieval Interpretations of *Ikhtilaf* and Its Modern Islamist Expressions As Pluralism

Classical and Medieval Interpretations of *Ikhtilaf*

The history of Islam has witnessed differences and pluralistic views because of multiple interpretations of the text and changes in economic, scientific, social, and political conditions. The text has been interpreted in many ways and at various levels and from different perspectives. Understandably so, for its manifestations include the exterior and the interior, the real and the metaphorical, the certain and the uncertain. All these indications were used historically to justify one view or another, one school or another, one trend or another. Around the sacred text the Qur'an, many sciences and schools of language, traditions (Hadith), exegesis (*tafsir*), jurisprudence, theology, Sufism, and ethics were shaped, developed, legitimized, and delegitimized. The text was not related only to jurisprudence or theology, and a Qur'anic truth could not be absorbed once and for all. The text was thought of as richer than reality, since there were always new developments that the Qur'an was invoked to interpret, especially given the Islamic belief that the text is an eternal guide for all people.

Differences on Interpretative, Qur'anic, Philosophical, Sufi, and Theological Matters

The Qur'an is very clear on a fundamental principle, which is the freedom to believe or not to believe. There are clear texts in the Qur'an that outlaw coercing people into a specific belief. One verse speaks generally to the Muslims: "There is no coercion in religion, it has been made clear what is guidance from falsehood." Another verse speaks to the Prophet about the nature of belief: "If your Lord had wished, all of those on earth would have surely believed. Do you then coerce people until they become believers?" On pagans: "If God had wished, they would not associate God with others." And elsewhere: "If your Lord had wished, He would have made people into one nation."[1]

The Prophet's role, then, is to guide people to metaphysical truth and to inform them about it, but not to force them to believe. The Qur'an made that clear when it informed the Prophet: "If they become Muslims, they are guided; if they shy away, you only have to inform. God discerns [the affairs of] the people." It also told him: "If they shy away, We have not sent you as a keeper but only to inform."[2] Furthermore, the Qur'an is clear that freedom of belief is guaranteed for all people; while it disagreed with many beliefs of the Jews and Christians, it nonetheless did not call for their forcible conversion but for dialogue with them. It even allowed them to set up their places of worship and to conduct their religious, personal, and social affairs as independent groups within the same community.[3]

The Qur'an as a text for guidance contains instructions and bases for evaluation and classification. In the main, it classifies things as legal or illegal, moral or immoral, and good or evil. It also puts forward arguments for its adherents and against its opponents. However, the text's importance goes beyond this level of instruction and cannot be viewed from one perspective only. While it is the most categorical text for Muslims, most of its implications are not altogether categorical, but show flexibility. The worldview and the culture offered by the text were not to be separated from the realities of Muslims at a specific time.

To cite the authority of text in an attempt to legitimize one opinion over another is never wholly conclusive, as the text's meaning may be argued and reargued. The plasticity of the text, and not its specificity, is what keeps the text alive, and any attempt by a group of Muslims to claim exclusive validity for their representation of the text has been historically countered by other groups and claims. Put differently, the text does not lend itself to being controlled, especially at an epistemological and philosophical level, by specific claims or interpretations. Qur'anic legitimacy cannot be seized by one group of people; strict classifications of people are also beyond the powers of religious institutions. Every Muslim is, in principle, a legitimate interpreter and reader. The agreement of a group of people on one interpretation or reading does not make it the authoritative one. Insofar as a reader does not specifically deny the text or interpret it in opposition to the text itself, that reader is free to read from or into the text whatever is necessary and convenient to the well-being of his individual and communal life. The reader or the interpreter may depend one day on the text, another day on consensus, opinion, reason, evidence, or interest—for all of these ways are themselves sanctioned by the text.

While the text as a divine revelation is a source of different interpretations, it has itself justified differences, diversity, and pluralism. Quite a few Qur'anic verses speak of differences, both natural and political. While they speak negatively of political disunity, they speak positively of the diversity of tribes, sects, nations, and peoples as well as races and languages. Also, they acknowledge the natural differences in the intellectual and physical capabilities of human beings. They view the different ways of living as a natural and even a divine aspect of creation. Therefore a forcible unification of people is not called for.[4]

A main factor in establishing the legitimacy of pluralism, differences, and diversity was the Qur'anic text itself. Because the meaning of text was open to diverse interpretations, no authority could categorically claim to have produced the correct understanding.[5] Divergent interpretations and understanding as well as methodological differences were natural outcomes of the text's nature. Thus, while Islam as a belief system and a law united the community, it also provided avenues for difference, pluralistic understanding, and even opposition, especially if one read the text into a specific context. The text could be understood in a continual process of change, and the reader of the text was not necessarily bound by previous readings but might be guided by his context. While Muslims tended to imitate their predecessors, this imitation was not textually demanded but was driven by social pressures and nostalgia for the past. The text itself did not preclude new readings. While divergent interpretations and readings of the text hinged on the same textual basis, they were indeed different views and, at times, systems of thought or ideologies.

The fundamental problem in the intellectual history of Islam was not in legitimizing the diversity of interpretations and readings, but in the finality that many schools pretended to have acquired. More precisely, intolerance was the main source of enmity and hatred. Each party looked on itself as the text's best practical representation, though no exterior criterion was used. This view led to deeper intolerance, then to strife and war and, in turn, to sharper political differences and more exclusive ideologies.

What was originally a practical or particular matter—like who should rule or the time of breaking the fast—acquired with time and argumentation an ideological or theoretical orientation, leading to the rise of different schools and sects as well as theories and discourses. Every party lost sight of the text and clung instead to its interpretation. This process of difference without tolerance brought about exclusive consciousness and sectarian identities. These identities became closed circles and developed close discourses that ultimately replaced the formative power of the text and the freedom to read it. While the text's original objective was to unite the community and allow its development and change in practical terms, the narrow interpretations developed about the text weakened and contradicted its significance.

In this fashion, most schools of thought rejected the others' views and saw themselves as the authority in religious matters. They not only excluded the others but branded them heretics or infidels. While all schools accepted the idea of difference, they did not push the argument to its logical limits. The original view on pluralism in Islam rests on the premise that every opinion that results from the fullest use of reason (*ijtihad*) is correct.[6] Because human reasoning cannot reach the status of the absolute, all judgments made by it are of a tentative nature and subject to correction and change. When an individual claims his judgment's validity and the others' error, this is only in relation to the evidence presented and cannot be but tentative, according to al-Ghazali.[7] Differences at this level were acknowledged as diverse opinions in legal matters that change from one age to another and one community to another. Thus, jurisprudence has long been seen as a practical science that was subject to differences and pluralistic understanding, was dependent on circumstances and contexts, and was related to will and interest.

There was in principle no religious reservation about different theological interpretations. While the theological fundamentals of religion were looked on as very basic and were not subject to different interpretations, in reality theologians accepted the notion of differing interpretations even of theological principles. Because theologians recognized the difficulty of establishing religion on basic fundamentals that were subject to different interpretations, they agreed on the need to conform to one basic interpretation that was accepted by the majority of scholars and the public. The theological mind was of a defensive and unitary nature and employed categorical definitions. It represented the ideological orientations for uniting the community and rejecting disunity.

However, such a mental structure could not but produce real differences and different theological schools. Because every theological school considered itself the possessor of truth, the possibility of harmony and rational exchange was reduced and was replaced instead by categorical judgments of the others' falsehood. These schools identified their understanding of the basics of religion with religion itself and tried to discredit the views of the others. While al-Ghazali accepted the principle of different interpretations, he nonetheless rejected categorically the interpretations of others, like the Batiniyya and the philosophers, whom he accused of unbelief. Al-Ghazali originally meant to object only to the exclusiveness of the Shi'ites and the philosophers, but he ended up rejecting the others in principle.[8] It is thus apparent that whenever an individual or a group has attempted to make itself the representative of pure Islam, it has tended to reject the principle of pluralistic understanding in favor of the notion that truth can have only one meaning or representation. This is why most differences in Islam have ended up being embodied in opposition movements that claimed opposite theologies. The history of theology and that of schism are one and the same.[9]

The stage of theological dialectics and the rise of theology are a good example of tolerance and, at times, intolerance of pluralistic views. The Mu'tazila believed that reason can lead to belief and fought a long battle with the traditionalists. While they defended religion, they developed theology as an independent science during the second and third centuries of Hijra. Jurists did not look favorably on this science and doubted its authenticity, yet most of them, like Ahmad ibn Taymiyya, participated in the raging debates of the time.

Abu al-Hasan al-Ash'ari, the founder of a new school of theology, argued that his views represented the views of the Companions of the Prophet and their followers as well as the views of *ahl al-Hadith* and *ahl al-Sunna*. He made theology (*'ilm al-kalam*) a recognized Islamic science. He even sanctioned the scholar's engagement in it, and thus opened up the legitimacy of arguments and counterarguments about God and His attributes, predestination and free will, and other theological topics. Abu Hanifa had no reservations about branching out into theology because the Mu'tazilites were Hanafites and because he adopted "opinion" as a basic methodology in lawmaking. Al-Baqillani, as a Malikite, helped in recognizing theology as a religious discipline. The only school that did not recognize the legitimacy of theology was the Hanbalites, who downplayed the role of reason. However, the Ash'arites allied themselves with the Sufis and gained a great reputation and a recognition of reason's power to investigate divine issues. The Hanbalites believed themselves to be following the literal and authentic traditions of good ancestors.

When al-Ghazali appeared in the fifth century, two problems presented themselves to the Ash'arites: the religious view on theology and the religious view on Sufism. Al-Ghazali argued that theology was not for the common people, though it could be used as a medicine to clear doubts about creed. Individuals who had certain beliefs did not need theology.

Anyway, he doubted the power of reason to understand ultimate knowledge or God. Theological views for al-Ghazali could be false or true, and theological methods per se did not lead to undoubted truth. Thus the development of the four legal schools and the commitment of the majority of Muslims (*ahl al-Sunna*) to the Ash'arite theology and their doubt of the role of reason led to narrowing the role of *ijtihad* and reason and ushered in the phase of traditional imitation.[10]

The Shafi'ites were the first jurist school to adopt Ash'arism. The views of its founder, al-Shafi'i, were in the middle between the views of *ahl al-Hadith* represented by Malik and *ahl al-Ra'y* represented by Abu Hanifa. Ash'arism was the middle ground that struck a balance between the text and reason. It believed that ideas followed a specific course with rules, and there was no room for accident. It believed as well in the existence of opposite values: a thing was either right or wrong, true or false, good or evil, happy or miserable, virtuous or sinful, legal or illegal, and legitimate or illegitimate. Such a dichotomy led to political and theological splits between jurists and Sufis, Sufis and Hanbalites, Hanbalites and Mu'tazilites, Mu'tazilites and Shi'ites, Shi'ites and Sunnites, Sunnites and Kharijites, and so on.

While these divisions originally represented pluralistic attitudes toward religious understanding within Islam, with the weakness of the Islamic world and internal jockeying for power, they turned into competing factions that aimed at either political or ideological dominance. During the reign of Caliph al-Ma'mun, a seminal event took place that showed the danger of political interference in the making of religious and political ideals. This incident, known as the Ordeal (al-Mihna), was a kind of court of inquisition conducted by the caliph, who had adopted Mu'tazilite views and ordered the people to adhere to them. Those scholars and jurists who did not yield to the religious ideology of the ruler and the Mu'tazilites were tried and jailed. Ahmad ibn Hanbal was one of these scholars. However, with the ruler's turnabout and adoption of the opposition's religious ideology, counterrepression took place, and the Mu'tazilites were not even allowed to have debates or teach and were treated as outlaws.[11]

Another *mihna* that testified to the danger of the state's adopting a religious ideology was the ordeal of Ghulam al-Khalil, in which the Sufis suffered tremendously at the hands of the Hanbalites. Ghulam al-Khalil, a Hanbalite, accused the Sufis of heresy and turned the public against them. The caliph arrested more than seventy Sufis. The Sufis' ordeal ended with the execution of al-Hallaj in A.H. 309.

With time, however, such ordeals decreased and the general public as well as the political authority tended again toward tolerance and pluralism. Sufism became ultimately a mainstream movement within Islam, after it had been cleansed of al-Hallaj's inexplicable expressions of union with the divinity. Sufism started adhering to the *shari'a* and followed the path that was developed by al-Ghazali in his *Al-Munqidh min al-Dalal*. The sects that pitted Muslims against each other became less dominant, as Mu'tazilites and Hanbalites adhered to exclusive views about reason and the text, respectively. Most Muslims opted for more middle-ground ways in theology and jurisprudence that were mainly represented by Ash'arism and Maturidism. The former in particular found support in the intellectual centers of Baghdad, Nishapur, Basra, Ispahan, and Mosul, thanks to the effort of Nizam al-Mulk, the illustrious minister of Alp Arslan who established the Nizamiyya schools in order to fight the Shi'ite propaganda.[12]

Islamic philosophical discourses were in principle more open than juristic and theological discourses. Ibn Rushd, for instance, allowed dissent against *ijma'* in theoretical matters while insisting on following *ijma'* in practical matters. He believed that religion was subject to many interpretations depending on the individual's intellectual capabilities. Allegorical interpretation must be used to resolve apparent contradictions between the text and philosophy. Allegorical interpretation opened the way for differing, and pluralistic, views since it led to widening the role of reason in understanding the text. Ibn Rushd pushed the role of interpretation to its utmost by arguing that Aristotle discovered the truth.[13]

Before Ibn Rushd, al-Farabi had postulated the different ways of arriving at the truth. Al-Farabi considered that the truth was one but its representations were diverse, and so were its symbols. Every community or sect used its own representations of the truth depending on its circumstances, customs, and language. What was comprehended in the mind was one and the same, but what was presented to the imagination varied from one individual to another, and from one community to another. That is, reason was one, and imagination was multiple.[14] And since all claims were basically made by imagination, truth could not be claimed by one community only. Unity of mind thus did not deny diversity of opinion. The philosophers, however, created their own division of mind, and of community. The philosophical mind divided humankind into two basic camps: virtuous and nonvirtuous. Individuals and communities were classed as either virtuous and happy or ignorant and unhappy. Those that were ignorant and unhappy were the unrecognized and ignorant cities. They, therefore, lacked legitimacy and were in need of reformation.

This philosophical openness was exceeded only by the Sufi openness. Sufi theories accepted not only different epistemological interpretations but the existential as well. The existential focus of Sufism obliterated in the final analysis all man-made classifications like the virtuous and nonvirtuous. The idea of difference in the Sufi mind represented the very fabric of existence, because it meant not only accepting diversity in social and political domains but also accepting the coexistence of contraries. For instance, God was the one and the whole, the one and the many, the first and the last, the internal and the external, the unseen and the present. Truth was unfathomable.[15]

The Sufi united himself with all religions, and recognized God in every belief system. He identified himself with inanimate and animate objects as well, and with animals and humans. Existence was one picture reflected through many mirrors. The Sufi identified himself with the believer and nonbeliever as well as the Buddhist, the Jew, the Christian, and of course the Muslim. No body or idea was excluded, since the truth was either an apparent or an allegorical expression of truth.[16] The Sufi mind had, therefore, rejected strict identification with sectarian orientations as well as legal and theological schools that were capable of overcoming the Sufi mind. After the victory of these legal and theological schools, the Islamic mind tended to adhere to categorical classifications about the truth, and to narrow sectarianism, which were not conducive to dialogue. Thus a theological absoluteness was added to Islamic thought in the form of a system of beliefs and disbelief that later crippled the development of Islamic civilization.[17]

Differences on Legal and Political Matters

Muslims may differ on a particular issue even when there is a religious text, because people read into the text different things and have different experiences. People's right to differ with each other has been accepted by Islamic jurisprudence. Islamic history is full of such differences in politics, jurisprudence, language, and even history. In an environment of diversity, the ruler acted as the arbitrator among the different views. His adoption of a particular view made that view a legal and political judgment, which precluded the escalation of differences among Muslims. However, the legal aspect of his judgment was never identified with the law itself but with its absence. A good example in this context is the disagreement between Abu Bakr and ʿUmar ibn al-Khattab on how to deal with the people who stopped paying alms to the state after the Prophet's death. ʿUmar held that these people were Muslims and should not be fought, especially as they were not a large group that threatened the state. Abu Bakr's view was that these people had recanted Islam when they stopped heeding a legal pronouncement, and therefore should be fought. Of course, Abu Bakr's view triumphed because he was the ruler; it was simply a political decision.[18]

The ensuing fighting became known as the wars of apostasy (ridda). These wars, launched by Abu Bakr against Arab tribes, were mostly conducted not because of the tribes' refusal of Islam but because they refused to pay their taxes. Abu Bakr considered this an act of treason against the state. The dissenting tribes contended that taxes due to the Prophet did not have to be paid to the caliph. Abu Bakr believed that the right to exact that tax belonged to the state. This was not a religious argument of a categorical nature, and many Muslims objected to the wars. 'Umar ibn al-Khattab questioned the caliph's right to impose his view on other Muslims, saying, "Do you fight people who acknowledge that there is no god but God?" However, the wars of apostasy established the power of the caliphs to interfere in the community's private affairs. While originally the difference between Abu Bakr and the tribes was a difference in interpreting a Qur'anic verse about the Prophet's right to certain shares of money, Abu Bakr created a precedent. That precedent allowed the caliph to interfere in the interpretation of verses that were linked to the execution of state financial policies. Here the "apostasy" charge was not due to denying any basic tenet of Islam but simply to disputing the administration and distribution of taxes.[19]

Differences also developed over the status and distribution of the land that the Muslims occupied after taking control of Iraq, Syria, and Egypt. One view was that it should be divided among the soldiers who fought there; another, that it should become a tax producer, with the proceeds to be divided among orphans and widows. While 'Umar ibn al-Khattab insisted that making it tax land was only a matter of opinion, he nonetheless enforced that as ruler. Again, it was a political decision based on the ruler's prerogative and the silence of law.[20] Thus, while it is true that Islamic law was the supreme law, the absence of injunctions on many issues, new and old, gave the ruler great power to enact his opinion. This was especially true when there was no obvious contradiction to Islamic law, and when the scholarly circles were not organized in such a way as to pressure the ruler on a specific matter. Legal, economic, and administrative aspects of Muslim life were all affected.

The Prophet encouraged his Companions to deliberate on a broad range of topics during his life. Many of the Companions exercised ijtihad over many issues such as the call to prayer, without any resentment felt by the Prophet. These issues even included Islamic religious duties. The Prophet always commended the people who thought about how best to perform certain duties. During his life, he legitimized not only the textual sources for law, the Qur'an and the Sunna, but also opinion, or *al-ra'y*. After his death, the caliph started to sound out opinion through a process of consultation with the Prophet's Companions on specific issues that were raised. If the Companions agreed or had a consensus, he would yield to their ruling. If they did not agree, the caliph would make a ruling. Differences were, then, legitimate. For the Companions, *ijma'* became normative without terminating the power of opinions or the validity of differences (*ikhtilaf*), since multiple views were the standard. In the absence of a clear-cut consensus, one opinion was as valid as any other opinion. In his famous letter to Abu Musa al-Ash'ari, 'Umar ibn al-Khattab asked him to rule first by the Qur'an and the Sunna, and then by opinion on those matters upon which the Qur'an and the Sunna were silent.[21]

During the Companions' age, Abu Bakr and 'Umar, as caliphs, used to meet with all the tribes' chiefs for consultation. If they agreed on one opinion, they would execute it. If not, the tribes and groups were not bound by opinions that were not agreed upon. However, the caliph used to enforce his own opinion. While it was very obvious that consensus for the Prophet's Companions was a source of legislation, the absence of solid collective agreement, which was normally the case, sanctioned pluralism and diversity. In practice, the consensus of the Medina community was especially important, since Medina, where most of the Companions who were jurists resided, was the Muslims' legal capital. The consensus of Medina reflected the consensus of most of the learned Muslim scholars. Nonetheless, the Companions in their turn urged the public to express their opinions in order to complete the consensus and to remove the possibility of later dissension. Ibn Khaldun mentioned that during the Prophet's life, the Qur'an and the Sunna were the sources of authority. After his death, the Companions agreed that consensus was as authoritative as the two. The jurists generally looked on consensus as unerring and binding.[22] But, again, there was seldom a solid consensus without any dissenting voices—not even on the collection of the Qur'an and the caliph's function.

The Companions' followers also accepted the Qur'an, the Sunna, and consensus as the sources of authority. Discussions took place over the nature of consensus and whether it should be the consensus of jurists or of all the people. 'Umar ibn 'Abd al-Aziz saw the impossibility of a universal *ijma'* and accepted the *ijma'* of a specific country. Put differently, he sanctioned different collective views that were popularly held. He accepted the first step in the making of a universal consensus, that is, the agreement of a group of people in a specific country and the community's acceptance of it; if other countries or communities accepted it, then it became more universal. A group of people cannot act on behalf of all the others. At that time, four cities were well known for their scholarly and legal standing: Mecca, Medina, Basra, and Kufa. Most prominent scholars of the period like al-Uza'i, the jurist of al-Sham, and al-Shafi'i, the systemizer of jurisprudence, acknowledged both the formative role of consensus and the legitimacy of divergent views. Thereafter, phrases like "the imams of the Muslims [accepted]" and "the community agreed on it" and "the majority of scholars accepted the matter" entered circulation in scholarly circles and books.[23]

Furthermore, the founders of the four authoritative Sunni legal schools accepted the validity of consensus as well as pluralism. Al-Shafi'i, who was the first jurist to write extensively on the fundamentals of jurisprudence, saw tacit consensus as the agreement of all of the community, both scholars and the public. While he acknowledged that this agreement was practically difficult, it was theoretically the highest kind of consensus. The scholars' consensus was binding, but to a lesser extent. Any such consensus suffered from the same difficulty: it was very unlikely that you could not find a scholar who would oppose it. In other words, differences and pluralism were, in one way or another, legitimate even when a semblance of consensus existed. This was probably why some jurists put forward the idea that a group of scholars may claim a "silent" consensus.

The diversity of Islamic jurisprudence was institutionalized as its legal schools were made the bases of the state's judiciary system. During the Mamluk period, judges became very influential and were put in charge of the legal schools and supervised the appointment of state and religious employees. Medieval jurists, however, disliked being attached to the state because it led to the exploitation of knowledge by political authorities, to the scholars' subjection to the sultan's interest, and to increased jealousy among scholars. They believed that scholarship should serve religious objectives, not politics. Politics was dangerous for knowledge, and government should not interfere in scholarship.

The development of political jurisprudence was the outcome of social interactions between the scholars and other segments of society. Though it was civil in nature and removed from the authority of the state, it dealt extensively with political matters, from the doctrine of good government to the community's defense. Such topics were freely taught at mosques. If a scholar attracted many followers to his lessons, he became a prestigious personality whose authority sprang from social acceptance and not from any political appointment. In fact, most political doctrines and religious issues were settled in such places, away from the intervention of governments. When a legal opinion of a scholar became widely accepted in society, it became a part of the community's legislative compendium that the government had to honor and to fulfill. This is why the Muslims did not formalize their legislative processes but kept them away from political authorities until the nineteenth century, when Europe imposed its own views of legislation as well as its mechanisms. Since then, in the Muslim world as elsewhere, legislation has become part of the state itself, manipulated to justify its tyranny.[24]

Nonetheless, the Ottomans could not incorporate completely the institution of *'ulama'* in the structure of government or force people to follow the state's declared legal school (the Hanafi), for the community had accepted the equal validity of various schools. The *'ulama'* proved resistant to absorption or disintegration until the collapse of the Ottoman Empire, though some of them became state functionaries like Shaykh al-Islam in Turkey and Shaykh al-Azhar in Egypt. Basically, the historical role of the scholars' institution has always been of intermediaries between the state and segments of civil society, especially as a majority of the *'ulama'* also took part in the crafts or commerce, and thus exerted economic power.[25]

Also the moral and political duty of *hisba,* to enjoin the good and forbid evil, was shouldered by civil groups and not by the state. If the community neglected this duty, it was considered that a social ill had befallen society. This duty entailed the right of society to participate in public debates, to give its opinions, and to criticize public actions and governmental policies. It went further than the abstract notion of citizenship and demanded the active involvement of diverse segments of society in running the affairs of society and state. The duty being a religious one, those who participated would earn divine reward, but those who, though capable, did not perform that function would incur the penalty for impiety.[26]

Another evidence of the deep-rootedness of civil society in the history of Islam is the role that the nobility (*al-ashraf*) played between individuals and the state. This informal civil section of society cushioned relations between society and the state. Its members were descended from the Prophet, which gave them tremendous standing among other segments of society. Their leader (*naqib al-ashraf*) commanded a wide civil influence and intervened on the individuals' behalf with the state.[27]

Other powerful civil forces were the professional or craft organizations. A complex web of commercial interrelationships linked the craftsmen with the notables, who depended for their authority on local economic and social ties. Indeed, a craft would often have a notable as its *shaykh* (leader). All of this unified the local structures and rules on which the political authorities depended to facilitate their exercise of power and relations with society. These structures and rules, in addition to blood ties and tribal organizations, played a central role in protecting individuals and social segments from the state's arbitrary exercise of power. The leader of a craft or professional group was charged with administering the affairs of its members as well as solving their problems and supervising the implementation of contracts and agreements. The leader usually had direct access to judges for the purpose of registering contracts and bringing the complaints of the craft against other crafts. Also, the leader was the avenue through which the local governor contacted the craft's members. Internally, the craft's organization followed a very strict hierarchy, working up from initiation to the attainment of full craftsmanship. An awesome ceremony was held to bestow membership on a craftsman who would swear allegiance to his master and to the rules of the craft, which involved perfect work, honesty, fair prices, and, above all, solidarity with fellow craftsmen. It was more a fraternity than a business club.[28]

Sufi orders too were connected with the crafts and the notables. This reflected the right of civil segments to conduct their work and even their worship in the manner they deemed appropriate—a further indication that the exercise of social authority in civil society was conducted away from political authorities. Sufi and notable and professional intermediaries had thus created a multilayered framework of belonging for the local community, and then connected this framework to the general ideal of the Islamic nation (*umma*). Relations with local and national authorities revolved around taxation and law and order, while the interconnection of crafts and religious movements played a very important role in social stability.[29]

However, the civil role of the crafts and the religious movements started to deteriorate by the late nineteenth century, and was demolished completely by the nineteen-twenties with the emergence of modern states and trade unions. Islamic markets were increasingly absorbed into international markets. The traditional markets and crafts were lost, along with the civil society that they had created. The Islamic city saw the disappearance of its authentic civil institutions and their replacement by governmental associations that have not been able to play the independent role of the crafts, the Sufis, and the notables or to create a true civil society.[30]

Of the many other civil groups that existed in Muslim society, one last, but not least, group will be discussed here—the minorities that flourished under adherence to their own laws and scriptures. The leaders of these religious minorities played for their own people the same role that Muslim scholars did, for they were accorded great latitude in running their internal affairs.

While pluralism is mostly needed in the construction of identity, which requires the acknowledgment of differences between one individual and another or one group and another, it has become a universal issue. Every human grouping includes diverse opinions. Put differently, it is very natural that people differ, while unity is a rational construction. In this sense, any culture is a project to organize human beings in order to unite them. Any discursive reading of human culture and civilization shows that diversity is the principle and origin of development.

Rejecting the validity of political difference or diversity is one of the most glaring problems in Islam. Difference, and not uniformity, has been the major characteristic of Islamic social and political organization and thought. Right after the Prophet's death, differences over the nature of political rule arose and soon developed into full-fledged ideologies or political tendencies that are still today part of the modern consciousness of Islamic communities. Controversies over the caliphate produced a diversity of views on its nature and its linkage to the political community—for political legitimacy is not derived from power but is dependent on social bonds that seek power for their fulfillment. Nonetheless, political legitimacy in Islam needs its religious as well as its rational justifications. Thus the main Islamic text, the Qur'an, becomes a tool of legitimacy that is impervious to sheer power. The text has in fact justified the rise and fall of political parties, which later expanded into legal and theological schools. Over the centuries, the text in Islam stood for diversity and justified different discourses that were tied to the power and interests of different groups and their social organizations. Since no social group had any intrinsic right to rule, all were equally entitled to propound the best way to rule and the qualifications for government and the nature of political organization, obligation, and freedom.[31]

Islamic law commands the believers to change evil conditions of human living, whether produced by an individual, a group, a party, or a system. The Prophet also ordered the believers to change their own conditions for the better. Further, the Prophet declared that those who do not enjoin the good and forbid evil are not part of the community: those who do not struggle for the sake of society, he explained, are not true believers.[32] Thus people's involvement in the community's affairs is religiously required. The community is ordered to oppose evil and wrongdoing related to society and government. The best example in the past was the development of legal and theological schools as well as Sufi orders, which are equal to our modern understanding of political parties. Parties that express innovative attitudes toward social and political issues and aim at the good of society are a modern must for the religious fulfillment of the command to enjoin the good and forbid evil.

The term "party" as a political entity was not in circulation in Islamic political literature until late in the nineteenth century, though in the oldest constitution of Islam the term "party" was used politically. It was mentioned in the Qur'an to make a distinction between the party of God and the party of Satan. The party of God, Hizb Allah, included those individuals who believed in God and his messengers; it is the party of *tawhid*. Hizb al-Shaytan included those individuals who forgot God and fought the Prophet and aimed at division of the community.[33] However, it apparently applied only to a group that belonged to a nation, a religion, or a tribe. It was also used to denote the groups that fought the Prophet. Thus the term "party" seemed to be reserved to those who did not accept the Islamic system and fought it.[34] The word *millet* was used to describe the followers of a religion, a principle, or intellectual pursuit; *nihla* was used to denote the followers of a specific view within the *millet,* while *firqa* was used to indicate either of the two.[35] These terms functioned as equivalents of our "party." However, the word *hizb* was not used as an indicator of political difference or political pluralism.

Public Opinion and Pluralism

One of the five main fundamentals that the Mu'tazilites upheld was the community's duty of enjoining the good and forbidding evil. A group of Muslims can, however, perform that duty on the condition that forbidding a specific evil not lead to a greater evil.[36] The principle became ingrained in the consciousness of Muslims as the legitimizing rule for loyalty or opposition, individual, social, or political. According to the Qur'an, enjoining the good and forbidding evil is a duty upon which the superiority of Muslims as a historical entity is dependent.[37]

The third century of Hijra was one of the richest centuries in Islam because it showed all sorts of attitudes toward religion, politics, and society. The Islamic society viewed and dealt with public opinion in terms of legal concepts like consensus, opinion, and preference as well as the majority and the community. It was worked out before and after Islam through venerable institutions like the elders of the tribe or the council of *shura*. Islamic thought tried to reduce the tribe's input and to replace that with the community's input. While the issue of the caliphate after the death of the Prophet was the first major test of the formation of public opinion and its diversity, the division of public opinion led to the rise of political and legal schools.[38]

Public opinion during that period was basically expressed in the political organizations, religious movements, revolts, circles of literature and arts, as well as sects and different social groups. All groups, whether theologians, Sufis, jurists, or thinkers, were classified in terms of their relations with the political authorities. Public opinion on the government and the political system was divided, which in many cases led to revolts and strong opposition movements such as the Khawarij and the Mu'tazilites. Divisions over class privileges also produced sharp social unrest, as with the Shu'ubiyya, and conflicts between Arabs and non-Arabs. All these factors weakened the central authority and led to the rise of reform movements.[39]

Public opinion was generally divided along Arab and non-Arab (especially Iranian and Turkish) lines. The latter were, in turn, divided by social, economic, and political systems. While Islam was the focus of the Islamic state, these nationalities competed with each other and had national ambitions. Each nationality included groups that either opposed or approved of the government. At times, price rises were sufficient to bring about political upheavals, not only in the ranks of the opposition but also among the loyal and even the military. One time a minister would be fired, another time a revolt would take place. The Zinj, Qaramita, and Babikiyya revolts were originally triggered by opposition to economic policies such as the collection of revenues by the 'Abbasids. Bribery was also condemned publicly through the circulation and recitation of poems about some officials.[40]

Public opinion had many centers. During that century, the 'Abbasid prisons were basically filled with political opponents. Most prisons were made for political prisoners as well as for those who fell afoul of the economic and social system. Al-Ma'mun, for instance, during the Ordeal imprisoned those scholars who refused to acknowledge the createdness of the Qur'an. Another important place for the formation of public opinion was the market, a complex net of professions and relations in the center of the city where both locals and foreigners would visit, buy, and converse. Many opposition movements and revolts were nurtured there, like the Zinj opposition movement.[41]

Mosques too were centers of public opinion. While the mosque remained a place of worship and religious studies, it became the center for the administration of state social and political policies, as well as the place for weddings, funerals, dialogues, discussions, and other social activities. When Ahmad ibn Hanbal died, for instance, it was reported that 860,000 people attended his funeral, which, even if it was not true, indicated the popularity of Ibn Hanbal and his school.[42] During major crises, mosques became pivotal for voicing different opinions.

At a theoretical level, Islam sanctions freedom of opinion both as a right and as a duty. It could be considered a fundamental principle of the *shari'a*. The Qur'an itself indicates the need for free opinion and prohibits its suppression.[43] It is established in Islamic teachings that freedom of opinion is necessary to freedom of belief, which is essential for believing in God. Free opinion allows the individual to probe his belief and leads to solid convictions. Indeed, many scholars have held that belief acquired through imitation is imperfect belief.[44]

Furnishing the conditions for freedom of opinion is also religiously required. God in the Qur'an censures those who do not create favorable conditions for voicing their views, and visits His punishment on those who accept and yield to falsehood without doing what is necessary to change their conditions and free themselves from oppression. The Qur'an even calls for migration in order to attain that freedom. It makes the spread of free opinions a call for enjoining the good and forbidding evil and a strong basis for social unity and coherence. In fact, suppression of free opinions, by preventing the creation of a united and coherent society, actually leads to social and political disunity and division.[45] At the same time, however, Islamic law sets limitations on freedom of opinion. Since freedom aims at uniting the people and finding an avenue for expressing their views, any act that endangers that unity is in principle outlawed. First, any opinion must be based on true information before being circulated. Morally, it must not be harmful or libelous.[46]

The first centuries of Islam saw widespread freedom of opinion and the rise of juridical and theological schools as well as opposition movements. Muslims benefited from opening up to other civilizations and borrowing ideas and methods from them, especially as they followed the same general framework of ideas and had a common worldview. When al-Ghazali launched his critique of Greek philosophy, he stated that his aim was not to prove the truth but only to show the falsity of Greek philosophical methods from a general Islamic point of view. At the same time, he discredited the prevailing Islamic theological methods as also producing unconvincing knowledge.[47]

In the medieval history of Islam one can sense that whenever freedom of opinion was suppressed, there was an intellectual shift toward the strict discussion of minor matters and away from global or universal thinking. Jurists went from being great thinkers to imitating the founders of their schools and busied themselves with extravagant details that were unrelated to the pressing issues of their time. They turned to writing commentaries on commentaries, instead of studying the text and linking it to their daily life and social, economic, and political institutions. The limiting of freedom led to the limiting of genuine and committed scholarship. After the fifth century of Hijra, when political tyranny reached its apex under the semi-independent Islamic states, *ijtihad* was not truly exercised; Sufism, as an escape, spread, while scholars were immersed in details of jurisprudence, developing new juridical theories. Muslim sciences became defensive rather than inventive, notwithstanding the rise now and then of great individual scholars. The general intellectual environment was dead and removed from the realities of the time. It had lost its freedom to deal with these realities.

While the Islamic religious mind is, in theory, free from institutional overseeing, the political repression of opposition pushed the Islamic mind to move to Sufism. If Muslims felt that they could not affect their political life, they tended toward idealism and preservation of traditions—hence, traditionalism. Jurisprudence became a traditional and theoretical science. As one can observe from al-Mawardi's political treatise, jurisprudence crafted the realities of the time onto idealistic and traditional views without an attempt at reworking either.

The original freedom of opinion, manifested clearly in the development of jurisprudence, theology, and philosophy in a free intellectual atmosphere, was replaced by narrow sectarian intolerance. Muslim unity during the first four centuries, when a multiplicity of views and methods covered the Muslim world, was far stronger than in the centuries that followed, when sectarian schools of thought dominated and state oppression increased. In the first instance Muslims, whether philosophers, theologians, jurists, or the common people, may have disagreed, but within one frame of reference. In the latter instance, the attempts to force an ideological and theological unity led to political disunity.

More important, rational opinion, or the use of reason to arrive at an opinion (*al-ijtihad bi al-ra'y*), is one of the fundamental sources of legislation, and was used to produce legal principles and general understanding of religion. It is still in theory a source for understanding the ultimate causes for and meanings of revelations as well as the objectives and details of the *shari'a* and the interests of individuals, societies, and nations.[48] The Qur'an itself used reason to explain the causes for certain commands and judgments, which opened the way for the jurists and scholars to use the same logic. That a legal order or a theological view is accorded justification in the Qur'an itself testifies to the legitimacy and necessity of opinions that are rationally developed in order to enjoin the good and forbid evil. The ultimate significance of legislative Qur'anic aspect must be logically developed and used for guidance. The logic of a specific text goes beyond the text itself to effecting social constructions and institutional developments. This is more obviously true because Islam speaks not only to the Arabs who know Arabic but to non-Arabs and to illiterate Arabs. Islamic legislation and philosophy of life cannot just be derived from the Qur'an, but must be tailored to a specific reality in terms of its changing needs or contexts.

Thus *ijtihad*, and the opinion it generates, is essential for understanding the scope of the text as well as its significance. It has had much usage. First, on those issues where there was no textual authority, the jurists developed analogical deduction (*al-ijtihad al-qiyasi*) to help in producing new opinions. This kind of *ijtihad* is also used to develop the renewed interests (*al-masalih al-mutajaddida*) of individuals, society, and the state. Second, it is employed to draw up the policy for legislation (*siyasat al-tashri'*) that is required to keep pace with development and, especially, with emergencies. This policy should aim at implementing justice, the *shari'a,* and general safety. Finally, it is the method used for theoretical renewal or development of the legal system in order to make the *shari'a* applicable to different times and conditions.[49] Also, opinion is needed for proper application of the *shari'a* to daily life, not just to theoretical questions. Specialized or expert opinions are needed, especially in dealing with public issues that might not be strictly religious but require technical skills, like public health. Thus, proper implementation of social, political, legal, and legislative systems requires opinions.[50]

Islam sanctioned intellectual diversity in understanding religion and reality, for the meaning of both the text and reality may differ from one individual or group to another. When the Prophet said that there would be at the beginning of each century a person who would renew religion, this was understood to mean that we need to renew our understanding of religion. This implies, of course, renewal of the intellectual edifice and of the legal, legislative, social, and political systems in line with the evolving interests of the individual, society, and the state. Since the text is fixed and opinion is not, logically the former is interpreted by the latter. Thus opinion, scholarly or public, is a religious requirement and a human necessity.[51]

Opposition in Islam

Opposition manifested itself as intellectual endeavors that took the shape of theological and philosophical schools and political differences that took the shape of legal schools and opposition movements. Opposition (*mu'arada*) was used in Islamic terminology to indicate intellectual differences throughout the history of Islam. The meaning of the term differed from one age to another, depending on the issues that were dealt with at a specific time. However, general characteristics shaped the behavior of the opposition. First, it must be ruled by the precepts of the *shari'a* such as the conditions for the breaking of a contract. Second, it is loose and does not have to have a solid organization; it is often individual, since the individual is the focus of the Islamic discourse for enjoining the good and forbidding evil. In fact, opposition reflected a political phenomenon in society that aimed to achieve the ideals of Islam as both an intellectual school and a political movement.

Al-Ghazali argues in his *Ihya' 'Ulum al-Din* that enjoining the good and forbidding evil is a Qur'anic duty. This duty, which perfects people's belief and life, may be performed either by an individual, a group, or the community. The Qur'an made the distinguished status of the Muslim community dependent on enjoining the good and forbidding evil. This command applies to individual, social, and political spheres of life.[52]

While the community's total agreement or consensus was not realistically possible in most cases, the jurists referred to the idea of majority (*al-jumhur*) as a practical replacement for consensus. Al-Ghazali, for instance, accepts the imamate of the persons who receive the approval of the majority, which is equal to the modern-day idea of democratic rule. Opposition usually surfaced as minority views, which were expressed freely most of the time.[53] The Islamic system of government accepted the principle of opposition; the important issue was the scope of opposition that Islam allowed. Opposition requires accepting the legitimacy of the free expression of different opinions in a context of tolerance.

The Qur'an laid down many principles that regulate the relationship between the ruler and the ruled, whether loyalty or opposition. The ruler is one individual from among the believers, and therefore is subject to the command "enjoin the good and forbid evil." *Shura* is another principle that regulates the relationship. Obedience to the ruler is not absolute but conditioned on obedience to the *shari'a*.[54] Legitimate opposition is linked to observance of the same law. The term *mu'arada* (opposition) is not mentioned in the Qur'an, but allied concepts such as conflict, difference, dissent, and argumentation are mentioned.[55] The Qur'anic acceptance of such concepts among the community is an acknowledgment that no single opinion or method is expected of the community. The concepts go beyond mere opposition to include different methods of ruling as well as accepting philosophical, interpretative, and political differences. If religious matters are subject to differences and interpretations, it stands to reason that worldly matters are subject to at least the same level of differences and interpretations. The Qur'an, then, does not stand against the principle of opposition but makes itself the ultimate legitimizing tool of opposition.[56] A clear Qur'anic verse, for instance, does not by itself resolve a conflict between communities. The Qur'an asks the faithful to resolve their differences by referring to Qur'anic teachings and the Sunna. However, such an act cannot be performed by the Qur'an itself, but requires a body of people or scholars to do the referring.

If there is no clear Qur'anic verse or Prophetic tradition, again a body of people or scholars is needed to look into the issue. *Shura* is one way of resolving controversy; different arguments and opinions may be circulated to inform the public on divisive issues. While in an Islamic state there is no legitimate opposition to the Qur'anic creed, all issues that relate to human interactions are subject to opposition. If opposition means denying a religious command, it is prohibited, since Muslims are asked to submit to Qur'anic commands.[57]

Also, disunity is not accepted as a legitimate tactic of opposition. Of course, if opposition arises in response to a violation of divine law, then it is a duty and falls within "enjoining the good and forbidding evil." However, most opposition is related to issues and differences that are permissible by religion and should in principle be subject to *shura*.

In sum, then, the Qur'an legitimizes opposition insofar as it does not infringe on the basic doctrines of religion. Opposition is considered to be a natural or intuitive matter and unavoidable. It is doctrinally bound and justified by *shura* and the command to enjoin the good and forbid evil.

The Prophetic Sunna, the second foundation of religious law, likewise legitimizes opposition. When the Prophet laid down the first constitution in Islam in the form of a contract between different groups and individuals, he allowed dissent or opposition there as well if the terms of the contract or the articles of the constitution were not respected. On religious principles the Prophet was uncompromising, but political and social matters were subject to opinion, *ijtihad,* and *shura.* The Prophet was often asked whether his views were part of revelation or his own. He was many times opposed, especially in political and social matters. He is quoted as saying, you know better the matter of your world, but I know better the religious matters.[58]

While the legitimacy of opposition is based on *shura* and the command to enjoin the good and forbid evil, and while jurists have agreed that *shura* is a pillar of Islamic rule, they have disagreed on its practice by the ruler, whether commended or obligatory. This is why many scholars link it to *ijtihad,* which demands the views of the experts. However, *shura* as a communal duty is an essential step in the process of electing the ruler when divergent views are expressed before elections. The failure of *shura* to produce a consensus or a majority view gives the opposition legitimate cause for dissent. In political life and communal administration, *shura* thus becomes the linchpin.

The command to enjoin the good and forbid evil, later institutionalized as *hisba,* is a comprehensive principle that legitimizes opposition not only in the communal and political arena but in matters of ethical behavior.[59] It is both an individual and a state duty because the Qur'an postulates its necessity for good community.[60] *Hisba* was the political interpretation of this religious principle, where the community and the individual as well as the state were capable of expressing their views as part of *hisba.* The duty falls more on the ruler, who is responsible for furthering the good and preventing the harm of the community.

Islamic opposition often invoked the same principle when standing against the political system and state policies, for Muslims are asked not to be silent against the harmful but to change it to what is good. As a legitimizing principle it has historically provided the opposition with a strong Qur'anic weapon for use against a ruler or a government that is seen to act counter to Islam or the community's interest. It is a religious principle powerful enough to be set up against another principle, obedience to the government. Furthermore, it provides groups within the Muslim community, especially the opposition, with a higher value system whose legitimacy does not spring from the political system, for the basis of legitimacy is to rule according to the community's general interests with no contradiction to Islamic law.

The Prophet clearly ordered enjoining the good and forbidding evil by actions and behavior, by speeches and opinions and, at least for the weak, by passive resistance of evil. Thus there are two levels of opposition, positive and passive. Positive opposition involves actual actions to bring about change; passive opposition does not involve actions but the intention to bring about change. The jurist Ibn Hazm argues that the community agreed on the duty to command good and forbid evil. However, differences were related to the method of fulfilling this command. A group of *ahl al-Sunna* preferred passive opposition and, at most, preaching, but saw a need for active involvement only when the government was threatened. Put differently, they did not allow armed resistance against the government in order to enjoin the good and forbid evil.[61] Other Sunnis as well as the Mu'tazila, Khawarij, and Zaydis saw it as their duty to fight to fulfill that command—provided they could overcome the ruler.[62] They thought that it was better not to fight the ruler if there was no possibility of winning, for bloodshed and social disruption would follow. Briefly, enjoining the good and forbidding evil could, equally as well as *shura,* be the basis of legitimate opposition. Either could be used by internal and external opposition, whether in effecting a change of state policies or a change of ruler.

While the caliphate represented the first model for political rule, which later turned into a form of kingship, another model of political rule, the idea of the imamate, represented the first model of organized political opposition. Later in the history of Islam, the caliphate and the imamate came to be synonymous.[63] Around the doctrine of the imamate many groups, like the Khawarij and the Shi'a, crystallized their opposition. Sunni opposition mostly took the form of passive attitudes toward the state; since the Sunnis had in mind the interest of the community at large, they were not easily moved against the state. Intellectually, the Sunnite opposition was always present, but not in revolutionary forms as was the case with the Shi'a.[64]

The Sunni opposition usually saw its opposition as a form of enjoining the good and forbidding evil. It linked its views of a caliphate to the caliph's application of the *shari'a,* not to his intrinsic faculties. For this reason the Sunnites opposed most views of the Shi'a on the imam's personality. Instead they postulated general qualifications for the caliph, his lieutenants, and *ahl al-hal wa al-'aqd* and conducted many studies to organize the systems of *mazalim* (appeals), *hisba,* and the judiciary.[65] Generally it may be said that Sunni opposition took institutional forms within the system, while Shi'ite opposition took place outside it. For instance, the

Sunnites who did not accept the imam's infallibility found that society's elite, or *ahl al-hal wa al-'aqd,* had the power to remove him. Not every mistake is a good enough pretext, especially if there is a possibility of chaos or anarchy. But the imam is wholly responsible for his actions, and major misrule, like damaging the community's interests or suspending the law, can legitimize major opposition against the ruler.[66]

Sunni political thought tended always to favor patience out of fear of disunity. None of those theories that advocated armed resistance sounded well to the Sunnis because they threatened the stability of society. Sunni scholars focused more on the security of society than on the issue of strict legitimacy. Ultimately, enjoining the good and forbidding evil is a principle that draws the line between loyalty and opposition. Forbidding evil takes precedence over enjoining the good because preventing harm must rank above bringing about improvement. Enjoining the good may take many forms but should not lead to violence, civil wars, dissension, or other dangerous consequences.[67]

Modern Islamist Expressions of Pluralism

During the Ottoman rule, the diversity of religious scholars became threatened, for while the state acknowledged the legitimacy of the four Sunni legal schools, it tried to impose the Hanafi legal system by tying it to the state organization and the judiciary. The attempt to unify the organizations of scholars into one Ottoman system was partly successful but could not altogether do away with diversity in the scholarly centers of the Muslim world. Egypt, for instance, did not yield to the Hanafi system and maintained its own center of al-Azhar. At this time the Ottomans' organizational plan depended on reordering society according to professions, religions, and regions, with the characteristics of each group acknowledged. A direct consequence was the rise of strict professional associations that followed strict rules, and this included the religious scholars.[68]

The scholars of Egypt and Syria, among others, resisted having their profession subjected to the Ottoman state's necessities—and its sectarian and racial preferences. During the sixteenth century, the rules of any city depended on the dominant legal school that governed interactions in the market, the mosques, and society. The development of the Islamic city corresponded to the development of jurisprudence. However, the new regulations of the central Ottoman government dissected the city into smaller professional and religious groups. Contradictions between state laws and the religious law led to marginalization of the religious law and its interpreters, the jurists; the city found itself undergoing reorganization both at the state level and socially. State regulations accentuated group differences within cities, diminishing their unity. The jurists naturally opposed policies that bred disunity, even as they themselves were becoming an important professional group with its own interests and structures. For instance, families that were deeply rooted in the religious establishment were able to bequeath their jobs to their children.[69]

It was argued that the intervention of Western powers on the Christian side changed the balance of power within the Ottoman Empire and led to degrading intercommunity relations. Furthermore, the spread of European education, an education spearheaded by missionary schools, highlighted the differences between Christians and Muslims. More important, Western powers encouraged sectarian and racial claims—for instance, Armenian and Kurdish—in order to weaken the Islamic state.[70]

The Ottomans, who fought the Byzantine Empire and other European powers and seized Constantinople and expanded into Europe and Africa and many other areas, also suffered from internal problems related to legitimacy. While claiming that the 'Abbasids had conceded the caliphate, the Ottomans in reality acquired it by force—another addition to the historical antimodels of rule by seizure. The Ottomans ruled as both sultans and caliphs and joined religious power to political power. While the Ottomans adopted the *shari'a,* they also introduced the concepts of civil law. Law (*al-qanun*) was considered to be the sultan's will, and not that of God or the people. Suleiman al-Qanuni abolished the four judgeships that represented the four schools of law in Egypt and replaced them with a military judge.[71]

The period of Sultan Suleiman was considered the golden age of the Ottoman Empire, because of its scientific renaissance and its superiority over the West. The empire even expanded then, into Serbia, Iraq, Armenia, and other areas, and developed a navy that controlled the seas. However, the Ottomans were weakened by their battles with the Europeans and by difficulties in governing the empire's diverse ethnic and confessional groups. The military (*al-hashshashin*) took over; so did corruption, injustice, and immoderate taxation.

The commercial competition between the empire and Europe, at a time of massive political and economic changes like the discovery of America and the depreciating of the Ottoman economy, was reflected in the poor administration of its territories. The empire started falling behind Europe and ceding one thing after another, first signing peace treaties with European powers and finally granting special concessions. The Europeans adroitly exploited the issue of *ahl al-dhimma,* turning the empire's minority problem into a process of extracting concessions, not only for minorities but for European foreigners. Europe also revived the issue of racial distinction between the Turks and other races, especially the perception that the Ottomans had discriminated against non-Turks for a long period. In a 1916 circular for the revolutionary movement against the Ottomans in the Hijaz in Arabia, some of the Arab complaints centered on attempts to end using the Arabic language in schools, ministries, and courts in order reduce the literary, intellectual, and military influence of Arabs. Also, the Ottomans confiscated Arab funds by moving many rich Arab families to Turkey.[72]

The Ottomans tried to include intellectuals in the political establishment, in line with earlier policies of the Seljuks. However, contention arose between the state and a large segment of the *'ulama',* while other segments became more involved in local social structures. While the Ottomans increased centralization, politics was still subject to a range of pressures from the diverse communities that constituted the empire. During its early period, the empire was largely accepted even in European lands; in Germany it relieved people of the European feudal system. Everywhere they expanded, the Ottomans tried to impose the rule of institutions that were underpinned by the *shari'a.*[73]

The Ottomans' acceptance of a constitution—promulgated in 1876, suspended in 1878, and reinstituted in 1908—signified a major transformation in political thinking with the adoption of representative political bodies and elections.[74] While the communities' experience was not based on election, elections reveal the harmony between the communities' political image of themselves and their powers, i.e., *shura* and consensus. This image is opposed to the authoritarian nature of the Ottoman rule and its changed attitude toward its citizens. Six parliamentary elections were held, and if they were not conducted in the ideal manner, they did respond to people's demand to participate in decision making in political life. While the constitution reorganized the *millet* or confessional system, no real religious or political objections were raised against the concepts of a constitution and elections, except by the sultans themselves and their entourage who would have preferred business as usual. In 1912 in Syria, for instance, we are told that the elections were hotly contested, not only because they provided fertile ground for a newly emerging partisan discourse that appealed to ethnic sentiments and made political use of Islam but also because the race appeared close, and a good turnout on one side could swing the vote. In Syria, religious-sectarian discourses entered the campaigns in a negative way by reinforcing the appeal to Muslim voters rather than by soliciting the non-Muslim vote. "Sectarianism was stronger in those parts of the Empire where the non-Muslims were numerically stronger. . . . This apparent concern to court the minorities turned into mutual accusation of disregarding religious precepts and favoring the non-Muslims."[75]

Even while codifying the *shari'a* according to the recognized four schools of law, the Ottoman Empire left local authorities to decide which school was to be followed, for the empire included diverse ethnic and religious ties. The Ottomans acknowledged each minority's right to conduct its religious practices and personal laws and religious endowments in accordance with its own laws. This gave the religious leaders of minorities, who acted as intermediaries, privileged positions vis-à-vis the government—especially as the Hanafi school of law, which was followed mostly by the Ottomans, considered all People of the Book a genuine part of the community.

After World War II, the West sought to further its control of world markets and cheap material. This economic advantage was coupled with the West's military occupation of the Middle East, bringing about the rise of nationalism as an ideology of resistance. The nationalists were finally able to liberate their land but failed to bring about democracy and liberalism. Both secular liberal trends and Islamic modernist reforms were curtailed and were mostly replaced by authoritarian secular ideologies.

Nowadays, the moderate and pluralist discourse of the Muslim Brotherhood in Egypt, still the most profound Islamist movement, is prominent in the understanding of pluralism. This discourse, however, has become the basis of two contradictory discourses: one that is very radical, antiliberal, and militant, and another that is very moderate, liberal, and nonmilitant. The liberal development of the inclusivist discourse of Hasan al-Banna and the Muslim Brethren was not a possibility under the authoritarian governments of 'Abd al-Nasir and his successors. More logical was the transformation of this discourse into a radical Islamist discourse, of which the most exclusive is that of Sayyid Qutb; the ideologues who followed him set up armed radical groups.

However, most Western and Middle Eastern media as well as scholars have in general treated modern Islamist discourses as consisting of only one negative and radical interpretation of the religion of Islam. Worse, many analysts and politicians even make Islam and Islamism interchangeable, turning Islam into an easy target as a strategic enemy for the West.

Now it is common currency that a green, or Islamic, threat has replaced the red threat of communism. While it is true that many Islamic movements are radical in the sense that they are alienating to and alienated from their societies, others are moderate, open to compromise, and involved positively in their societies. Still Islamic fundamentalisms—and even Islam itself—are all read through the lens of Islamic radicalism, while other religions are read through the lenses of their moderate views.

Islamism is, however, an umbrella term for a wide variety of discourses and activist movements that range from a high level of moderate pluralism, and thus inclusive democracy, to extreme radicalism, intolerant unitarianism, and thus tyrannical majority rule. While some Islamist groups are pluralistic in terms of inter-Muslim relations and between Muslims and minorities, others are not. Again, while some Islamists are politically pluralistic but theologically exclusive, others are accommodating religiously, but direct their exclusivist programs to the outside, the West, or imperialism. Even at the scientific level, some Islamists argue for Western science and technology as Islamicly sound, while others exclude them because of their presumed un-Islamic nature. Also, while the majority of Islamists call for pluralistic democracy and argue for it as an essentially Islamic point of view, the radicals brand it unbelief.

In modern times, many movements that call for a return to the fundamentals of Islam have flourished throughout the different regions of the Muslim world. These movements seem to be a continuation and development of the earlier Islamic response, or modernism, that was aborted. Leaders of such movements have felt that the Islamic spiritual dimension can aid in developing a clear portrait of the enemy, condemn moral corruption, and mobilize Muslim societies. The contrast becomes brighter and sharper when the perceived corrupted present is contrasted with a perceived glorious past full of ethical purity. This idealized past is being used today to reactivate Muslims' energies to establish a new civilization, to reconstruct their identity, to absorb modernity, and to develop their discourses on human rights, pluralism, and democracy.

Although Islamists agree on the usage of the foundations of religion, the Qur'an and the Sunna, and develop similar philosophical superstructures, I argue that it is the incompatible policies of most Middle Eastern states—by turns inclusive democratic and exclusive authoritarian—that create the dual nature of Islamist political behavior. While Arab regimes hold the international order responsible for their harsh situations, the Islamists attribute the states' economic, social, and political failures to the structure and ideology of the regimes. They view the regimes as a conduit of global conflicts between dominant world powers and the ambitions and hopes of the indigenous populations.

Islamists in general believe that their governments do not serve the ideological, political, or economic interests of their peoples but those of the dominant world powers. Imperialism, colonialism, exploitation, and materialism—all these are charges brought against the West. Liberalization, whether economic or political or cultural, social justice, political freedom, and democracy are major demands of both radical and moderate Islamist groups. Modern national states have been viewed by Islamists as the link between what is unacceptable and inhumane in both Western and Eastern civilization, namely Western materialism and Eastern despotism. An Islamic state, they believe, can withstand and even correct Western materialistic domination and Eastern political authoritarianism. This notwithstanding, we must know how an Islamist theoretician or movement creates its discourse and argues for the active method of setting up that state, the manner of conducting politics therein, and the state's basic ideology before we can classify that theoretician or movement as an exclusivist, nonliberal, radical antagonist of pluralistic democracy or an inclusivist, liberal, and moderate protagonist of pluralistic democracy. The rest of this chapter, therefore, sets up a preliminary typology of Islamism on pluralism.

Radical Views

The Iranian constitution accepts the command to enjoin the good and forbid evil as the doctrine that organizes relations between individuals and groups as well as the government. However, it should not lead to threats against military, economic, cultural, and political independence. All individuals, the community, and the government are responsible for maintaining freedom, independence, unity, and safety. Freedom cannot be exploited to threaten independence, and independence cannot be exploited to threaten freedom.[76]

'Abbud al-Zumar, an army intelligence officer, the military leader of Tanzim al-Jihad, and a founder and leader of Jama'at al-Jihad al-Islami, follows Sayyid Qutb's rationale in stressing the importance of active involvement in total opposition to the state. The program of action should focus on a workable Islamic vision that contributes to uniting Islamic movements within one framework and leads members to forgo individual and public differences. Employing a key Qutbian political term, *ma'alim al-tariq* (signpost of the road), he urges the Islamic movement to concentrate on its basic objective, the Islamic state. This requires an uncompromising and exclusive attitude toward the *jahili* systems and societies as they relate to all aspects of life. The alternative is a radical transformation or total Islamization of all facets of life and the unwavering rejection of secularism, nationalism, and parliamentary life. All this change has to start, however, with dethroning current rulers who do not adhere to the *shari'a.*[77]

In adopting an uncompromising and exclusive attitude toward the *jahili* systems, societies, and religions as they relate to all aspects of life, Islam's objective is to eradicate unbelief and paganism, including nationalism, patriotism, and incorrect religious creeds. Al-Zumar rejects the idea that jihad is launched for a defensive purpose and argues that Muslims have agreed not only to defend themselves from unbelievers but to invade them as well and to force them either to accept Islam, pay *jizya* (head tax), or be killed. This is why God sent his Messenger, to raise the banner of jihad. Peace or coexistence is not allowed if Muslims can fight the unbelievers, though their temporary deception is permitted. Jihad will remain a permanent Islamic duty until the day of judgment.[78] In line with his exclusive radical ideology, al-Zumar tried to kill President Sadat; though he failed, Sadat was later killed with al-Zumar's aid by members of Tanzim al-Jihad.

Muhammad Abul Salam Faraj, the general secretary of Tanzim al-Jihad, believes that the reason why Islam lost its universal place is that Muslims do not pursue jihad anymore. Tyranny on this earth will not disappear without force, and it is the Muslim's religious duty to establish God's rule on earth. Faraj also argues that the abode of Islam is that land that is ruled by God's law, and the abode of unbelief is the land that is ruled by other laws. Today the so-called Muslim lands and Christian lands are both the abode of unbelief. The law that rules over the whole earth is the law of unbelief. Rulers are raised up by "Crusadism, communism, or Zionism," and are like the Tatars who borrowed law from Judaism, Christianity, and Islam.[79]

As to jihad, which relates to the self, the devil, the unbelievers, and hypocrites, Faraj again argues like previous thinkers that it is made for the spread of the divine message, and it could be both defensive and offensive. First, however, the message of Islam should be spread peacefully so that people can adopt Islam willingly; if not, then it is either *jizya* or war. Fighting is a duty of all Muslims without exception. Those who do not fight have renounced their faith.[80]

Salih Sirriyya (1947–74), originally associated with Hizb al-Tahrir and later the leader of another radical and militant Islamist group, Tanzim al-Fanniyya al-'Askariyya, likewise fell under the spell of Qutb. His exclusivity can be seen in his categorization of mankind in three groups only: Muslims, infidels, and hypocrites. Any neglect of an Islamic duty makes the individual an apostate and subject to death. Multiparty systems and diverse legal schools negate unity and lead to substantive conflicts.[81] Sirriyya allows the temporary use of democracy in order to set up an Islamic state. If activists are persecuted, then they can secretly infiltrate the political system and even become cabinet ministers. However it may be pursued, the struggle to topple un-Islamic governments and any irreligious entity is a religious duty until the day of judgment. Sirriyya cites the defense of un-Islamic governments, participation in un-Islamic ideological parties, and adhering to foreign philosophies and ways of life as obvious instances of unbelief that incur death. The fact that sovereignty belongs to God is used by Sirriyya to divide mankind into the exclusive Hizb al-Shaytan, consisting of all individuals and institutions that do not believe in or practice Islam, and the exclusive Hizb Allah, consisting of those who struggle to establish the Islamic state. Out of this logic, Sirriyya attempted a coup d'état against Anwar al-Sadat and was executed in 1974.[82]

Sirriyya refuses to see religion as only a way of worshipping God. The Christian concept of religion as a private relationship between man and God is becoming current in the Muslim world, but this understanding of religion is wrong because it denies the appropriateness of Islamic law to life. Those who hold such beliefs are unbelievers. Sirriyya argues that the West wants to separate religion from politics because it wants to isolate Islam from political life, as happened to Christianity in the West. However, unlike Christianity, Islam will not be cornered.[83]

More radical and fundamental is the ideology of Sayyid Qutb that spread throughout radical circles in Islamic countries. Qutb argues that self-interest, for instance, weakens communal solidarity, while mutual responsibility (*takaful*) strengthens that solidarity, itself a religious duty on all of the society. Although Qutb argues that this responsibility is social in nature, it may turn into a political responsibility carried out by the state—such a responsibility extends to education, health, proper jobs, and the like. While the state's interference must be limited, in reality and in practice, any failure of society to take care of its own affairs would lead to the state's moral responsibility to dominate society. Again, while the state's actions are of a supplementary nature, they ultimately exclude and then replace the institutions of civil society. Interest groups are allowed only if their objectives are broad, such as caring for the poor or the sick. Others such as women's liberation movements on Western models are not welcomed or included, for their freedom to pursue their personal interests away from the family weakens society.[84]

Again, because Western political systems to Qutb are false both practically and theoretically, he excludes them and prohibits group formation along Western lines. A good society, then, is composed of groups sharing similar interests and perceptions of life as well as unified political orientations. A particular problem for Qutb in adopting Western models of unions and federations, and the cause for their exclusion, is their selfish and materialistic nature. In Islam *al-naqabat* or unions, which were originally the models for their Western counterparts, are based on brotherhood and solidarity. Thus Qutb sees only mutual exclusivity between the philosophies, ideologies, and institutions of the West and those of Islam. The former are *jahili* and, as such, belong to the party of Satan (Hizb al-Shaytan); the others are Islamic and, as such, belong to the party of God (Hizb Allah).[85]

For Qutb only an Islamic ideology may be represented in a political party (the vanguard or *tali'a*). His book *Ma'alim fi al-Tariq* (Signposts on the road) is specific about the mission that this vanguard should carry out with an exclusive and uncompromising attitude to all other ideologies, societies, and ways of life. However, the establishment of an Islamic system permits the involvement of different institutions in political processes so that the public will may be known in the context of an Islamic ideology and in exclusion of other ideologies.[86]

Qutb excludes the legitimacy not only of multiparty systems but also of one-party systems and replaces them with a religious vanguard whose job is first and foremost salvational. Any ideological group or system not based on Islam is not allowed to operate. Minorities are included religiously in that they may keep their faith, but they are excluded politically, with no right to form political parties or even a "vanguard." Qutb also links valid free expression to the parameters of Islamic ideological understanding. All those societies and parties that do not conform to such an understanding are described as *jahili* or paganist.[87]

Shukri Mustapha (1942–1977) was arrested in 1965 while distributing pamphlets against the regime at the university in Asyut. Mustapha was released in 1971 and continued his studies. As an inmate with Sayyid Qutb, Shukri Mustapha accepted the former's views and established the exclusivist radical Jama'at al-Muslimin (Community of the Muslims), notoriously known as al-Takfir wa al-Hijra, as a fulfillment of the Qutbian vanguard. In 1977 his group kidnapped a former minister of endow-ments, Shaykh Mahmud al-Dhahabi, who had earlier criticized its ideol-ogy. It asked for money and the release of some fundamentalist prisoners from Jama'at or Tanzim al-Fanniyya al-'Askariyya. When its demands were not met, the minister was executed. Mustapha and others were tried by the Higher State Security Court, found guilty, and executed.

Mustapha denied the legitimacy of pluralism and called on people to adhere only to the Qur'an and the Sunna of the Prophet. In his trial before a court martial in Egypt, he explained the exclusivity of his group. It re-jects all theories and philosophies that are not textually derived from the Qur'an and the Sunna of the Prophet, for these are the only criteria of legitimacy and truth. Therefore, the government is in violation of God's governance. Furthermore, Mustapha branded as unbelievers all other Muslims who did not view Islam in his own manner and turned migration from the Egyptian society into a religious duty—thereby making his iso-lated community the only true Muslim society. Prisons in Egypt played an important role in Qutbian radical education, of himself and of others.[88]

Al-Jama'a al-Islamiyya al-Jihadiyya, a branch of Tanzim al-Jihad in upper Egypt, was headed by 'Umar 'Abd al-Rahman (1928–). He gradu-ated from al-Azhar University in 1965 and became a religious scholar. He was appointed imam in a state mosque. His sharp speeches attracted the interest of people. The year 1968 was a turning point in his life as he started moving into political Islam; he described Jamal 'Abd al-Nasir as a "pharaoh." The police secret intelligence and the administration of al-Azhar both warned him against making provocative statements and threatened him with imprisonment and expulsion, respectively. 'Abd al-Rahman was arrested for eight months because he issued a legal *fatwa* prohibiting the death prayer for 'Abd al-Nasir in 1970. When released, 'Abd al-Rahman continued his graduate studies and received a Ph.D. In 1977 he was appointed a professor at al-Azhar University in Asyut. Then he held a teaching position in Saudi Arabia for four years at Riyadh (later King Saud) University. When he returned to Egypt, he was tried for insti-gating by a legal *fatwa* the killing of President Sadat but was released in 1984. In 1990 'Abd al-Rahman emigrated to the United States of America, and in 1993 he was implicated and in 1994 sentenced to life imprisonment on charges of involvement in the World Trade Center explosion in New York.

He condemns the Muslim Brotherhood for its acceptance of minorities' rights, pluralism, and democracy as legitimate tools for political action and the establishment of the Islamic state. By contrast, al-Jama'a al-

Islamiyya denies the rights of minorities and the regime's legitimacy and publicly follows a course of total confrontation. Rejecting integration in democratic institutions, ʿAbd al-Rahman calls for adopting a course of forcible resolution of basic issues of identity, ethics, value system, and the like.[89]

Such a view leads al-Jihad to declare war against the Egyptian Parliament: the parliament has given itself the constitutional right to legislate and permits democracy, a concept that treats believer and nonbeliever alike as citizens.[90] ʿAbd al-Rahman argues that the democratic system in Egypt wants the Muslims to enter into party politics in order to equate Islam with other ideologies. However, the Islamic movement believes in its distinct superiority and does not respect the *jahili*-positive law. ʿAbd al-Rahman further rejects any role for representative bodies as instruments of Qurʾanic interpretation and adjudication. Qurʾanic legitimacy stands on its own. Any violation of Qurʾanic texts leads a ruler to *kufr* punishable by death. ʿAbd al-Rahman himself was viewed as the instigator of Sadat's assassination, especially since he argued that illegitimate rulers deserved death. Also, in line with Qutb's argument, he describes any system that adopts foreign principles as belonging to *kufr* and the *jahiliyya* and legalizes its overthrow.[91]

ʿAbd al-Rahman divides Islamic movements into two trends. The first, spearheaded by the Muslim Brotherhood, accepts the existing regime as legitimate and therefore accepts pluralism and democracy as legitimate tools of political action for the establishment of the Islamic state. The other movement, spearheaded by al-Jamaʿa al-Islamiyya, denies the regime's legitimacy and publicly follows a course of total confrontation. ʿAbd al-Rahman accuses the Brotherhood of complacency because of its work with Sadat and Mubarak, its condemnation of Sadat's death and of violence, not to mention its visits to the Coptic pope and the like. He further rejects its inclusive and compromising attitude in allying itself with the Wafd party as well as al-ʿAmal and al-Ahrar. He calls for replacing the Brotherhood's inclusivity with the Jamaʿa's exclusivity. Also, in line with Qutb's argument, he describes any system that adopts foreign principles as belonging to *kufr* and the *jahiliyya* and legalizes its overthrow.

Moderate Views

As opposed to the radical trend, al-Turabi views the individual as religiously responsible for acquiring freedom and religiously justified in fighting oppression. Ultimate political authority is reserved by al-Turabi to the community, which makes a contract with an individual to lead the community and organize its affairs. However, this is done only through delegation of power for the community's well-being. Al-Turabi accepts any state structure or institution that is bound by, and is based on, contractual mutuality, where the ruler never transgresses against the individual and communal freedom provided for by the Qur'an—for the main Qur'anic discourse is directed primarily not to the state but to the people, and especially to the individual.[92]

This is why a proper Islamic constitution must guarantee all sorts of individual and communal freedoms. The ruler and government must set proper representative bodies. Al-Turabi looks on the freedom to reorganize and establish political institutions as the absolute prerequisite for an Islamic revival. A reformation that lacks true philosophical and political reformulation of Islam will not propel the sought-after cultural revolution. Again, mere religiosity along traditional lines would not be conducive to revolution. The revolution, however, must be based on religion and supersede temporal interests and be underpinned by social consensus.[93]

While the *shari'a* is pivotal to al-Turabi, he does not exclude non-Islamic doctrines and institutions, especially if an Islamic society needs them. Consensus must be the product of communal interests, and the social setting is the environment that enables the individual to exercise his freedom. Al-Turabi exhorts the Muslims to keep in mind the objectives of religion. Justice, for instance, does not have a constant meaning throughout history; individual interpretations of it may change with time and place, insofar as there is no direct opposition to a Qur'anic text.[94] Al-Turabi explains the "true" Islamic position on woman by arguing that Islam has provided her with complete independence. The Qur'anic discourse speaks to her without a male mediator; her belief like the male's could not be meaningful without her sincere conviction. If the Qur'an postulates her complete religious freedom, it follows that she is free in other aspects of life as well, in society and the state, in economics and politics. She has equal rights in public life. While al-Turabi acknowledges the historical lower status and mishandling of women, he attributes all of this to misinterpretations of Qur'anic verses on women and to the social environment. These two aspects must be rectified both theoretically by a rereading of the text and practically by giving women their proper place in society.[95]

This kind of change cannot take place through minor adjustments, but requires comprehensive mental and social restructuring of the community's experiences within a modern program that leads to redressing not only the particular grievances of woman but all other contemporary inequities as well. The starting point, however, relates to freeing individuals and groups to pursue what they consider promising new means toward development. The historical experience of Muslims is now defunct and could not be of major use to Muslims today, for they are experiencing things they themselves did not develop; simply, it is a new world that requires new thinking.[96]

This leads al-Turabi even to call for the founding of a modern jurisprudence based not on past history but rather on modern experience. A modern Islamic jurisprudence, one that is based on freedom of research without past restrictions imposed by the jurists or a limiting state interference, seems to al-Turabi capable of providing Muslims with the necessary instruments for the onset of revival. In this process, the state's role should be formal—that is, to conduct *shura* and to codify communal opinions. It must refrain from forcing its views on the public and must allow a new breed of *'ulama'* to develop and restructure Islamic thinking. Official institutions have no right to seize the communal rights of legislating and thinking.[97] Al-Turabi further postulates comprehensive freedom as a fundamental right and formative principle in the life of all people. More specifically, he denies the government any right to impose even recognized legal views on the community, for such an action constitutes an uncalled-for interference by the state in the community's life and a breach of *shura*. Again, enjoining the good and forbidding evil is the source of the legitimacy of the superiority of the people over the state.[98]

This does not mean for al-Turabi that the community should hold a single unanimous view. On the contrary, he believes that the existence of only one public opinion may constitute an obstacle to progress and inflexibility about change. While public opinion expressed in the media or by other means does not constitute an alternative to *shura*, policy makers should take it into consideration. Again, while the jurists' *ijma'* on a specific issue is not binding on the community, the state should not dismiss it altogether. However, the community should be subject neither to jurists nor to clamorous public opinion. A democratic interpretation of Islam requires in al-Turabi's view the existence of proper and free relationships between the state, individuals, and the community and its institutions.[99]

The original freedom includes the freedom of expression, to believe or not to believe. For God convinces and does not force man to believe. Again, if this is the case with religion, so should it be with political matters. For al-Turabi, without freedom man loses his and religion's true nature and becomes indistinguishable from animals. From an Islamic point of view, therefore, tyranny cannot be justified and the *shari'a* calls on people to voice their views. However, today's powerful rulers force the people to follow this ideology or that, this political program or that, contributing to the people's marginalization. Because the only normative individual commitment is to Islam, which frees the individual from having to accept or yield to imposed principles or ideologies, al-Turabi stands against the individual's identification with the state. The individual's original freedom cannot be given to institutions and to society; any institutionalization of freedom means its destruction.[100]

Al-Turabi cites a few examples of the powers that Islam has given to both the individual and society. Muslim society, for instance, has the power to legislate and to impose taxation. Al-Turabi argues that while the West has surrendered such powers to the state, Muslim societies have reserved them to themselves and made no delegation as such. Strictly speaking, they are social powers and not political. Their surrender to the state negates the possibility of independent social development and links it to the state and the rulers. As a modern manifestation of the social power to legislate, al-Turabi gives the example of political parties or legal schools. A political party expresses the individuals' cooperation and unity; multiparty politics may be the expression of *shura* in a structured system.[101]

However, such freedom should not lead to breaking the Muslim society into combatant ideological groups, as has happened in the history of Islam, where the community is basically split into Shi'ism and Sunnism. While pluralism is recommended by al-Turabi, its good practice revolves around its consensual context where a set of principles is agreed upon that will guarantee the indivisibility of society and where equilibrium between freedom and unity is maintained.[102] Al-Turabi cites the mosque as a place that exemplifies the true spirit of Islamic democracy. It is a place formed by ideological bonds and a place of unification of social and political orientations. More important, it is a prototype for communal unity, solidarity, unified organization, communication, and leadership. The democratic aspect of religion is so obvious that even leadership in prayer is subject to people's selection and cannot be legitimately forced on the community. Also, in spite of color, origin, wealth, and language, equality permeates all aspects of religious life. This is an example that should be copied in politics—see al-Turabi on this below.[103]

Al-Turabi reduces the state's authority to a minimum and maximizes the individual's—a view actually unprecedented in the history of Islamic thought. He believes in making *shura* obligatory in determining social, economic, and political issues as opposed to the advisory nature of elitist *shura*, to bring forth the community's power in a new and modern religious form. Any *ijma'* that is attained in such a manner, and without contravening any basic text, can then provide formative and normative principles. *Shura* could also take many forms and shapes: a parliament, a constitutional council, or any other form of representation. However, there must always be an institution that can look into the decisions taken by representative bodies and ensure that they do not violate any clear-cut religious principles.[104]

It is obvious, thus far, that al-Turabi's acceptance of democracy is formal, and not completely substantive, because he does not ground it in rationality alone or historical development. On the contrary, he grounds it in religion itself, which has been assumed to be pretty much incapable of furthering democratic notions. In the Middle East, it seems that such a grounding of democracy may strengthen it popularly, while its secularization may pit the state against it and the people against governments that pretend to be calling for secular democracy. That the Qur'anic text is the ultimate founding and justifying power of democracy makes it a solid social and political instrument of evaluation to be applied to both society and the state, both the ruler and the ruled. The state's machinery is seen to be dependent on the represented and always subject to a higher law than its own. This is in fact one of the reasons why al-Turabi Islamized democracy. *Shari'a* in this context becomes a popular power, higher than the law of the state, and is developed popularly, not by the state. This being so, state institutions and policies are balanced both by social institutions and society's will.[105]

In this fashion, the discourse of pluralism is validated by the formative—indeed, the interpretive—power of the text and its reading within a specific era that is dominated by the West and its discourse. However, for al-Turabi this discourse on pluralism is also made with a view to establishing common ground with the West that may lead to dialogue. Al-Turabi believes that it is the duty of the modern Islamic movement to open up to the whole world, so as to transmit its message after a period of isolation. The Muslim world cannot be isolated from the rest of the world, and in directing the Islamic discourse to the West, the Muslims who are the West's followers are also addressed. The West then has the choice of dialoguing with the Muslim world or giving credence to the well-publicized new confrontational doctrine of the "clash of civilizations."[106] Al-Turabi concludes that the real conflict in the world is not a political one between East and West but rather a metaphysical conflict between *tawhid* and *ishrak* (polytheism) and between human *jahiliyya* and divine *hakimiyya*.

The modern Islamic movement, as the leader of revival in Islamic societies, must prepare itself to start a fruitful dialogue with the world, and on all levels: the economic, the social, the political, and above all the intellectual.[107] Muslims should deal with others in terms of others' discourses and languages. Both Muslim and Western societies should transcend their history of conflict and bloodshed in order to bring the diverse parts of the world closer to one another. Al-Turabi's agenda for dialogue includes the freedom to discuss all issues of culture, civilization, politics, economics, information, society, arts, and even sports. The dialogue between the West and the Islamic movement on the political front should deal substantively with two main aspects: first, Muslim political society and its political dimensions including false representation of people, suppression of freedoms, political oppression, political unrest; second, the Islamic political system and issues of change of man and society, *shura* and democracy, Islamic revivalism, and the new world order. For al-Turabi, there is now no "end of history," and the "clash of civilizations" is not the destined fate of mankind, that is, not if mankind seeks salvation from its miseries and catastrophes.[108]

The leader of al-Nahda in Tunisia, Rashid al-Ghannushi, is not far off from the views of al-Turabi. Al-Ghannushi argues the need to maintain both public and private freedoms as well as human rights, which are both called for by Qur'anic teachings and ratified by international covenants. They are not contradictory to Islam and involve primarily the freedoms of expression and association as well as political participation, independence, and the condemnation of violence and of the suppression of free opinion. Such principles for al-Ghannushi may become the center of peaceful coexistence and dialogue between society and the state and between rulers and the ruled.[109]

Al-Ghannushi ties the legitimacy of a political system to its provision of freedom for all political parties and segments of society that could compete peacefully on social, political, and ideological agendas. Such a system must provide free elections to all representative councils and institutions so that they may contribute to state administration. If this takes place, the Islamic movement lends its popular support to the system, and since the popular authority, grounded in God's governance, is the highest authority in society, the system then carries political legitimacy. Accepting freedom of association leads al-Ghannushi to accept even those parties that do not believe in God, such as the communists.[110] Some citizens may find it in their best interest to form parties and other institutions that might be nonreligious. This does not constitute a breach of religion, since pluralism—or to believe or not—is itself sanctioned by religion. The sacred text represents a source for, a reference to, an absorption of the truth, while its human interpretations are grounded in diverse methods representing different understandings of changing social, economic, political, and intellectual complexities. Unfettered possibilities of systematic development should be encouraged.[111]

Before al-Turabi and al-Ghannushi, al-Banna argued that where religion is acknowledged as an essential component of the state, political conflicts ought not to be turned into religious wars and must be resolved by dialogue. Individuals enjoy equal rights and duties of a religious, civil, political, social, and economic nature. This principle of individual involvement, to enjoin the good and forbid evil, is the origin of pluralism leading to the formation of political parties and social organizations or, simply, the democratization of the social and political process. Again, al-Banna's system includes different social and religious groups such as Christians and Jews who along with Muslims are united by interest, human good, and belief in God and the holy books.[112]

For al-Banna, the natural condition of life is peace, not conflict. At times, however, when faced with individual and collective ambitions and greed, one has to fight. Defense of the self and the nation, of life and property as well as religion, is legitimate. Also, Muslims may defend their creed from ideological attacks and fight those who break their contracts and agreements. In addition, Muslims may launch war in order to defend oppressed people wherever they are. Apart from this, Islam prohibits war.[113] Al-Banna argues further that while Islam fights colonialism, it does not accept dominating other people, for people are born free. Islam calls for *jihad* in order to defend the nation and to secure the spread of God's message, if it is opposed by force. Again, Islam encourages peaceful solutions when there is goodwill, and the Prophet accepted peace agreements and accepted the arbitration of non-Muslims.[114]

One of the followers of al-Banna's logic was Taqiy al-Din al-Nabahani (1909–1977), the founder of Hizb al-Tahrir in Jordan and Palestine. Al-Nabahani studied at the University of al-Azhar in 1932. He was a schoolteacher from the West Bank, worked at the *shari‘a* court, and became a judge in 1945. He fled to Syria in 1948 after the war in Palestine. He returned to Jerusalem as a judge in the Appeals Court and stayed until 1950 when he resigned. He flirted for some time with Ba‘ath ideology and wrote his *Inqadh Filistin* (Liberation of Palestine). He was a member of the Muslim Brotherhood in Palestine before establishing Hizb al-Tahrir al-Islami in 1952.

A good party life, said al-Nabahani, must be based on a set of principles that commit the community to act. Only in this manner can a real party first rise and then represent the people and push for major positive development. Without popular support, civil institutions cannot work properly.[115] In his *Al-Takatul al-Hizbi* (Party formation), while accepting multiparty politics as a contemporary counterpart for the duty of "enjoining the good and forbidding evil," al-Nabahani laments the loss of many opportunities for political movements, due to the lack of proper awareness of the parties' renaissance.

Al-Nabahani imagines a gradual, threefold process of development: first, propagation of the party's platform and principles; second, social interaction to sharpen people's awareness on essential issues; and third, the quest for power in order to rule in the people's name. The party should always play the role of watchdog and not let itself be absorbed into the structure and machinery of the state. Its independence from the government is essential for its credibility. While the government's role is executive as it represents the people, the party's role is ideological. The party should always watch the government, so that the government does not isolate itself from society and become unresponsive. The party, even if it is represented in government, must remain a social force that supervises government actions. Put differently, the civil institutions of society are above the government, which must yield to public demands and interests. And of course, at no time may they act in contradiction to any Islamic principle.[116]

Other thinkers, like the distinguished Muhammad Salim al-ʿAwwa, a former member of Egypt's Muslim Brotherhood, go beyond these general statements and directly address the issue of pluralism. Starting from al-Banna's discourse, al-ʿAwwa elaborates on the absolute necessity of both pluralism and democracy. Al-ʿAwwa sees Islam as falsely accused of opposition to pluralistic societies. Pluralism is the tolerance of diversity—political, economic, religious, linguistic—and such diversity is natural; even the Qur'an allows differences of identity and belonging.[117]

Al-ʿAwwa identifies six features of Islam that make it tolerant and pluralistic: Islam does not specify a particular social and political system but provides general ideas; any ruler must be elected by the people through *shura;* Islam permits religious freedom, making all other kinds of freedom likewise legitimate; all people are equal in terms of both rights and duties; God's command to enjoin the good and forbid evil is a communal religious duty; and, finally, rulers are accountable to their communities.[118] However, the legitimacy of pluralism hinges for al-ʿAwwa on two conditions: first, that it not contradict the basics of Islam, and second, that it be conducted in the people's interest. If these conditions are met, individuals and groups may associate with each other in any manner they deem necessary or appropriate, especially in political parties, which could become a safeguard against limitations of freedom and the onset of despotism.[119]

For al-ʿAwwa, a civil society exists when institutions aiming to affect political life are free to function and to develop without interference from the state. Because the institutions of society change with time, al-ʿAwwa does not specify what kinds of institutions make a Muslim society a civil or pluralistic society, but he links this to the function of institutions. In the West, unions and clubs and parties have such a civil function; in the Muslim world, mosques, churches, religious endowments, teaching circles, professions, craft organizations, and the neighborhood function similarly. However, all these institutions are important not in themselves but as instruments. Muslims ought to develop whatever is conducive to a pluralistic life; their institutions do not have to be imitations of Western models in order to be effective civil institutions.[120]

That despotism was the general practice of the historical Arab-Islamic state is indisputable, but this does not mean that Islam, by its very nature, is opposed to pluralism and democracy. Al-ʿAwwa uses his own historical examples, like the first state in Islam founded by the Prophet, to show that despotism as a political concept, though tolerated, has not enjoyed any credibility with the general populace. Nor could the historical state claim sole legitimacy to impose its opinions on the people. For al-ʿAwwa, the first step to major change is the reorganization of society in a way that allows civil institutions to develop freely without any state control. Current conditions hinder the development of pluralistic societies, while real civil institutions would serve the interests of groups all across the spectrum. The institutions now present in Islamic states have been created so as to preclude the functioning of real representative institutions and to force them to go underground. Thus al-ʿAwwa calls for the revitalization of civil society to free the people from the grip of the state and its unrepresentative institutions.[121]

3

The Classical and Medieval Roots
of *al-Huquq al-Shar'iyya* and Its Modern
Islamist Conceptions As Human Rights

Classical and Medieval Roots of *al-Huquq al-Shar'iyya*

Human rights in Islam are human, social, economic, and political doctrines that are considered to be one of the objectives of Islamic law. For
instance, they include self-preservation as both a right and a duty. The
obligatory nature of human rights is derived from the *shari'a* itself. Put
differently, human or "legal" rights (*al-huquq al-shar'iyya*) are not philosophically or humanly developed but are, from a classical Islamic perspective, religious rights that should be guaranteed by the state. As an example, freedom is not an objective in itself but is a means of fulfilling the
objectives of the *shari'a*. Furthermore, these rights are not merely individual but are replete with social functions that take into account the
rights of others. Thus the "legitimate" human rights include both individual and communal interests in an attempt to balance individualistic
extremes with communal controls. Human rights in Islam are creedal
rights that seek the fulfillment of the main objectives of human existence.
Man, from this perspective, is not born free but is born to be free from
whims, instincts, and desires through proper shouldering of responsibility
toward himself, the community, and humankind.

Human rights in Islam cover what are historically referred to as *al-
darruriyyat al-khams,* or the five necessities: the preservation of religion
(*al-din*), the self (*al-nafs*), reason (*al-'aql*), family (*al-nasl*), and money (*al-
mal*). They are called necessities because, as much as they are the rights of
individuals, they are individual duties. For instance, the right of self-preservation (*hufz al-nafs*) includes the responsibility of personal integrity,
both morally and materially. The human being does not own his life; it
belongs to God. Man, therefore, cannot legitimately kill himself or damage part of his body, let alone kill others or damage their bodies.[1]

Freedom is an instrument that man uses to preserve and develop his five rights as well as others. This instrument cannot be taken away because it relates to the five necessities and thus becomes, like them, a necessity in and of itself. If freedom is the necessary condition for the preservation of man's rights and the fulfillment of his duties, it is the duty of the individual, the community, and the state to preserve that condition. The proper web of good human relations requires as much, for fulfillment of the objectives of the *shari'a*. Man's rights therefore become comprehensive rights. They include all aspects of human existence and produce derivative rights, like *shura,* freedom of worship and creed, free speech, and free education. Al-Imam al-Ghazali even provides moral rights for relatives, friends, neighbors, the weak, and the poor. These rights include moral and practical good treatment, advice and help, as well as forgiveness, sincerity, and similar qualities.[2]

These rights are duties or obligations because they represent the social function of rights, which leads to human, social, political, and economic mutuality, all of which in turn enhance the quality of human life. Thus the obligation to preserve and develop religion, life, the self, the family, and wealth requires a reconsideration of the meaning of "right" as well as its development in line with the material and moral development of humankind. While these human rights are fixed in principle, their material existence is changeable from one context to another and from one time to another. The proper implementation of that obligation means the flexible exercise of that right within multiple contexts. It also means that derivative rights can increase or decrease in light of the context. In certain contexts, equality may be the main right; in others, free speech. The scheme that medieval thinkers developed for derivative rights in Muslim societies may not be feasible today, especially as the moral and material contexts of rights have changed not only in Muslim societies but all over the world and among all religions and cultures. Today's rights must reflect today's realities.

While human rights in the West are based on individualism, human rights in classical and medieval Islamic thought were based on the general interests of society.[3] Not that medieval Islamic thought denied individual rights, but it stressed that proper human rights had to be socially contextualized, or else individuals and their society would clash head on, which is not in the general interest of either. Justice was seen as concomitant to freedom. Individual freedom that did not take into account the community's general interest was perceived as being unjust. Individual interest, which freedom serves, should not be an obstacle to the general interest. A balance among individual economic interests should be struck, and another balance is needed between individual interests and the general interest.[4] If freedom, for instance, does not serve the preservation and development of man, then it negates its original objective and loses its legitimacy. Freedom must confer benefits and deter harms.[5]

This does not mean, however, that a "right" is only a social function, for if that were the case, then it would lose its meaning. It is proper to say that a "right" is normative when it seeks both the individual's and the others' interests. For instance, the right to own property is fundamental, but its regulation ought to take into account the community's general interest. Also, while not developed according to modern arguments nor expected to be so, the rights of women, as traditionalists view them, were acknowledged from the beginning of Islam. Islam viewed men and women as springing from the same origin and therefore as equal morally, educationally, socially, and religiously before the law. A woman had independent existence that gave her rights of inheritance and ownership. However, all of this was linked to a social system whose basic unit was the family.[6]

Some scholars argue that human rights in Islam are not only political rights of citizens or natural rights but are also, because of the people's vicegerency, legal rights derived from divine law that belong to all human beings qua human beings. Islamic deterrents, or al-hudud, like cutting off the hand of the thief or stoning adulterers, are stipulated to protect the human rights of the weaker parties. Thus the harder the punishment, the more secure the right.[7]

Justice was one of the doctrines that engaged Islamic political thought, and therefore influenced the development of human rights, in the classical period. While individual rights were attached to and derived from the legal rights, certain social rights were also postulated, like preventing espionage, aggression, and injustice, as well as ethical rights like prohibition of jealousy, arrogance, and humiliation. Such a scheme of rights made the state responsible for the implementation of rights. Freedom, which had existed as a doctrine and a right, was linked to the doctrine of justice and law. The Qur'an linked proper government to proper application of justice.[8] This comprehensive doctrine was not related only to Muslims but included all human beings. For instance, a just distribution of alms meant dividing economic aid among all those who deserved it, including non-Muslims.[9] An instance of the jurists' view on justice was Ibn Taymiyya's statement that if a ruler acted not justly but according to racial, linguistic, sectarian, and other preferences or prejudices, he was a traitor to God and His Prophet.[10]

Thus the state, which is responsible for securing people's rights, must work within a just context. For instance, the right to privacy—the prohibition of espionage or intruding in the private life of people—cannot be secured without such a context. Al-Mawardi summarized the jurists' views on this by saying that the privacy of people could not legitimately be invaded if there was no apparent misconduct or violation of the law.[11] The sanctity of privacy was earlier postulated by the Prophet himself as well as the Qur'an; the Prophet prohibited entering any residence without the owner's permission. And Hanbali, Hanafi, Shafi'i, and some Maliki jurists agreed that a person can defend his privacy and even hurt the offender without incurring punishment.[12]

Furthermore, a context of justice is needed because Islam prohibits torture, which goes against the dignity and vicegerency that God granted to man.[13] Most jurists agreed that just and exact punishments were to be imposed, including the legally severe ones like *hudud*, for Islam provided very specific legal punishments for capital offenses; regular punishment should be less severe. In no case should punishment turn into torture, which was perceived to be of a quite different nature.[14] Ibn Khaldun argued that aggression and injustice led to the ruin of civilization and the destruction of the state. The usurpation of any ownership, thing, or right constituted injustice, and the state that allowed it was paving the way for its own and civilization's demise. For this reason the prohibition of injustice was central to Islamic law.[15]

Minorities

The Prophet's state was based on religious freedom. The Qur'an told the Prophet that there was no compulsion in embracing Islam,[16] so Islam did not force people to adhere to its beliefs. Islam also provided freedom of political opposition on the condition that it not endanger the community. And it provided social freedom where individuals and groups were free to organize themselves as they deemed fit. As to justice, it was the basis of government and covered all groups and individuals. The doctrine was based on many verses and included all aspects of living.[17] History witnessed Muslims' positive acceptance of minorities, especially Jews and Christians, on the basis of Islamic law and customs that governed relations between the different communities that constituted the Islamic community at large. Islamic thought provided freedom of religion to non-Muslims and protected their religious practices, though historical political practices did not often conform to the standards laid down by Islamic jurisprudence.

Ahl al-dhimma, or the people of contract and security, are those groups of non-Muslims that lived in the Islamic world under a contract between themselves and the Muslims. *Dhimma* means simply security, and a *dhimma* contract means that non-Muslims became members of the Islamic state and enjoyed equal rights and incurred equal duties. This contract made by Islamic authorities and non-Muslims was based, like any other contract, on mutual agreement.[18]

Such a contract obliged the Islamic state to protect and defend minorities in exchange for *jizya.* Those non-Muslims who fought alongside the Muslims—that is, became an organic part of the Muslim community—did not pay *al-jizya.* However, those who lived on the margins of Muslim society and were protected by that society had to pay this specific tax.[19] Put differently, non-Muslims were like naturalized citizens or permanent residents who had certain rights and duties depending on the level of their naturalization. The Armenians, for instance, built their own army under an agreement with Caliph Mu'awiya that stipulated self-rule for Armenia and the suspension of *jizya* for three years, after which the Armenians would pay whatever they decided and no Muslim troops or princes would be sent to reside in Armenia.[20]

Islamic jurisprudence made it a general rule that the peoples of the lands the Muslims occupied were, like the Muslims, bound by the contracts they agreed upon. They became, in most cases, part of the Islamic land and state, though treated as semi-independent entities. Such entities were no longer acknowledged when their peoples broke the contract. Still, the contract should be respected, which is why al-Imam al-Uza'i chastised the governor of Baalbek for dealing unjustly with the Christians of Mount Lebanon for tax purposes. He told him that Qur'anic rule and the Prophet's will called for respecting the contract and not overburdening *ahl al-dhimma* with taxes.[21]

Most jurists except the Hanafis viewed *jizya* as compensation for protecting the minorities. The Malikite jurist Ibn Rushd, for instance, viewed *jizya* as a yearly payment for protection and security whereby the minorities did not have to fight the state's enemies, inasmuch as payment of the *jizya* was conditioned on the existence of an Islamic ruler who protected minorities. Al-Mawardi, a Shafi'ite, also looked on *jizya* as a source of protection and security for minorities.[22] Only Hanafi jurists saw *jizya* as a punishment for not adhering to Islam. If this were the case, however, most jurists argued that it would have been imposed on all members of minorities, and not only on the rich. Also, it would not have been legally abrogated when members of minorities defended the land of Islam along with the Muslims or when the Islamic state could not protect the minorities.[23]

In pre-Islamic terminology the *dhimma* contract, the contract of protection that Jews and others entered into, was the highest sort of contract given by a stronger party to a weaker one.[24] Thus, under Islam, diverse non-Muslim groups were given the *dhimma* of God. W. Montgomery Watt tell us that under such a contract "these small groups were said to receive the 'protection of God and his messenger' and they retained their internal structure of government and in return they made a payment, usually in kind." All minority groups had arrangements of this sort—protection from external enemies, internal autonomy, and payment to the treasury; indeed, *ahl al-dhimma* originally meant, according to Watt, "people of security-undertaking." These protected minorities were usually *ahl al-kitab*, the people of the Scripture, or more specifically Jews and Christians.[25]

The Prophet applied the ordinances of *ahl al-dhimma* first to Jews and Christians in Arabia, then to the Magi in Bahrain. He also asked that the Copts of Egypt be treated well. The rightly guided caliphs generally followed the Prophetic Traditions in treating the religious minorities. While the minorites paid *jizya*, they nonetheless benefited from the aid that the state gave. As an example, it is worth mentioning the oft-repeated tale of 'Umar ibn al-Khattab, who one day passed by an old blind man begging. He asked the poor Jewish man about his condition. The man answered that he had reached this state because of *jizya*, need, and age. 'Umar took him to his home, gave him some money, and ordered the keeper of state funds: "Look after this man and the people who are like him. We have not been fair to him, we have taken some of his money in his youth, and we have not helped him when he has reached old age." On his deathbed 'Umar, who was assassinated by a Magus, said: "I recommend to the caliph after me [to take care of the people] of the *dhimma* of God, to defend them and not to burden them [with *jizya*]."[26]

Non-Muslims could legally determine the method of arbitration in their legal, social, and religious affairs, but Muslims could not. They had to submit to the Prophet's revealed legislation in most cases. When his authority on religious affairs was in question, as when the Jews or the Christians proclaimed the salvation of only Jews or Christians respectively, his human judgments were always supplemented by divine texts as revealed in Qur'anic verses, though these were never legally enforced. The political judgments, however, were subject to implementation, since they were grounded in political agreements.[27] In Medina there was a great need for a supreme judicial authority.[28] At times Prophet Muhammad used to apply the Jewish laws to the Jews. One day, we are told by Ibn Hisham, some rabbis, who met to rule on the adultery of a married Jewish man with a married Jewish woman, decided to send the two to Muhammad to be judged. The Prophet, asking some rabbis about Jewish law on this matter, was told that the penalty was stoning to death, but that this law was not followed anymore. However, the Prophet ordered them stoned, as a fulfillment of Jewish law.[29]

The legal status of non-Muslims, or the *dhimmis,* was later developed under the Umayyads in line with the positions of noncitizen groups in the Eastern Empire. According to N. J. Coulson, "By the contract of the *dhimma,* which embodied the notion of fides in Roman law, the Jewish and Christian communities, or *dhimmis,* paid a poll tax in return for the guarantee of protection and the preservation of their rights under their own personal law administered by their rabbinical and ecclesiastical tribunals."[30] Friction between Prophet Muhammad and the Jews is attributed usually to the Jews' hostility toward the Prophet because of his claim to prophecy, and to fear of the spread of his power, manifested in the Jews' alliance with the hypocrites against the Muslims (see below). In other words, it was a political struggle for dominance. The change of *qibla* (direction of prayer) signified a change in relations with the Jews, both intellectually and politically. However, the actions of the Prophet against the Jews were reactive rather than premeditated. Watt tells us that "in so far as the Jews changed their attitude and ceased to be actively hostile, they were unmolested"; the Jews had "opposed Muhammad to the utmost of their ability, and they were utterly crushed. In this case, both Muslims and Jews missed the opportunity of co-existence and religious autonomy.[31]

Muhammad wanted to establish peace among the different factions that constituted the people of Medina and was able, because of the breadth of his conception of the *umma,* to establish Islamic dominance over Medina and among the neighboring tribes. The *dhimma* contracts that he established with Jews and pagan Arabs as well as some Christians made the Islamic community of Medina a truly pluralistic society. While the state enjoyed religious foundations, this did not preclude non-Muslims from participating actively in state affairs. While he preached and, at times, demanded conversion to Islam in his capacity as Prophet, as the leader of the community that aimed at securing its very existence, he even contracted tribes on secular bases, mainly defense and taxation. Further-more, when Muhammad entered Mecca victoriously, he did not demand the conversion of the Meccans, and many of them took part in the battle of Hunayn without being Muslims. When Muhammad expanded to the north into Iraq and Syria, he again did not exclude non-Arabs but made alliances with them.[32]

Another major indication of the religious tolerance of Prophet Muham-mad and the early Muslim community was the decision allowing the coex-istence in Medina of an organized opposition to the Prophet among those who already professed Islam. This group, the movement of the hypocrites (*al-munafiqun*), headed by 'Abd Allah ibn Ubayy ibn Sallul, was plotting against the Islamic community from within. It was in fact a kind of apos-tasy, and its profession of Islam was pronounced mostly in order to protect itself and to retain certain privileges. 'Umar Ibn al-Khattab, among others, wanted to kill the hypocrites, but the Prophet forbade it because they witnessed that there was no god but God. By this attitude the Prophet, as a statesman, stopped short of open conflict with the extended tribes of the hypocrites who allied themselves with some Jewish and pagan Arab groups against him. On the religious level the Prophet, by allowing the movement to coexist within the Islamic community, prevented Muslims from investigating each other's belief and accepted the formal profession of religion as indicative of belief, even when he knew the insincerity of the hypocrites. While everyone in Medina knew of Ibn Ubayy's case, espe-cially after he withdrew from the battles of Uhud and al-Khandaq, the Prophet refused to accuse him and his group of unbelief or apostasy. Later, while the movement politically followed the Prophet's policies, it always distinguished itself from the rest of Muslims. On the day of Ibn Ubayy's death, the Prophet visited him, signaling the acceptance of differences and toleration.[33]

The Prophet's authority as an arbitrator was sanctioned by the revela-tion. One finds quite a few Qur'anic verses dealing with judgment of vari-ous sorts as well as showing the Prophet's role as a judge and the scope of his arbitration.[34] First, the Prophet became a world judge among different religions.[35] This idea has been based on Qur'anic verses that said: "Man-kind were one community, and Allah sent [unto them] Prophets as bearers of good tidings and warners, and revealed therewith the Scripture with the truth that it might judge between mankind concerning that wherein they differed. And only those unto whom [the Scripture] was given differed concerning it, after clear proofs had come unto them, through hatred one of another."[36] Second, the Prophet became an interreligious and supranational judge within one community, such as between Muslims, Jews, and others in the first Islamic state. When the Jews preferred their own laws to those of God and tried to arbitrate the matter with Muhammad, so that he would carry the burden of the judgment of a Jew who killed or committed adultery, God revealed the following: "If then they have recourse unto thee [Muhammad], judge between them or disclaim jurisdiction. If thou disclaimest jurisdiction, then they cannot harm thee at all. However, if thou judgest, judge between them with equity. . . . We did reveal the Torah, wherein is guidance and a light, by which the Prophets who surrendered [unto Allah] judge the Jews, and the rabbis and the priests [judged] by such of Allah's Scripture as they were bidden to observe, and thereunto were they witnesses."[37]

Moreover, Ibn Kathir makes any valid judgment dependent on justice, equity, and fairness among all. As an interreligious arbitrator, Muhammad arbitrated between nations and religions by using their own divine laws since he was not permitted to judge arbitrarily or by mere preference. He had to shun mere interest, prejudice, and ignorance and follow justice and the divinely ordained laws of all peoples as well as accepting the particularities of nations and religions.[38] This argument is based on a Qur'anic text that says: "And We described to them therein: The life for the life, and the eye for the eye, and the nose for the nose, and the ear for the ear, and the tooth for the tooth, and for wounds, retaliation. However, whoso forgoeth it [in the way of charity] it shall be exception for him. Whoso judgeth not by that which Allah hath revealed: such are wrongdoers. And we caused Jesus, Son of Mary, to follow in their footsteps, confirming that which was [revealed] before him in the Torah, and we bestowed on him Gospel wherein is guidance and a light, confirming that which was [revealed] before it in the Torah—a guidance and admonition unto those who ward off [evil]. Let the People of the Gospel judge by that which Allah hath revealed therein. Whoso judgeth not by that which Allah hath revealed: Such are evil-livers."[39]

While the Qur'an sets the Prophet as a judicial arbitrator, as Ibn Kathir puts it, judging primarily between people according to textual authorities, Muhammad must use his own reasoning (ijtihad) if no such textual authority exists and must seek evidence in order to arrive at just and reasonable judgments. This is based on the Qur'anic text that says: "Lo! We reveal unto thee the Scripture with the truth, that thou mayst judge between mankind by that which Allah showeth thee. And be not thou a plunder for the treacherous." Similar arbitral judgments covered religious disputes between different groups, Jews, Christians, and Muslims, especially when their own holy books were not the grounds for arbitration.[40] For the Qur'an says: "Hast thou not seen how those who have received a portion of the Scripture invoke the Scripture of Allah [in their disputes] that it may judge between them; then a faction of them turn away, being opposed [to it]?"[41]

The first nonprophetic political contract or pact with minorities was the pact of 'Umar Ibn al-Khattab (*al- 'uhda al- 'Umariyya*), which became a model for contracts between Muslims and minorities. Concluded between 'Umar and the bishop of Jerusalem, it provided protection of their life and money, churches, and crosses. The guarantee for respecting this contract was the *dhimma* of the Prophet, the caliphs, and the believers.[42] Similar contracts were made with the peoples of Damascus and Egypt. While *jizya* (poll tax) was imposed, certain solid rights were secured: rights of life, equal treatment under the law, maintenance of specific customs like wine-drinking and pork-eating, respect, personal law, and religious rituals. Caliph 'Umar ibn 'Abd al-'Aziz tried to obtain from a leading jurist, Abu al-Hasan al-Basri, a *fatwa* to prohibit minorities from having wine and pork. Al-Basri's response was that insofar as *ahl al-dhimma* paid the *jizya* they were free to believe whatever they wanted and that the caliph should follow the religious regulations on these matters.[43]

Under different Islamic states, relations between Muslims and the Jewish and Christian minorities went through ups and downs, depending on internal and external conditions. For instance, during the first century of Islam, minorities' buildings were not allowed to be higher than the Muslims'. The justification was that this prevented people from watching each other's households.[44] At the same time, many state employees were members of the minorities, and many Muslims complained about the high level of state employment of non-Muslims. When 'Umar ibn al-Khattab learned that Abu Musa al-Ash'ari had a non-Muslim secretary, he asked him to replace him with a Muslim. During the third century, however, the army was commanded twice by Christians, which brought displeasure to many Muslims.[45]

Usually the movements that resisted the expansion or prominence of minorities in state service had the goal of curbing their influence. In A.H. 235, Caliph al-Mutawakkil issued a decree prohibiting employing non-Muslims in departments that were mainly concerned with Muslim affairs. Then things changed again, and in 296, when the number of Christians in state administration had greatly increased, Caliph al-Muqtadir ordered their removal. Still his minister, Muhammad 'Ali Ibn al-Furat, maintained four Christians among his nine secretaries, who used to dine with him as well.[46] Later too, some caliphs like al-Ta'i' (363–81) and ministers like 'Iz al-Dawla (357) maintained Christian employees in sensitive places.[47]

Minorities in the Islamic states enjoyed in theory and in practice many political rights. They were employed at all levels of the state, with the exception of those posts that required Islam as a condition, like the caliphate, which was supposed to protect both the state and Islam. The Qur'an and the Sunna did not prohibit the employment of non-Muslims and linked such employment to efficiency. The Prophet himself employed non-Muslims to teach some Muslims reading and writing skills. Muslim jurists allowed non-Muslims to be executive ministers, tax collectors, advisors, and the like.[48]

In practice, minorities participated along with Muslims in running the Islamic state. For instance, when the Muslims occupied Egypt, they left state administration to the minorities. The Umayyads until the caliphate of 'Abd al-Malik ibn Marwan appointed Christians in almost every department because they were known to be good administrators. Mu'awiya, for instance, appointed as his secretary Sirjun al-Rumi, who stayed in his post until the caliphate of 'Abd al-Malik ibn Marwan. Al-Rumi's son and, eventually, his grandson succeeded him.[49] Much later, most of the Ottoman ambassadors were non-Muslims.[50]

The Umayyads' policy toward *ahl al-dhimma*, the Christians and Jews who lived in the Islamic state with a permanent contract of protection, was kind and gentle and allowed freedom of worship. Minorities were free to practice their rituals and maintain their churches and temples, and payment of taxes was dependent on the conditions of the payer. The Christians of Syria had a very good working relationship with Mu'awiya and the Umayyads who, when they took Damascus as their capital, liberated the local Christians from the injustice of their rulers and religious persecution by fellow Christian sects. The good relations were favored by the fact that most of the Christian tribes were Arabs who had migrated originally from southern Arabia, especially Banu Kalb. But the Umayyads included in their government non-Arab Christians as well. The caliphs did not restrict any of the rights that Christians could enjoy and treated them like the rest of their subjects. Some of them even worked in the *dawawin* (ministries). Mu'awiya himself had a Christian doctor, who was put in charge of the revenues of Homs, and his son's tutor was Christian as well. The Umayyads employed many Christians because of their skill and experience in running the affairs of the state.[51]

The religious freedom that Christians and Jews enjoyed under the

Umayyads was great especially because Muslims believed that there was no compulsion in religion. The Muslims during that period neither destroyed others' places of worship nor forced non-Muslims to convert to Islam, for the contract of *dhimma* protected not only individuals but also their ownership and worship. Furthermore, Mu'awiya married a Jacobite Christian who gave him a son, Yazid, who later became caliph. The Muslims did not interfere in the internal affairs of *ahl al-dhimma*, who would select their own leaders; these chosen leaders were usually confirmed by the ruler as official appointees. Put differently, they were independent but part of the state apparatus. The minorities were not forced in the least to change their religions. They publicly celebrated their holidays and Muslims participated in them. And Christians, for instance, went on building their churches.[52]

It was not only the Jews and Christians that paid *jizya;* the Umayyads even made the converts to Islam pay it. When 'Umar Ibn 'Abd al-'Aziz assumed the caliphate, he rescinded that. Told that state revenues would not be sufficient, he answered that God had sent Muhammad as a guide, not as a tax collector.[53] He disliked the power that the *dhimmis* had enjoyed under previous caliphs and tried to replace them with Muslims. Nonetheless, there was no religious argument against working with or employing Christians and Jews and other people of Scripture; usually the arguments put forward against their political power were related to misuse of power and/or discriminating against Muslims.[54]

Though Christians and Jews were integrated into the political establishment, they suffered at times, as during the reign of Caliph al-Mutawakkil, from the rulers' idiosyncrasies. If a Christian died without an heir during the Umayyad period, the state inherited. Later, however, under the 'Abbasids, the Christian community would inherit. Jews and Christians lived all over the Empire, especially in Damascus and Aleppo, in Iraq, in Ispahan, Shiraz, and Khurasan. They enjoyed high status under many—though not all—governments in the ninth century. Some Christians were even in charge of the army and thereby wielded considerable power. Because of their role in the administration, a question was raised as to the legitimacy of appointing a non-Muslim minister, and there were divergent *fatwas* on the matter—an indication of the lack of categorical textual authority prohibiting Christians and Jews from dealing in politics.

Their power brought jealousy and conspiracy against them, especially under the Fatimids. Al-Hakim bi Amri Allah ordered the religious minorities to do and to stop doing many things, like not to ride horses and to dress differently and not to employ Muslims. Many Christians and Jews then converted to Islam in order to avoid discrimination and to enjoy the privileges of being Muslims.[55]

Under most Fatimid caliphs the minorities enjoyed much better treatment, and most ministers and advisors were Christian and Jews. But under al-Hakim bi Amri Allah they were forced to convert to Isma'ilism if they wanted to be employed in the state apparatus, and were persecuted if they did not. Al-Hakim bi Amri Allah even tried to demolish al-Qiyyama Church, one of the most important churches and supposedly the place where the crucified Christ was buried. He did abolish some churches in Egypt. Jews and Christians were also forced to wear distinctive clothing, usually black, and were prevented from celebrating their holidays. Their endowments became part of the official *diwan* or ministry. They were subjected to other prejudices and cruel customs, like having to ride donkeys instead of horses. Finally, large groups of minorities were forced to migrate from Egypt. We are told that after the fall of the Fatimids many returned; in only one day, seven thousand converted back to Christianity.[56]

Jurists made it a duty of the Islamic state to defend minorities against harm from both within and without because of the *dhimma* contract, which made minorities part of the Islamic state and, therefore, entitled to freedom of expression and movement. Jurist Abu Yusuf advised Caliph Harun al-Rashid to make sure that the minorities were living well and were not mistreated.[57] Muslims accepted the minorities' right to follow their religions, to educate their children accordingly, and to meet at their places of worship. They also generally viewed them as part of the Islamic state, for while they paid *jizya,* at the same time they had rights. 'Umar ibn 'Abd al-'Aziz, for instance, ordered his lieutenants to look for the needy among the minorities and to aid them from state funds. From this example and others, the jurists concluded that the Islamic state had the duty to care for its needy members, including the minorities, and that like the Muslims, minorities should have certain claims on and guarantees from state funds.[58]

The *dhimmis* (people of contract), or *ahl al-kitab* (people of the Book), were affected by the process of Arabization of the languages of administration and financial transactions. Under 'Umar ibn 'Abd al-'Aziz, many Christians and Jews were fired from their governmental posts in finance and administration, though the caliph and the state depended on them, a situation that persisted during the 'Abbasid rule.[59] Other restrictions were imposed. Under 'Abd al-'Aziz, Christians could not carry arms and had to use specific roads and animals for transportation. At the same time, he intended to give back part of a church that was used to expand the Great Mosque in Damascus, an intention that brought expressions of displeasure from Muslims.[60] Again, he lived the last years of his life near a monastery, Dayr Sim'an, and provided Christians with allowances from state funds.[61] It seems that the oscillation between moderation and radical behavior by the Muslims was part of the process of formation of Muslim society and its links to non-Muslims within that society and the distribution of wealth and power.

Relations between Muslims and non-Muslims were governed as well by relations between the ruling power and the opposition. For instance, when Muslims were the rulers and most of the population was non-Muslim, Muslims were very strict in religious observance relating to social affairs in order to assert their identity and their ascendancy over the non-Muslim majority. When Muslims were the rulers and when most of the population was also Muslim, Muslims were very tolerant of the non-Muslims and emphasized the features common to Islam, Christianity, and Judaism. Also, when the Muslims split into warring factions and sought the support of minorities, the minorities usually sought the help of foreign powers and revolted against the Muslim rulers.[62] In short, the dialectics of tolerance and intolerance was subject to the ups and downs of both Muslim communities and minorities and their attitudes toward internal and external circumstances.

Muslims in turn met with similar or worse treatment. At least the Muslims acknowledged the communal identity and the religious essence of both Christianity and Judaism, while Christians and Jews did not accept Islam as a legitimate or revealed religion. The fall of Granada in 1492 put a huge Muslim population under Christian rule, which pursued violent policies toward the Muslims. In 1502, Muslims as well as Jews were hauled before courts of inquisition and were given the choice of expulsion or conversion. Muslims who converted to Christianity, called Moriscos, were not allowed to wear Islamic dress, to build public baths, or to use Arabic or possess books written in Arabic; eighty thousand books were burnt.[63] We are told:

> The christening of Muslim slaves settled, so to speak, their complete assimilation. After all, having received this sacrament, they fell under church discipline, including the Inquisition. This formed a considerable impediment to maintaining a Muslim religious conviction. The socially enforced conversions to Christianity that took place on

a large scale among Muslim slaves led in practice, however, to the continuation of Islamic religious life in secret, in other words, to form a crypto-Islam, comparable to the crypto-Islam of the Moriscos in sixteenth-century Spain, preceding their deportation at the beginning of the seventeenth century.[64]

Bernard Lewis, whose negative views of modern Muslims are well known, could not but concede in one of his books that Islam was an egalitarian religion. When he compares the Muslim world in medieval times with the caste system of India or with the aristocratic privilege of Christian Europe, he concludes that Islam did indeed appear to have been an egalitarian religion in an egalitarian society. There was far greater social mobility in Islam than in Christian Europe or Hindu India. Even when Islam put certain limits on mobility, these limits were not intrinsic or insurmountable. For instance, the unbelievers' inferiority was not racially oriented or socially classified, it was optional. Adopting Islam made the unbeliever a member of the dominant society and canceled his inferiority. So there was an element of choice.[65]

Lewis further tells us that while Christians and Jews tended to live in their own quarters, these were a natural social development, unlike the legally enforced ghettos of Christian Europe. Minorities tended to master certain professions—diplomacy, banking, commerce, brokerage, espionage—and were later associated as well with lower jobs like tanner, butcher, and hangman.[66]

During medieval times, the Jews of Europe looked to the Jews of the Islamic world for inspiration. For instance, the Jews of Egypt lived side by side with Muslims and Christians, not in ghettos. They lived like other members of Egyptian society and participated in its affairs. They worked in public administration at all levels, and many Jews converted to Islam and held high positions under the Fatimids, like the minister Ya'qub ibn Kils, or like Maimonides, who worked in the court of Salah al-Din al-Ayubi. Jews also owned property and participated in the economic life of Egypt. And in their cultural life they comfortably used Arabic. The internal affairs of Jews as well as Christians were independent of the state. The heads of religious minorities were part of the official hierarchy, but selected by their respective communities.[67]

The *dhimma* system was developed later by the Ottomans into a confessional (*millet*) system by which groups and peoples were recognized as self-autonomous groups but under the central state authority. When Western powers intervened on behalf of Christians within the Ottoman Empire, they influenced intercommunal relationships, for the establishment of missionary schools and the spread of European education led eventually to heightened racial and sectarian tensions.[68]

Modern Islamist Conceptions of Human Rights

In discussing the doctrines of human rights, this section also sheds light on modern theoretical developments in Islamist views of Christianity and Judaism. While minorities have solid foundations in the Middle East, the issue of religious minorities has been especially explosive since the rise of independent nationalist states, specifically in the second half of the twentieth century. This study does not deal with the histories of Judaism, Christianity, missionary schools, orientalism, or Islam, but focuses on the theoretical analyses of Christianity and Judaism by some Islamist movements. The first objective of this section is, therefore, to show the contexts within which Islamism has arisen and its opposition to the traditionally held views on religious minorities. The second objective is to show how the negative relationship with the West, and its perception as a protector and manipulator of religious minorities in the Middle East, have led to a theoretical revision of traditional views. The third objective is to show that many Islamists as well as ordinary Muslims nevertheless share with Christians and Jews common concerns about pluralism, tolerance, the nature of the political order, ethics, morality, and coexistence. Christianity in the Middle East has witnessed an Islamist-style revival, indeed, in Lebanon, the Sudan, and Egypt. The Coptic revival, for instance, has contributed strongly to politicization of the Egyptian Coptic Church.

The Christian missions have sought since the fourteenth century to educate both Christians and Muslims. While the Ottoman caliphate did not acknowledge the Catholic Church, it did maintain good relations with the Orthodox Church, whose patriarch enjoyed an exalted status in Constantinople. The missions took different forms ranging from orders of monks to, later, educational institutions. Most European powers established very influential centers in the Ottoman territories and in Constantinople itself.[69] The missionary societies that were set up in these territories exerted intellectual influence by, first, separating the Arabs from the Ottoman state and, second, downplaying the role of religion in politics. Mount Lebanon, for instance, was put under a special administrative unit and was divided into two sections, one for the Druze and another for the Christians. The English supported the Druze and the French supported the Christians, especially the Maronites. Civil unrest escalated in 1860 to civil war. While the Ottomans attempted to stop the war, French forces landed in Beirut, and Lebanon was made a special concession with a semiautonomous administration headed by a Christian.[70] In this context, Robert M. Haddad provides us with a sobering reflection on the effects of the missions even among Christians themselves:

> In the span of some hundred years, then, the Latins succeeded in all but doubling the number of Syrian Churches and in destroying the tolerance and mutual accommodation which, on the eve of missionary penetration, seem to have characterized their relations. The bitterness and suspicion which stood between the Uniates and their parent Churches not infrequently erupted into violence in the eighteenth and nineteenth centuries and to this day has yet to be entirely dispelled. Any meaningful and consistent unity of action had been irretrievably lost.[71]

Europe succeeded in playing on the internal problems within the Ottoman Empire. *Ahl al-dhimma,* which were considered autonomous entities within the Muslim community, were used by Europeans to give themselves the right to interfere in the internal affairs of the Ottomans. The *millet* system, which organized minority affairs, became incapable of dealing with the new intercommunal conflicts and interconfessional tensions. With the intrusion of Europe, the minorities became the arena where new limitations could be imposed on the Ottomans. As a result, many states in Europe revolted in the name of religion against the sultanate—Romania, Bulgaria, Serbia, and others. Many Christians were also given European citizenship that made them subject to the conditions of a "foreign concession." France "protected" the Catholics, especially the Maronites of Lebanon; Russia demanded the right to protect the Orthodox. Thus began political differentiation between Muslims and Christians. Christians were soon considering themselves citizens of European states, though still residing in the Ottoman Empire. Muslims for their part perceived many Christian sects as agents of the West that wanted to destroy the Muslim world. Thus, the modern problem of minorities took shape as the minorities became suspect in the eyes of the majorities.[72]

Haddad puts the matter very succinctly and perceptively:

> [The Ottomans] failed utterly to comprehend that the Latin advance represented an early and enormously important aspect of Western penetration and that its success was a partial index to the extent of the breakdown of Ottoman polity and an early example of regroup-

ing of Near Eastern society around European and certain indigenous sources of authority, notably the heterodox Lebanese princes.

Nor was the effectiveness of the missionary unrelated to economic considerations. For as the seventeenth century drew to a close, the Melkite men of commerce . . . had grown acutely aware of the intimate connection between consular protection and membership in the Unia.[73]

Radical Views

The Islamist radical trend makes the essence of Islam a protest against all non-Islamic phenomena. Sayyid Qutb's discourse on Judaism and Christianity in the Middle East and in the world represents the intellectual framework for radical groups and movements. Qutb believes that the whole of the universe is living a life of paganism; false gods of materialism, atheism, secularism abound, and the forces that fight true religion are alive and well. Even among Muslims, the spiritually inferior, powerless under the pressures of miserable conditions, look on Islam as just a belief, not a system of life. Relations between Islamic society and non-Islamic ones are based on attempts at mutual annihilation, or at least subjection. While Qutb believes that Christians and Jews may be allowed to worship in their own ways, they must submit to Islam as the sole universal foundation for positive interaction—which, for Qutb, is indicated by paying a head tax, or *jizya*. Only Islamic law could be the legitimate law governing the relations of Islam with Judaism and Christianity. Any other law brings all of society into a state of total disbelief. If this is applicable to Muslims, it is also applicable to Jews and Christians.[74]

According to Qutb, it is applicable to all. Christianity, for instance, lost its true essence when it created a church that allied itself with the Roman Empire, where man became naturally a sinner. The introduction of Greek mythologies and idols into the body of Christianity corrupted its essence. Although Christianity originally saw man as good by nature, it then tainted him with original sin, making the whole of the human race guilty. While the Church looks on Christ as the savior, no true salvation in fact occurred. Man's instincts and sexual desires became a sign of "dirtiness," and self-awareness a sign of sin.[75]

According to Qutb, paganism and polytheism were introduced by hypocrites who pretended to be Christians and held high positions in the Roman Empire. Also, Emperor Constantine was unjust and did not follow sincerely the teachings of the Church. Christianity then could not uproot paganism but became intermingled with it, which produced a new Christianity—whereas Islam radically uprooted paganism. Constantine, manipulating Christianity for the sake of his personal power, combined Christianity and paganism into a new paganistic Christianity whose political manifestation was the Roman Empire and whose religious manifestation was the Catholic Church.[76]

However, this new Christianity could not, adds Qutb, move Europe away from its materialistic and paganistic life. It led to unnatural reaction represented by monks who repressed natural and instinctual human desires and energies and created spiritual conflicts. It led as well to social and civilizational apathy. Finally, Europe revolted against the Church and its doctrines and moved away from dogmatism to reason—and thereby made reason into the new god that must control all aspects of life. Positivism followed in the nineteenth century and blew away the power of reason. Now it was believed that matter created man's ideas and his reason, and man was nothing more than an imprint of nature. Darwin, Freud, and Marx dealt the final blow to any religious conception of life by arguing either that man's impulses were all sexual in nature or that man was only an economic instrument of production, the real source of all history and ideas.[77]

Thus Westerners' dislike of religion is in general due both to the Church's misuse of authority and to its view of man. Islam has not had the problem that the West has had, whether in politics or ethics. This is so because from its beginning Islam has not looked down on man's needs and desires nor allowed any religious institution to rule in God's name. Nor has it sanctioned life isolated from social interaction.[78] The original version of Protestantism is, from Qutb's perspective, closer to Islam, for Protestantism as developed by Martin Luther in the fifteenth century attacked "the devil's teachings"—the teaching of popery, the Trinity, and the Catholic Church—and denied the validity of salvation through the authority of the pope. Luther made the highest authority the text (the Bible) and called for freedom of interpretation, while arguing as well for the priority of faith over reason or nature. As for Calvin, Qutb adds, like Luther he made the Bible the highest Christian authority and denied the doctrine of the Trinity. Religion became a subject of contention for Europeans. Qutb attributes Luther's revolt against the Church and other principles to the effects of Islam, whose teachings were carried to the West through the Crusaders and Spain.[79]

Qutb's discourse is built on the premise that Christian theology is pagan in origin. The Roman Catholic Church has been opposed throughout history because it does not represent the divinely inspired "true Christianity" but only a human development within certain periods and for specific political goals. It has even gone against the essence of religion and used the worst kinds of tyranny and torture. The conflict between faith and reason is indeed the conflict between Catholicism and human thought in European life.

For Qutb, while all messengers of God from Noah to Jesus taught the pure oneness of God (*tawhid*) and the centrality of man's position in the universe, only Islam stayed pure and true to its origin. Those who do not follow Islam are, he says flatly, holders of incorrect religious views. As an example he discusses the essence of Judaism. Like Christianity, the religion of the people of Israel is full of paganistic and nationalistic features. Though the children of Israel received a pure message of *tawhid* along with the Law of Moses, they have corrupted them by including in the Old Testament elements that are no better than Greek myths. Abraham called for pure *tawhid*, but only a few Jews followed him, while the rest insisted on worshipping idols and broke the Covenant with God. Furthermore, they believed that their god was a national god and not universal, thus justifying the use of one moral code among themselves and another with non-Jews. The Old Testament is full of references to selectiveness (the God of Israel) and unseemly depictions of God (Adam hiding from God, God's sadness, feeling of guilt, and the like).[80]

Qutb uses the purity of *tawhid* as the only measure of the truth of any divinely inspired religion. While he acknowledges the divine origins of both Christianity and Judaism, he nonetheless equates them in modern times with unbelief. He believes that Islam is the only religion that has protected its message from theological myths and economic and political corruption. The Islamic text for Qutb is beyond any doubt the word of God and divinely constructed, but other divine texts are at best dubious and man-made constructions.[81]

Muslims are therefore, for Qutb, called on to apply an Islamic method that brings man to his true nature by worshipping God alone, liberating him from all other methods and religions. In Islam, God is the only universal lawgiver and governor; no other gods, lawgivers, or governors are legitimate. Both Jews and Christians—and actually most Muslims—have committed the gravest sin in accepting legislation from political authorities and representative bodies, for they are thereby mixing the divinely ordained texts with human interpretations. When priests and rabbis legislated or made laws, he argues, they and the people who accepted their legislation and laws deviated from the oneness of God. Only Islam did not give this right to any group of human beings. It is incumbent upon "true" Muslims to achieve God's pure method on earth by adhering to divine governance and negating human paganism. Human acts of legislation cannot by definition be neutral or universal, since human legislation is affected by time and place. Thus Christianity, Judaism, and nontextual Islam should not be observed or even respected but must be demolished.[82]

Al-jihad (struggle)—which is commonly and wrongly translated as holy war—becomes mankind's instrument for achieving purity and submission to God. For Qutb, Christianity and Judaism may be tolerated, but only under the umbrella of Islam. Since its main objective is the unity of mankind under the doctrine of *tawhid,* Islam does not acknowledge any sort of difference as a source of distinction, be it color, race, language, or wealth. Its distinctions, and therefore its rights and duties, revolve around the purity of doctrines and adherence to divine governance and negation of paganism. The believers conduct jihad, including war, in order to establish the just and straight system, or Islam. While individuals are allowed to be equally Muslims or non-Muslims, for Islam prohibits forcing people to believe in God, the superiority of an Islamic system and the need to establish it is incontestable to Sayyid Qutb. The abode of Islam (*dar al-Islam*) is the land whose law is Islam, whether the citizens are Muslims or non-Muslims; conversely, the abode of war (*dar al-harb*) is any land whose law is not Islam, also whether the citizens are Muslims or non-Muslims. Interestingly enough, Qutb allows peace treaties and nonbelligerence between the two abodes, if the intentions of the abode of war are good, nonaggressive, and nontreacherous. However, if any of these intentions is present—and for Qutb, these are the intentions of the West—then war must become decisive in resolving conflicts between the two.[83]

If one brings together his political views about the Christian world (or now the West) and about Judaism (or now Israel), one can predict the relations of Muslims with Christians and Jews. His political discourse about Christians and Jews is more exclusive than his theological views, for while he tolerates the existence of Christianity and Judaism under an Islamic order, he believes that Islam cannot coexist under a non-Islamic political order and especially under Zionist, imperialist, and colonialist domination. He argues that Western colonialism has occupied almost all of the Muslim world and imposed itself on it. Colonialism has attempted by all means to eradicate the Islamic creed, but to no avail. Now the Islamic creed is being revived in order that the Muslim world may regain its power. This requires, however, sublimation (or psychological superiority) because dignity is related to belief and not to superior material force. Muslims must resist and struggle to establish this sublimation or superiority, because God is the ultimate power. All of the Islamic world has fought the colonialists and worked for its liberation, because the unity of the Muslims and independence are inseparable.[84]

Qutb further argues that Western Orientalism was created in order to rewrite Islamic history in a manner suitable to the mentality and objective of the colonialist West. Europe is made the historical center of civilization, while other civilizations are intellectually subordinated to the West, even when it was backward and without any major scientific and intellectual achievements. Thus political domination created intellectual domination.[85]

The Muslim world cannot get rid of this Western intellectual domination, according to Qutb, without first getting rid of Western political domination. The West has "eaten up" Muslims individually and carved up their world into dependent states and created within each a fifth column or a minority that is allied with the West and its interests rather than the people and their interests. The modern West has sunk so low in its destruction of the Muslim world that its behavior is unprecedented in history, unequaled even by the Tatars or the Crusaders. Moreover, the Eastern bloc that pretended to be without religion was still pursuing the objectives of the Russian Empire. While the Muslim population of the empire was around 42 million in the czarist era, under Marxist rule it diminished during a period of thirty years to 26 million: on Russian soil alone, 16 million were annihilated. Also, Yugoslavia and Albania witnessed religious and ethnic cleansing. Qutb argues, therefore, that "the spirit of Crusadism" is still alive and behind the dealings of the West—both the Eastern and Western blocs—with the Muslim world. To prove this he quotes a French officer who represented General Catroux as saying on entering Jerusalem in 1941, "We are the offspring of the Crusaders; whoever does not like our rule can leave." For Qutb, this is the spirit of Europe, as well as the United States and the communist countries. They all hate Islam and adhere to the Crusaders' discrimination. The West sucks Muslim blood, and the national state serves its interests. Qutb even goes back to 1909 and tells us of a conference held by missionaries at the Mount of Olives in Palestine. When the conference coordinator said, "Our efforts have failed miserably, because no one converted to Christianity except one or two," a priest stood up and said, "Our mission is not to convert Muslims to Christianity, our mission is to make them non-Muslims. . . . In this sense, we have succeeded completely, for every school graduate, and not only the graduates of missionary schools, left Islam."[86]

In a case like this, jihad becomes a necessary tool to defend the Muslim world as well as to spread the true message of God. From Qutb's perspective, all modern wars have been made for nationalist interests and exploitation, taking away from people their natural resources and making them dependent on, and markets for, the West. The two world wars for Qutb were direct results of the spiritual bankruptcy of mankind.[87] While the first objective of jihad is to protect Muslims so that they are not attracted away from Islam by foreign thought and power, the second objective is to maintain the freedom of propagating Islam, and the third is to establish God's authority over the globe and to defend it. Therefore, Islam does not look for peace at any price, but requires, in addition to all of the above, total justice. This means that Muslims should not placate the earth's tyrants, whether individuals or groups or classes, or accept enslavement or exploitation. What Muslims should accept from non-Muslims is one of three things: conversion to Islam, jizya, or war.[88]

For Qutb, paying jizya indicates either stopping resistance, the establishment of free Islamic proselytizing, or the abolition of the material force that stands against Islam. As to war, it is a reaction to resisting the Islamic call. Individuals who surrender after fighting become ahl al-dhimma (those who have a protection contract) and are treated equally with Muslims. Indeed, the jizya imposed on non-Muslims is equivalent to the zakat imposed on Muslims, both of which are needed for covering the expenses of the Islamic state so that all citizens enjoy justice, medical care, and retirement benefits. While zakat is an Islamic duty, jizya is not, but is an alternative tax imposed on non-Muslims. Also, non-Muslims do not have to fight the enemies of the state: fighting is a religious duty, so non-Muslims do not have to yield to it. However, if Christians and Jews choose to fight along with the Muslims, then they do not have to pay jizya. Therefore, to raise concerns and doubts about the status of minorities in the Islamic community is, for Qutb, a propaganda against Islam spread by some ignorant groups among minorities. At other times, it is done by people who have "Islamic names"—Muslims—but whose interest is not Islam but certain material gains received from foreign Crusadism.[89]

Similarly, because the Islamic state for Abu al-A'la al-Mawdudi is ideological, it splits its citizens into two categories: those who believe in its principles and those who do not. While the state may employ the unbelievers, they cannot be appointed to the central positions. However, the Islamic state provides guarantees to its minorities, as opposed to the national state, which either gradually weakens, through absorption, the collective identity of minorities, destroys and expels minorities, or makes them outcasts. The Islamic state gives the minorities equal rights and duties to those of Muslims that are religiously mandated, and no power can legitimately take these rights away, while in the national state the majority accords or denies minorities their rights.[90]

For al-Mawdudi Islam provides the following rights to minorities: preservation of the self and dignity, equality before the law, and maintenance of equal civil law—with the exception of allowing them to eat pork and drink wine and trade in them. He also includes respect for minorities' personal law and religious rituals and places, and fairness in applying the *jizya* and *kharaj*—religious taxes—in exchange for exemption from military service, since jihad is a religious function that non-Muslims are not asked to perform. Also, minorities have the right to write and preach, hold public positions, and take part in education, commerce, and trade. Minorities have no right to vote or to hold representative positions and ministries, but they can hold municipal positions because they do not then participate in the making of general state policies.[91]

According to the Iranian constitution the official religion of Iran is Islam and the official legal school is the "unreversable" Twelver Shi'ite. Other legal schools are respected, and their followers are allowed to practice accordingly in the fields of education, personal status, and civil court adjudication. In an area where the majority adhere to a specific legal school, local regulations should conform to that school.[92]

Furthermore, Jews, Christians, and Magi (Zaradusht, or Zoroastrians) are the only recognized religious minorities. They enjoy the freedom to practice their rituals, to follow their personal law, and to conduct their religious education. The Islamic constitution calls for treating non-Muslims justly and morally and for maintaining their human rights when they do not work against Islam or the Islamic state.[93]

Under the third chapter, People's Rights, the constitution provides fourteen articles on the rights that people enjoy in the Islamic Republic. They include equal rights and nondiscrimination in terms of ethnicity, language, and similar characteristics, and equal protection under the law. Other rights include women's rights to further their moral and material standing, the protection especially of pregnant and nursing women, and help for underprivileged women, especially widows, the old, and those who do not have sponsors. Furthermore, rights of property, work, and money are protected, and social guarantees and education are seen as public rights. On the political level, the freedom of association, whether in political parties or other groups, is guaranteed on the condition that it not contradict the stated bases of the Islamic Republic. This means that nonreligious political parties, for instance, cannot have legal status, nor could Christians form a religious political party.[94]

Like Qutb, Shukri Mustapha believes that the Qur'an exhorts Muslims to fight the people of the Book (*ahl al-kitab,* or Jews and Christians) because many of them want to turn Muslims against their religion. Fighting them stops only after they pay *jizya.* For him, Jews and Christians like pagans deserve death. Thus, when the Qur'an orders Muslims to kill the infidels, then Jews and Christians are included. When the Qur'an talks about their toleration, it is an exception to the general rule and for specific reasons. For Islam accepts nothing less than Islam, and the complete religion is no more than Islam. Muslims can coexist with non-Muslims either under their rule, when Muslims are in a state of weakness, or when non-Muslims pay *jizya,* or when an agreement is reached. As to the verses that call for noncoercion in religion, Shukri states that they have to be linked to the more general verses—for him, those verses that call for fighting. Formal submission to Islam is necessary whether people believe in it or not. So when Islam calls for allowing people to believe in whatever they want, this for Shukri does not include the formal aspect of religion, but only conscience. There is no freedom to express unbelief; when the Qur'an speaks of that freedom to the prophet Muhammad, it is telling him that he cannot force them to believe because he does not know their intentions, but still they have to conform to the rituals of Islam.[95]

Though belief at heart is for Shukri different from formal submission, nonetheless outside conformity is called for. While Muslims may not be able to make others believers, because no one can force faith, Islam calls for the spread of its message, whether people like it or not. Islamic law must be maintained whether people are Muslims or not, and Islamic rituals must be exercised. Muslims may fight non-Muslims who do not want to fight, because Muslims fight for the spread of the Islamic message; also killing is permitted if the message of Islam reaches non-Muslims and they reject it. For Shukri, dominion over the world should be the objective of Muslims so that the divine law and doctrines become supreme. This is why "true" Muslims must isolate themselves from their societies, then defend themselves, and finally overtake others—Jews, Christians, and even Muslims. Interestingly enough, Shukri argues that the Jewish occupation of Palestine is no different from any other occupation of land by infidels, which is characteristic of the whole world today. He does even not believe that fighting Jews is a priority, because the war between the Arabs and the Jews is not an Islamic war. An Islamic war is not launched to regain a land, Shukri goes on, but it is the war that spreads the message of Islam. The wars that are going on today in the world are human wars. While fighting Jews is a legal duty for Shukri, he makes fighting them similar to fighting Egyptian intelligence services, and he denies the legitimacy of fighting Jews under the aegis of the current regime in Egypt. He even prohibits his fellow members from joining the Egyptian army; for him all existing societies, Muslim, Christian, and Jewish, are equally infidels and should not be dealt with positively.[96]

Going further, Salim al-Rahhal, leader of a branch of Tanzim al-Jihad, argues that Muslims today are confronting the whole world and the enemies of virtue like international Crusadism, international communism, international Zionism, and their secular agents. The United States of America stands at the top of the list of the enemies of Islam because of its strategic alliance with Israel and its oppression of the people of world. His analysis of the objectives of the U.S. in the Islamic world leads him to attribute to the U.S. the deep "Crusaders' hatred" of Islam as well as an interest in raw materials. For the U.S. belongs to the Christianity of the Crusaders and perpetuates the historical enmity between Islam and Christianity. Hatred is what regulates U.S. behavior toward Islamic movements. After a detailed analysis of this, al-Rahhal argues that the U.S. supports religious minorities against Muslims, and gives the example of the Copts in Egypt. While Egypt is an ally of the U.S., still the U.S. supports the Orthodox Coptic Church and its illegal political party (which is legal in the United States). Also, the U.S. uses Egypt to bring Arabs into peace with Israel and to fight Islamic movements in the area, since Islam does not fit U.S. interests in the Muslim world.[97]

Moderate Views

Al-Banna, on the other hand, argues that Islam calls for respecting contracts, agreements, and pacts. However, *jizya* is a tax collected from people of the Book for the services provided by the state, protection, and defense. It was also collected from the people of the land that was won in war, since Muslims became responsible for their state affairs. Islam in this regard is like Christianity and Judaism; the three do not reject jihad and war.[98]

Al-Banna rejects the notion that an Islamic system denies religious minorities the right to exist or practice their rituals. On the contrary, he believes that all groups should cooperate in setting up a good and virtuous society. Islam postulates the need for protecting minorities and prevents Muslims from fighting others for no legitimate cause; all believers, Muslims, Christians, and Jews, constitute one community.[99]

Islam acknowledges the unity of mankind, all being the offspring of Adam, and only piety distinguishes one individual or group from others. The Qur'an addresses all mankind equally and establishes the divine origin of religions. The religious holy books are inspired by God, and the sincere believers in His books are saved wherever they are. Thus, people should not fight each other in God's name and must unite in religion. A Muslim should believe not only in the Qur'an but also in the other holy books and in all prophets without distinction. The teachings of Moses, Jesus, and Muhammad are based on the Abrahamic traditions. The Torah is a legitimate holy text; so is the Old Testament and the Bible. The children of Israel are the nation of Moses and Christians are the followers of Jesus. Therefore, relations between the three religions should be based on their common beliefs and interests, especially when no group overpowers the other and occupies its land. Muslims are asked to use good argument with the people of the Book because of the unity of the message. Islam does not want to create enmity with the believers, be they Christians or Jews. Al-Banna goes on to say that Islam has given all people spiritual rights, in addition to political and other rights.[100] However, the conflict with Western civilization is not religious in nature but political. The West is not fighting the East because it is Muslim, for the West fought within itself more severe wars than those with Muslims. It supports Jewish Zionism because that serves its colonialist objectives, but in fact the West dislikes it and committed murders against the Jews. Put simply, the West wants to control the East politically and economically. The materialist West wants to appropriate raw materials and oppresses the rest of the world after it has taken the leadership from the Prophetic traditions of Moses, Jesus, and Muhammad. The West is now unjust and repressive.[101]

Taking a related line, 'Umar al-Tilmisani, the former guide of the Muslim Brotherhood in Egypt, says that while the implementation of Islamic law in Egypt is necessary, he does not look on minorities and the West as enemies. As to the Christians and Jews residing outside the Muslim world, he believes that Islam makes international relations dependent on goodwill and justice. The Jews are included within this framework, but the conflict with the Israelis is a political conflict, and insofar as they do not hurt Muslims, normal and cordial relations can be developed and maintained. Now the Jews have expelled the Palestinians, and are enemies of peace and have controlled some Islamic holy places. In other words, they are the aggressor right now. However, minorities in the Islamic world have the right to conduct their lives according to their own laws.[102]

Yusuf al-Qaradawi, a contemporary leading thinker of the Muslim Brotherhood in Egypt and the Arab world, conditions relations with non-Muslims on, again, goodwill and justice—contingent, of course, on the absence of war and of persecution of the Muslims. Jews and Christians have a more favorable position in Islam than others, even though some of them have made some changes in their holy books. The Qur'an, adds al-Qaradawi, calls on Muslims to dialogue with the people of the Book, allows eating the animals they slaughter, and allows marrying their women, which means mixing Muslims and non-Muslims and thereby making non-Muslim women heads of Muslim families. This applies as well to Jews and Christians who do not reside in Muslim territories.[103]

However, al-Qaradawi continues, those Jews and Christians who do reside in Muslim territories are *ahl al-dhimma,* which refers to non-Muslim citizens of an Islamic society. *Al-dhimma* means security, guarantee, and contract, which are provided to them so that they can live peacefully. It is similar to today's naturalization where a foreigner becomes a citizen. In this sense, *ahl al-dhimma* belong to the abode of Islam and hold Islamic citizenship. This contract is eternal and guarantees that Muslims protect *al-dhimmiyin* if they pay *jizya* and accept Islamic law in nonreligious issues. Their rights include internal and external protection, physical, financial, and legal aspects as well as retirement guarantees. More important, their religious freedom, whether in terms of rituals or belief, is also protected and they may not be forced to change any of it. They enjoy as well economic freedom, whether in terms of work or selling and buying—excluding usury, pork, and alcoholic drink. On another level, they have the right to occupy any government post except those that are of an Islamic religious nature, like the imamate and the presidency, because these institutions represent the prophet Muhammad, and non-Muslims cannot represent him. However, they can be appointed as ministers and work as deputies.[104]

Al-Qaradawi then explains the duty of the people of the Book. He delineates three basic duties: (1) to respect the rituals of Muslims, (2) to adhere to Islamic law in civil interaction, and (3) to pay *jizya* and other taxes. *Jizya* is a compensation for not serving in the community's defense against external enemies, because fighting others may involve some religious aspect that non-Muslims do not want to honor. Jihad is in particular a religious duty that non-Muslims are not asked to perform, and if non-

Muslims fought for Islamic causes, this would be unjust. However, those Jews and Christians who fight alongside Muslims do not pay *jizya*, nor do clergy, women, children, the elderly, the blind, and the sick.[105]

As to tolerance, al-Qaradawi argues that Islam extended it to the point where those who do not believe in Islam are allowed by textual authority to hold their divergent views. Islam has never sanctioned forcing people to adhere to Islam and has always respected the rituals of others. While Islamic law has, for instance, prohibited drinking wine or selling pork, the prohibition does not infringe the rights of non-Muslims, for while Christians do not prohibit drinking wine, drinking itself is not a religious duty, nor is eating pork. Thus, by not eating pork or drinking wine, they are not committing any religious crime but would be sensitive to the feelings of Muslims. Therefore, he concludes, non-Muslims ought to respect the feeling of Muslims in matters that do not involve breaking a religious law. Tolerance of each religious group should go beyond the specifics of legal issues to include goodwill, gentle interaction, justice, mercy, and benevolence, most of which fall outside the scope of law.[106]

On the other hand, al-Qaradawi gives historical examples of the others' intolerance of Muslims. He asks his reader to study what the Muslims did when they invaded Spain, and what Christians did when they overcame Muslims eight hundred years later. He also discusses the Crusades and their consequences, which are like the communist revolution in Russia and Nazism in Germany. Muslims in Ethiopia, Russia, Yugoslavia, China, and other countries are today oppressed and killed. The history of Christianity testifies to the intolerant attitudes of Christians even with each other, which led to many wars and crimes. Al-Qaradawi's exposition shows that Christianity has historically been less tolerant than Islam, and that the very charges that are brought against Islam can be brought against Christianity. Now as in the past, Islam is essentially tolerant of the others' religions, but the others are intolerant of Islam.[107]

As to Islam's position on human rights, he argues that Islam from its very beginning provided humanity with rights that were divine and permanent. These rights include that of life, which makes no distinction between male and female, white and black, old and young, or the like. Other rights include dignity, honor, money, and subsistence for the needy; all these rights are based on the principles of brotherhood, equality, and freedom.[108]

Similarly, Sa'id Hawwa, the Syrian Muslim Brotherhood leader and thinker, argues that in an Islamic state all citizens are equal and protected from despotism and arbitrariness. The distinction between one individual and another should not center on race or belief. As to the exercise of power, it should be based on *shura* and freedom of association, specifically political parties, unions, minority associations, and civil institutions. The one-party system is unworkable in an Islamic state. Furthermore, he adds, the rule of law should reign supreme, and people should be able to have access to courts to redress their grievances. More important, freedom of expression should be guaranteed, whether on the personal or the public level.[109]

In particular, Hawwa shows sensitivity to the importance of arguing to the Syrian majority the case for equal rights for minorities. While ultimate authority should be within the confines of Islamic teachings, and while individuals from minorities can be members of cabinets or parliaments, political representation must be proportionate. However, the administration of their internal affairs and the building of educational institutions and religious courts are the domain of minorities themselves and should not be subjected to the control of others.[110]

Faysal al-Mawlawi, one of the leaders of the Sunni Islamic movement in Lebanon, believes that Islam sees women and men as equal, and therefore their rights and duties should be equal. Religious rights and duties are uniform because they belong to human beings per se. Both men and women have, for instance, the right to choose to believe or not to believe, and women's right to choose is equivalent to the men's at the highest level—as is the right to freedom, housing, opinion, belief, education, and social guarantees. In principle, then, women have the same rights as men. Any difference is related to the role each plays in society, which does not necessarily reflect unequal standing but different functions due to physical and sexual differences. Most important, since women shoulder the basic management of the home, their involvement and wielding of power is essential, since the family is the basic unit of Islamic society.[111]

As to the issue of men's right to marry more than one wife, al-Mawlawi provides ecological and biological as well as social reasons for that. First, there are more women than men; second, it protects women from exploitation by men; third, if some women cannot bear children, they are not inhumanely divorced; fourth, if some women become permanently ill, their husbands marry others without divorcing them. He believes that such a scheme is more dignified for women who might suffer from biological defects and ecological imbalance. Thus society's basic unit, the family, is preserved, and society's ability to maintain virtue is increased. For him this situation is by no means a degradation of women's rights and dignity.[112]

Hiba Ra'uf 'Izzat goes deeper in her study on women's rights to argue that the general Islamic worldview does not accept the idea of the social division of labor; women perform particular social jobs and men perform political jobs. The general objectives of the *shari'a* are the responsibility of all men and women. Women carry political responsibility as individuals in the community. Again, institutional division of labor is not limited to women or men. Efficiency is the focus of such a division, so women can belong to various institutions insofar as they can efficiently perform their jobs. The family's development is not merely a social function but is political as well. Women are thus eligible for political participation; in fact, it is a religious duty. However, the function of women in a specific society reflects the degree of social development, and women's function in Islamic societies did not reflect Islam's ultimate religious understanding of women's role, but rather reflected actual development.[113]

"The Statement of the Muslim Brotherhood on the Role of Women" in 1994 delineates these rights. On a woman's right to elect members of representative councils and similar bodies, it says: "We are of the view that there is nothing in the *shari'a* to prevent women from taking part in these matters. Allah says: 'The men believers and women believers are responsible for each other. They enjoin the good and forbid evil.'" On women's membership in representative councils and similar bodies, the statement says, "We are of the view that there is nothing in the *shari'a* texts to prevent this either. The views we cited earlier concerning their right to vote applies to their right to be elected as well. . . . We call for education and the enlightenment of both women and men, and the exertion of all possible efforts in this connection, this being an important objective and duty made binding by the *shari'a*." On the right of women to hold public office, the statement says, "The only agreed upon public office that a woman cannot occupy is the presidency or head of the state."

As for other types of public office, the woman can accept them as there is nothing in the *shari'a* to prevent her from doing so. Also, there is nothing to prevent her from working at what is proper, since public office is a type of work that the *shari'a* allows women to undertake. Women can work in professions such as medicine, or any field where she or the society may see a need.[114]

The views of the Islamist trend that legitimizes pluralistic civil society and democracy can be aptly derived from the circulated text of a pact (*mithaq*) that has been published and distributed by Muhammad al-Hashim al-Hamidi to other Islamists. He states that the success of the Islamic movement after it takes control of government hinges on its estab-

lishment of a just and democratic system in the Arab world. Lifting the
community from the tyranny that it has been plunged into necessitates
that any such movement establish limits and a program for justice, *shura*,
and human rights. The program must include the rights of life, justice, fair
trial, equality of women and minorities, and political participation as well
as freedom of thought, belief, expression, and religion. His suggestions for
basic principles governing the formation of parties and associations include the freedom to form parties and political associations for all citizens
without exception. Parties need not be licensed by the government. Internal party life must be governed by democracy. A call for dictatorship and
totalitarian rule may not be made in slogans or political propaganda or in
any manner. Furthermore, secular citizens, including the communists,
have the right to form parties, to propagate their ideology, and to compete
for power. Finally, racial, tribal, sectarian, or foreign affiliations cannot be
the basis of any legitimate political propaganda.[115]

On another level, al-Ghannushi recognizes the rights of minorities to
run for election and to be represented in the parliament of an Islamic state.
An Islamic state does not mean that all political institutions are limited to
Muslims, but rather that the law should be Islamic law and that all elements of society should be represented in parliament; a non-Muslim minority should participate in the administration of the state within the law
of Islam. Islam is thus not a condition of political representation, for citizenship with all its rights and duties is not the result of faith, but belongs
inherently to man. Of course, overall acceptance of the political parameters of the state is required.[116]

Openness and dialogue are essential, al-Ghannushi argues, not only
within the Muslim world but with all of the world, and the West in particular. The world has been transformed by scientific advancement into a
small village that can no longer tolerate war. This village has a common
fate, and its future needs serious rethinking—if its inhabitants are serious
enough about having a common fate. This presupposes, among other
things, putting an end to the abstract geographic and cultural division of
the world into East and West and the preconception that one is rational
and democratic, the other perverse and despotic. Such ideas are nothing
but a recipe for war. Any objective analysis testifies to the fact that among
the negative and positive values, the forces of goodness do exist here and
there. The forces of goodness are invited to dialogue and to search for
avenues of intercourse.[117]

4

Prospects for Pluralist Democracy

Classical, medieval, and modern Islamic thought, whether jurisprudence, theology, philosophy, or other disciplines of Islamic knowledge, contain concepts comparable to modern Western doctrines of democracy, pluralism, and human rights. While originally inspired by the law of natural rights, these doctrines are Islamicly based on textual authorities that derived from the Qur'an and the Sunna, and that lend themselves to arguments favoring democratic forms of government, pluralistic societies, and guarantees of human rights. However, the contexts that shaped the development of Islamic political thought have not been conducive to pluralistic democracy and human rights. The diverse theoretical trends of classical, medieval, and modern Islamic thought on these or similar doctrines have lately been acquiring different formulations through a process of deconstruction and reconstruction.

That the historic Islamic political orders had been composed of many religious and ethnic communities opens the road today to adoption of a pluralistic society. Unlike those who have been upholding the notion of a purely Islamic, or only ideological, state, I have argued that the fundamental law of the first Islamic state distinguished between religious authority and political authority. And although the religious authority had only to call people to religion, the political authority had to deal with social, ethnic, and religious organizations, political and economic development and changes, and human aspirations and needs. When the first Islamic political order—which was effectively a confederation of different religious groups—recognized the multiplicity of social, economic, ethnic, and political organizations, it unequivocally showed the original nondogmatic and pluralistic Islamic view of political life. This viewpoint allowed the minority non-Muslims full partnership in the political structure, even on the sensitive issues of war and peace.

The religious and even the divine were understood through the political—understandably, since religious matters became meaningful only through the agency of individual or collective human judgment, whether *ijtihad, shura,* or *ijma'.* From the majority's perspective, the inability of any human to ascertain his representation of God forced the community to accept *ijtihad, shura,* or *ijma'* as means of settling important matters, both political and religious. But while every member of the community acknowledged Muhammad's political authority in the first Islamic state, other religious communities like the Jews enjoyed complete religious authority.

It is very clear from the history of Islam that when an individual or a group claims a divine representation, then his (or their) positions turn into radical and absolute views. However, when even religious views are projected as political matters, then there is a possibility for compromise, at least in theory. For if politics is the art of the possible, which allowed the inception of the first Islamic state, then its religious counterpart, the art of the impossible, has most probably hindered the rise of any serious attempt to revive an Islamic political alternative. For instance, when Mu'awiya and 'Ali looked at their differences as political in nature, it was possible to find a compromise, but once the Khawarij introduced the impossible, or God's direct judgment, then all sorts of political problems were turned into questions of belief and unbelief and were thereby transformed into divine matters that were not subject to compromise. The humanization of the divine conditions it to the needs and requirements of life. Islamic history shows that any abstract and not-historical understanding turns the human into the divine, and consequently into a nonnegotiable metaphysical and metahistorical doctrine. But when the divine is filtered through a human agency and is subjected to human history, then it serves all of humankind. Hence, humanizing the divine turns it into a source of cooperation.

That the first Islamic state incorporated, among other things, non-Muslims and older structures indicates the need to adopt pluralistic intellectual and political models that incorporate freedom and fairness and shun prejudice and arbitrary judgment. Today too, the *umma* formative authority as an expression of the divine will and law can be employed to reorganize political orders. If it is the majority's view that political rule throughout Islamic history did not represent the divine will, then pluralistic understanding and tolerance become more likely. Inasmuch as the community is the human sovereign and the source of all powers, no individual or group of people—whether fundamentalist or modernist or traditionalist, military or religious—can have an exclusive claim to interpret the text or govern the people. *Ijma'*, then, whether through consultation or other means, is legitimate whenever the community, as the holder of such powers, conceives it to be so.

Political rule became a religious duty because the people, or a great majority of them, agreed on the matter. Similarly, *shura* was chosen by the people to settle the most important and formative events in Islamic history. Political rule rests on the people's power to make a contract, although its multiple interpretations have divided the community into many sects. While communal *shura* has been, in historical practice, generally waived in the interest of increasing the power of regimes and dynasties, its legitimate employment by the majority has become, in theory, almost incontestable. It can and should be employed today to humanize political legitimacy and democratize political power.

As a major source of communal power, *shura,* a form of democratic interaction, must be used to develop other doctrines of legitimacy and methods of action. Its elasticity can turn it into a democratic method of political life within and among states and toward world orders. Thus an old concept, deconstructed and reconstructed in line with modern democratic interpretations and reshaped by modern technology, should be postulated as a modest beginning for an authentic process of legitimate democratization in the contemporary Muslim world. *Shura* and *ijma'* are two key doctrines that Muslims can use today for the religious development of democratic notions of government and politics as well as protection of human rights, for they take away the divine perception of political government and restrict its legitimacy to the people's choice.

The revival of the doctrine of *ikhtilaf* opens up possibilities for accepting differing and even divergent understandings concerning the nature of power and government and, more important, social and religious organizations, including a multiplicity of religions and philosophies of life. Furthermore, doctrines on the legitimacy of opposition and the necessity of human or legal rights can be employed today in accordance with modern standards to develop economic, social, religious, and political life. These doctrines provide legitimate arguments, for majorities as well as minorities, against the tyranny of the modern state in the Islamic world, they constitute a method to reduce the traditionalism of Islamic establishments, and they open the way to elect governments freely.

Many Muslim political thinkers and jurists have tried mightily to turn rulers into good practitioners of Islamic law who abide by the basic notions of the *shari'a,* which could protect individuals and societies from state tyranny. Other thinkers and jurists have preferred to justify oppressive regimes by referring to the international, regional, and local conditions of Muslims. Nonetheless, compared to other civilizations during that period, classical and medieval Islam still offered the most advanced political discourse on basic human and political rights and duties and on the proper relationship between the ruler and the ruled. While this does not excuse the misuse of political power and the willful misconstruction of certain rights and duties, it places that discourse within its historical context. While Muslim scholars were discussing the human nature of political power and the need to reform it in accordance with *shura* and *ijma'*, the West was still believing in the divine right of kings. Again, while Islamic thought recognized the rights of minorities as a consequence of its recognizing Christianity and Judaism as revealed religions, the West did not recognize Muslims as a minority as a consequence of its not accepting Islam as a revealed religion.

Of course, the history of Islamic governments and dynasties testifies to many incidents of mistreatment, oppression, and even suppression of both Muslims and minorities. However, it also testifies to its tolerance and good treatment of both Muslims and minorities. What is important is that it left modern Muslims with fundamental views that are being developed today into a full scheme of human rights. Islamic political thought has closely examined the basic notions of human rights that existed during the classical and medieval Islamic periods. While these rights are not, could not be, and do not have to be identical to modern human rights schemes in the West, the very deep roots of such rights are, at least theoretically, acknowledged. In fact, these rights historically preceded modern Western schemes of rights and arose in response to the jurists' perception that they were religiously required and sanctioned by the fundamental objectives of Islam and the nature of social interactions.

The chance for developing liberal and democratic discourses in Islam is becoming greater because new and modern readings of Islam are developed as essential to a process of reformation. This process reexamines numerous Islamic doctrines and reforms the notions of political rule. It reinterprets important Islamic literature and challenges traditional institutions. Grounding fundamental doctrines like sovereignty in the Qur'anic discourse, it demands popular consent and insists on the legitimacy of popular discourses and institutions. Reinterpretation of the divine text endows the community with the only legitimate power; other existing powers and authorities are only secondary, and should be subjected to the community's approval. Thus the absoluteness of divine governance is counterbalanced by the divine legitimacy of human *shura*, and the honest observance of the former requires adherence to the latter.

Modern interpretations of *shura* normally absorb democracy within a religious context. Like democracy, *shura* should provide legitimate means of controlling government, since legitimacy is made dependent on popular approval. Finding no contradiction between, on the one hand, democracy and constitutional rule and, on the other, *shura* and divine law, modern reformist and Islamist thinkers absorb the principles of natural law in their reinterpretations of religious revelation. While the moderate Islamists show Islam to be a system capable of absorbing modern philosophy, politics, economics, science, and history without losing any of its validity, they also modernize interpretations of the Islamic texts and bring into Islam the doctrines of democracy, pluralism, and human rights.

The next basic element necessary to an Islamic revival is to reexamine and demystify history and to center responsibility on human actions. The crux of development lies within the scope of human power, not within a mythical history; humans can positively affect their future. Spiritual, intellectual, political, and economic revival is the proper domain of humans who are endowed by their Creator with the ability to act on His behalf. The process of revival cannot be frozen in history, but must be linked in practice to evolving sciences and changing conditions. Linking revival to the relative and the changeable without neglecting the revealed leads modern Islamic thought generally to reject traditional understanding and institutions, enabling it to accept democracy and turn it into a modern form of Islamic *shura*.

Today the demands for democracy, pluralism, and human rights are popular aspirations, and many Qur'anic arguments are made for their adoption. However, this requires two major practical developments: first, limiting government powers by filtering them through popular channels and representative bodies, and second, creating a tolerant political context that facilitates the development of tolerant intellectual, religious, social, and ethical interactions.

While examining classical, medieval, and modern Islamic thought as well as the practices of Islamic institutions, I have shown that the Qur'anic doctrines of *shura, ijma', bay'a, ikhtilaf,* and *al-huquq al-shar'iyya* are religiously demanded. However, the historical and institutional practice of these divinely inspired doctrines has mostly shown their manipulation by governments and elites. For instance, *shura,* a doctrine that demands the participation of the people in running the affairs of their government and society, came to be regularly exploited by political and religious elites to secure their economic, social, and political interests at the expense of other segments of society. Similarly, *bay'a,* a doctrine that should have been used to indicate people's voluntary approval of their ruler, became a compulsory act of formal subjection to the ruler.

Today *shura* is viewed not merely as a religious concept but as a reflection of the public will. A genuine state institutionalization of *shura* and *ijma'* provides the state with a normative role in making basic choices on behalf of the people. If the *shari'a* is also institutionalized in the state, all efforts should be made to ensure that legitimacy is a fact and not just a formality. More important, a political contract is required for the legitimate assumption of power. While Islam is the constitutional reference for modern Islamists, Islamic constitutionality should be upheld through public choices.

For radical Islamists, *shura* is more than a religious concept, more than a mechanism for elections, more even than a reflection of the general will—though this last is a concept much superior to individual freedom or social agreement. Above all, *shura* represents the divine will, and any deviation from the divine is a religious violation. The individual cannot but submit to this will; in fact, he is only an appendage to it, and his freedom depends on it. While his will may opt for a political contract with a ruler, it cannot, because of what it represents, allow pluralism and basic differences. The establishment of an Islamic state becomes for Muslim radicals the fulfillment of the divine will.

For the radicals, when the institutionalization of *shura* and *ijma'* is processed through the lens of the *shari'a*, it provides the state, which supposedly expresses the general will, with a formative role. The formal legitimacy that the state acquires makes it, in fact, unaccountable to anyone but God. Thenceforth legitimacy becomes an internal state affair, not a social and public issue. Therefore, as long as the state is not going against the *shari'a*, no measure can be legitimately used to overthrow it; indeed, in this manner the state supervises the morality of the people and the application of the *shari'a*. While the radicals transform individual religiosity into a communal public will, they transform the public will into state control, both political and moral. In this hierarchy they assign no intrinsic weight to parties, associations, and other civil institutions, which may operate only in a supplementary capacity. This view seems to demand an exclusively Islamic politics that rejects any pluralistic understanding of religions and marginalizes whatever is not Islamic.

The radical Islamists' employment of violence is not theoretical in origin, but their theory of violence is historically developed. Their theories that justify violence are outgrowths of the violence that they have been subjected to. They have transformed practice into theory, which has now a life of its own. Both radical groups and most regimes are dedicated to using intellectual and physical violence. Most violence, by both secular and religious groups, has been committed as a reaction to tyrannical practices of regimes. Islamists attribute the violence of the radical groups to the violence of their respective regimes.

On the other hand, moderate Islamists locate the root cause of violence in the lack of pluralistic societies and representative institutions. Even while they have not been allowed to participate politically, they have aimed to widen the political space and to bring into that space the doctrines of human rights, pluralism, and democracy as the proper instruments of good political life.

Moderate Islamist interpretive discourses on revivalism focus essentially on stripping the past of its sacred normative historical and systematic status. While the Qur'an and the Sunna, as the metaphysical and metahistorical formative and constitutive foundations of Islam, are exempt, they are subjected to unending interpretive and formative possibilities: *ikhtilaf* is pluralism or *ikhtilaf* is not pluralism, and so on. Authoritative texts have been cited in the interpretation of events. To moderate Islamists the two fundamental texts are nonhistorical but eternal, to be used to create good societies. While they depend on them to deny the existence, whether in the past or the present, of a perfect state—with the notable exception of the state founded by the Prophet—or of complete collective Islamic self-awareness, at the same time they employ these fundamentals to strive for modern, democratic Islamic societies and states.

Moderate Islamist quests for reinterpretation of basic Islamic doctrines rest on developing intellectual and formative discourses that rediscover the original connotations and denotations of the texts within the framework of modern life. Such discourses reformulate the religious fundamentals, or *usul al-din,* that are used to argue for a political theology. It is a political theology because it aims at social, economic, and political control rather than philosophical and religious understanding. Bypassing divine theology, it sees the important doctrines as political in nature, like the Islamic state, the community's choice, and individuals' rights. Again, the most important characteristic of divine oneness is manifested not in the individual's private conscience but in his commitment and actions toward the Islamization of state and society. For these moderate thinkers, deep theological commitment to Islam must involve the economic, social, and political concerns of society. Commitment to active Islamic politics signifies the deep-rootedness of belief, while weak commitment reflects weakened belief.

In this fashion, moderate Islamism marginalizes traditional jurisprudence and replaces it with a modern ideology. Now, politics informs all religious disciplines, and good politics depends on a consensual agreement through *shura*. However, this cannot be properly conducted without the machinery of the state. The historical experience of Muslims shows when the state is given the power to employ and execute the *shari'a* in the name of the *umma*, more substantial doctrines of the *shari'a* are overlooked to arrive at politically desirable rulings. To counter this, moderate Islamism transforms *tawhid* into a discourse, and formalizes *shura* into a fundamental form. Therefore, the discourse is interpreted by its form. Moderate Islamism compresses the religious discourse into a political ideology. Thus political belief depends on sound application of the divinely ordained textual *hakimiyya*; political unbelief results from depending on human *hakimiyya* alone.

While the moderate Islamists look on divine governance as an absolute political doctrine, they balance it with the doctrine of *shura*. Indeed, the good fulfillment of governance depends on the good exercise of *shura*. Moderate Islamism developed *shura* to accommodate democracy within Islamic political and religious thought. It has also argued for legitimate religious means of popular control of government. Seeing no contradictions between, on the one hand, democracy and constitutional rule and, on the other, *shura* and divine law, moderate Islamism postulates their harmony. This follows upon the Islamists' dismissal of historical Islamic discourses, which purifies basic Islamic doctrines and permits the introduction of Western philosophy, politics, economics, and science into modern Islamic thought. Thus *shura* has become for moderate thinkers and almost all of the moderate Islamist movements the source of legitimization of any authority, while the continuation of legitimacy hinges on the application of the *shari'a* and the people's approval.

A genuine democracy, grounded in the *shari'a*, paves the way for understanding between the East and the West. Moderate Islamism adopts liberal democracy in an Islamic fashion; radical Islamism adopts popular democracy in an authoritarian fashion. Moderate Islamism believes in the possibility of its inclusion in dialogues and cooperation whether with Arab regimes or the West. Moderate Islamists do not postulate a permanent or divine disaccord between Islamic institutions or systems and those of the West. When properly grounded, indeed, the Western becomes the Islamic. In this fashion, the moderate Islamists as well as the modernists bring together the East and the West by adopting and adapting Western schemes of human rights, pluralism, and democracy. They view East-West tensions as primarily political and economic, not religious and cultural, in nature. The East and the West enjoy common monotheistic backgrounds that pave the way for multicultural and religious cooperation and coexistence.

In most countries of the Muslim world, today's political contexts are not much different from medieval and classical contexts, and "democracy" is exercised as a form of ritual legitimization. While these countries have institutions like parliaments and parties that adhere formally to democracy, human rights, and due process of law, none of these is really observed. In fact, these institutions are used to cover up the tyrannical aspects of state manipulation. They serve only as window dressing for the outside world. Such posturing by Muslim regimes has led people to reject the sham institutions and seek indigenous institutions that can be used to counterbalance the oppressive nature.

One should regard the modern quest for democracy, pluralism, and human rights as a quest for liberation from tyrannical regimes. It is a liberation movement that uses religious doctrines that the state cannot safely challenge or visibly manipulate without the fear of losing legitimacy. If *shura* is a Qur'anic doctrine, and if the state does not defer to the people's choices, the state is then illegitimate. The Islamization of democracy in the form of *shura* is a quest for popular empowerment vis-à-vis the oppressive state. This form of popular empowerment, derived from a Qur'anic doctrine, offsets the coercive power of the state.

The modern Islamic trend that adopts democracy, pluralism, and human rights does not view these issues as an academic exercise. Rather it views them as a quest for liberation and freedom through democracy, for tolerance and acceptance through pluralism, and for respect and dignity through human rights. They are made as solid as the Qur'anic doctrines through their association with religion, interpretation in a religious fashion, and authentication in the Qur'an and the Sunna. Today the possibility that this trend can bridge the gap between the Islamic world and the Western world is real.

It remains now for the West itself to really support the quest for democracy, pluralism, and human rights, instead of supporting undemocratic regimes that flatten all opposition and flout all human rights. The West needs to lend its support on the international level to the process of democratization, sometimes at its own expense in the short run, in order to secure its interests in the long run. In a globalized world, the West cannot just sit back and imagine that the Islamic world is far from its borders or that its interests are secured by a few despotic regimes. The quest for democracy, pluralism, and human rights is now a global movement that is of concern not only to people within Islamic borders but across all borders. The mixture of high technology, high capitalism, and the quest for democracy may prove very explosive if it lacks the elements of fairness and justice, not only within countries but also among them. While these features are shaping the newly globalized world, they are not limited to the industrial countries but, surely, include the Muslim countries.

Notes

Introduction

1. About one-fourth of the information presented here is selected from my *Moderate and Radical Islamic Fundamentalism*.

2. This phrase is used by Professor Bulliet as the title for one of his books, *Islam: The View from the Edge*.

3. Ibid., 4.

4. Mayer, *Islam and Human Rights*, xi–xii. For a scheme of modern Islamic human rights, see, for instance, al-Sayyid, "Contemporary Muslim Thought and Human Rights."

5. Mayer, *Islam and Human Rights*, xv.

6. an-Na'im, *Toward an Islamic Reformation*, 40–58, 77–89.

7. See 'Ishmawi, "Shari'a in the Discussion on Secularism and Democracy," 133–38.

8. See, for instance, Zebiri, *Mahmud Shaltut and Islamic Modernism*.

9. Shams al-Din, *Fi al-Ijtima' al-Siyasi al-Islami*.

10. Jansen, *The Dual Nature of Islamic Fundamentalism*, xi.

11. Ibid., xiv.

12. Ibid., 2.

13. Ibid., 3.

14. Ibid., 6.

15. Kawtharani, *Mashru' al-Nuhud al-'Arabi*, 12–18. See also al-Jabiri, *Al-Khitab al-'Arabi al-Mu'asir*, chapter 2 on democracy.

16. Hamadah, *Bina' al-Umma*, 86–134; Kawtharani, *Mashru' al-Nuhud al-'Arabi*, 18–24. See also 'Amara, *Al-Din wa al-Dawla*, 151–72; al-Sharfi, "Mushkilat al-Hukm"; and al-Shawi, *Fiqh al-Hukuma al-Islamiyya*.

17. al-Mawdudi, *Nahnu*, 47–51, 23–25.

18. See 'Abdu, *Risalat al-Tawhid*, 17–51; al-Ghazali, *Tahafut al-Falasifa* and *Al-Munqidh min al-Dalal*.

19. See, for instance, al-Ghannushi, *Al-Hurriyyat al-'Amma*; al-Huwaidi, *Al-Islam wa al-Dimuqratiyya*; and *Al-Hayat*, 11 October 1996, p. 21; 12 October 1996, p. 21.

20. *Al-Hayat,* 4 August 1993, pp. 19, 25; 25 September 1993, pp. 14, 17. The series ran August 2–6. See also *Qadaya al-Isbu' 15* (10–17 September 1993): 1–2.

21. Djerejian, "One Man, One Vote, One Time"; Miller, "The Challenge of Radical Islam"; "Will Democracy Survive in Egypt?"; "The Arab World Where Troubles for the U.S. Never End"; Huntington, "The Clash of Civilizations."

22. Tibi, *The Challenge of Fundamentalism,* 4.

23. Ibid., ix.

24. Ibid., 53. On terminology relating to differences between fundamentalism, Islamism, political Islam, and others, see Moussalli, *Moderate and Radical Islamic Fundamentalism.*

25. Tibi, *The Challenge of Fundamentalism,* 25.

26. Ibid., xi.

27. Ibid. xi.

28. Ibid., 2.

29. Ibid., 39.

30. Ibid., 57.

31. Ibid., 70–71.

32. Ibid., 81.

33. Ibid., 111.

34. Ibid., 113.

35. Ibid., 13.

36. Ibid., 3.

37. Ibid., 17.

38. Ibid., 5.

39. Ibid., 7.

40. Ibid., 203.

41. Ibid., 207.

42. Ibid., 210.

43. Ibid., xv.

44. Shahin, *Political Ascent,* 4.

45. Ibid., 22.

46. Ibid., 25–26.

47. Ibid., 27.

48. Ibid., 32.

49. Ibid., 33, 69–70, 77, 79–80, 116–21, 131, 172, 174, 217, 222.

50. Ibid., 244.

Chapter 1. The Classical and Medieval Dialectics of *Shura* and Its Modern Islamist Constructions As Democracy

1. al-Ghazali, *Al-Iqtisad fi al-I'tiqad,* 215, and *al-Mustathhiri,* 62–63. See also al-Mawardi, *Adab al-Din wa al-Dunya,* 120, and Ibn Taymiyya, *Minhaj al-Sunna al-Nabawiyya,* 1:141.

2. al-Mawardi, *Al-Ahkam al-Sultaniyya*, 5, and *Adab al-Din wa al-Dunya*, 119–20. See also al-Durayni, *Dirasat*, 1:341–81.

3. al-Zabidi, *Taj al-'Arus*, 13:252–53, 384; Ibn Hisham, *Al-Sira*, 1:125, 2:192–99; and *Encyclopedia of Islam*, 3:72. See also al-Mas'udi, *Muruj al-Dhahab*, 2:286–89; Brockelmann, *History of the Islamic Peoples*, 43–44; and al-Musawi, *Dawlat al-Rasul*, 70–102. See also Watt, *Muhammad at the Medina*, 192–204.

4. Ibn Hisham, *Al-Sira*, 6:501–4; Brockelmann, *History of the Islamic Peoples*, 46; Watt, *Islamic Political Thought*, 4–14, 66–67; Watt, *Muhammad at the Medina*, 221–25; and al-Ahmadi, *Makatib al-Rasul*, 241–63.

5. Amin, *Fajr al-Islam*, 228–29; Sadiq, *Al-Firaq al-Islamiyya*, 9–15; Watt, *Muhammad at the Medina*, 228–38; and 'Ishmawi, *Al-Khilafa al-Islamiyya*, 83–86; and Ibn Hisham, *Al-Sira*, 6:548–54.

6. 'Ishmawi, *Al-Khilafa al-Islamiyya*, 87–90; Watt, *Islamic Political Thought*, 12–15; M. 'Ali, *Al-Mufassal fi Tarikh al-'Arab*, 635; and al-Zabidi, *Taj al-'Arus*, 8:252.

7. al-Shabani, *Nizam al-Hukm*, 67–83. See verses al-Nisa' 105 and 58, al-Shura 38, and al-'Imran 159 (all Qur'an translations are from Pickthall, *Glorious Koran*). See also Rosenthal, *Muslim Concept of Freedom*.

8. al-Shabani, *Nizam al-Hukm*, 16–20, and al-Sayyid, *Al-Umma wa al-Jama'a*, 83.

9. Amin, *Fajr al-Islam*, 235–36.

10. al-Mawardi, *Al-Ahkam al-Sultaniyya*, 15; Ibn Khaldun, *Al-Muqaddima*, 2:519; and al-Tabari, *Tafsir*, 1:199, 3:277.

11. al-Baghdadi, *Al-Farq bayna al-Firaq*, 210; al-Tabari, *Tafsir*, 1:147, 3:450; Ibn Khaldun, *Al-Muqaddima*, 2:519–20; al-Ghazali, *Al-Mustasfa min al-Usul*, 1:71, and *Al-Iqtisad fi al-I'tiqad*, 135; al-Shahristani, *Al-Milal wa al-Nihal*, 1:154–62; and al-Khalidi, *Ma'alim al-Khilafa*, 31–84.

12. al-Mawardi, *Al-Ahkam al-Sultaniyya*, 4, 135–37.

13. al-Shahristani, *Al-Milal wa al-Nihal*, 2:114–38, and 'Abd al-Khaliq, *Al-Mu'arada*, 256–57.

14. al-Mawardi, *Al-Ahkam al-Sultaniyya*, 12, and 'Amara, *Al-Islam wa Falsafat al-Hukum*, 54–68.

15. al-Tabari, *Tarikh*, 3:277; al-Mawardi, *Al-Ahkam al-Sultaniyya*, 7, 15; al-Iji, *al-'Aqida al-'Adwiyya*, 304; al-Sanhuri, *Fiqh*, 149; and al-Khalidi, *Ma'alim al-Khilafa*, 20–30.

16. Ibn Khaldun, *Al-Muqaddima*, 3:519; and al-Mawardi, *Al-Ahkam al-Sultaniyya*, 57. See also verses al-Baqara 30 and al-An'am 165.

17. al-Sayyid, "Mas'alat al-Shura," 29–37, and al-Muhasibi, *al-'Aql wa Fahm al-Qur'an*, 201–3.

18. al-Mawardi, *Al-Ahkam al-Sultaniyya*, 2, 4, 5, 6, 29; al-Sanhuri, *Fiqh*, 138–48; and Ibn Hazm, *Al-Fasl fi al-Milal wa al-Nihal*, 4:167–71.

19. al-Mawardi, *Al-Ahkam al-Sultaniyya*, 4, and Ibn Hazm, *Al-Fasl fi al-Milal wa al-Nihal*, 4:164.

20. al-Mawardi, *Al-Ahkam al-Sultaniyya*, 7; al-Iji, *al-ʿAqida al-ʿAdawiyya*, 304; and al-Sanhuri, *Fiqh*, 149.

21. Hamadah, *Al-Wathaʾiq al-Siyasiyya*, 83–85, 99, 102–5.

22. al-Mawardi, *Al-Ahkam al-Sultaniyya*, 14–16; al-Iji, *al-ʿAqida al-ʿAdawiyya*, 305–6; Ibn Hazm, *Al-Fasl fi al-Milal wa al-Nihal*, 4:170; and al-Sanhuri, *Fiqh*, 239–52.

23. al-Masʿudi, *Muruj al-Dhahab*, 2:331–48; Watt, *Islamic Political Thought*, 42–44; H. A. Hasan, *Al-Fikr al-Shiʿi*, 27–29, 213–16; Ibn Qutayba, *Al-Imama wa al-Siyasa*, 1:10–38; and al-Sayyid, *Al-Umma wa al-Jamaʿa*, 50–59, 69–87.

24. al-Masʿudi, *Muruj al-Dhahab*, 2:349–56; Juʿayt, *Al-Fitna al-Kubra*, 60–95, 125–29; and Hinds, "The Siffin Judgment Agreement," 93–98.

25. Sharaf, *Nashʾat al-Fikr*, 72–73, and al-Masʿudi, *Muruj al-Dhahab*, 2:356–74.

26. Sharaf, *Nashʾat al-Fikr*, 73–74; *Encyclopedia of Islam*, 3:72; Watt, *Islamic Political Thought*, 37–38; and Hinds, "The Siffin Judgment Agreement," 98–100.

27. al-Masʿudi, *Muruj al-Dhahab*, 2:374–92; Juʿayt, *Al-Fitna al-Kubra*, 52, 198–203, 224–27; ʿAbd al-Khaliq, *Al-Muʿarada*, 254–55; and Amin, *Fajr al-Islam*, 256–81.

28. See the Qurʾanic verse al-Hujurat 9.

29. Juʿayt, *Al-Fitna al-Kubra*, 207–10, 212–13.

30. Ibid., 213–14, and ʿAbd al-Khaliq, *Al-Muʿarada*, 257–58.

31. Watt, *Islamic Political Thought*, 54–55, and Juʿayt, *Al-Fitna al-Kubra*, 224–25.

32. ʿAbd al-Khaliq, *Al-Muʿarada*, 257–61, and Juʿayt, *Al-Fitna al-Kubra*, 226–27.

33. On ʿAli and judgment, see al-Masʿudi, *Muruj al-Dhahab*, 2:392–403, and Juʿayt, *Al-Fitna al-Kubra*, 207–10, 212–15.

34. On ʿAli's caliphate, see Sadiq, *Al-Firaq al-Islamiyya*, 34–58, 147–97. On the views and sects of Shiʿa, see al-Shahristani, *Al-Milal wa al-Nihal*, 252–55; Amin, *Fajr al-Islam*, 126–277; and al-Sayyid, *Mafahim al-Jamaʿa fi al-Islam*, 59–73.

35. Shams al-Din, *Fi al-Ijtimaʿ al-Siyasi al-Islami*, 185–95, 212–15, 241, 253.

36. Ibid., 75–76.

37. Ibid., 190–98; Ibn Qutayba, *Al-Imama wa al-Siyasa*, 1:180; and ʿAli ibn Abi Talib, *Nahj al-Balagha*, 1:91–102, 106–7.

38. ʿAli ibn Abi Talib, *Nahj al-Balagha*, 1:73–86.

39. al-Suyuti, *Tarikh al-Khulafaʾ*, 194–95.

40. al-Masʿudi, *Muruj al-Dhahab*, 2:387–92.

41. Ibid., 2:392–95, 398–411.

42. Ibid., 2:298–99, and Ibn ʿAbd Rabbih, *al-ʿAqd al-Farid*, 3:343–45.

43. Ibn ʿAbd Rabbih, *al-ʿAqd al-Farid*, 3:341; Ibn Qutayba, *Al-Imama wa al-*

Siyasa, 1:194–95; al-Mas'udi, *Muruj al-Dhahab*, 3:4–29; and al-Suyuti, *Tarikh al-Khulafa'*, 212–28.

44. 'Atwan, *Al-Fuqaha' wa al-Khilafa*, 7–35, and H. I. Hasan, *Tarikh al-Islam*, 1:484–93.

45. Ibn 'Abd Rabbih, *al-'Aqd al-Farid*, 4:147.

46. 'Amara, *Al-Islam wa Falsafat al-Hukm*, 506–13.

47. al-Jabiri, *Al-'Aql al-Siyasi al-'Arabi*, 231–43.

48. Ibn Abi Haddid, *Sharh Nahj al-Balagha*, 2:497.

49. Ibn Qutayba, *Al-Imama wa al-Siyasa*, 1:184–90, and al-Jabiri, *Al-Fikr al-Siyasi*, 244–60.

50. 'Ishmawi, *Al-Khilafa al-Islamiyya*, 129–34.

51. Ibid., 141–42.

52. al-Tabari, *Tarikh*, 5:34.

53. al-Mawardi, *Al-Ahkam al-Sultaniyya*, 23–24; Ibn Kathir, *Al-Bidaya wa al-Nihaya*, 7:79, 8:79, 217–323; al-Tabari, *Tarikh*, 4:325; and al-Khalidi, *Ma'alim al-Khilafa*, 124–31.

54. al-Khalidi, *Ma'alim al-Khilafa*, 292–311; al-Mawardi, *Al-Ahkam al-Sultaniyya*, 18–20; al-Shahristani, *Al-Milal wa al-Nihal*, 1:116; and 'Amara, *Al-Islam wa Falsafat al-Thawra*, 472–504.

55. al-Khalidi, *Ma'alim al-Khilafa*, 326–47; al-Asha'ri, *Maqalat al-Islamiyyin*, vol. I, 140; Ibn Khaldun, *Muqaddima*, 166; and Ibn Taymiyya, *Minhaj al-Sunna al-Nabawiyya*, 2:171.

56. Watt, *Islamic Political Thought*, 4.

57. al-Maqdisi, *Al-Murshid al-Wajiz*, 79–88, and Ju'ayt, *Al-Fitna al-Kubra*, 26–33.

58. al-Maqdisi, *Al-Murshid al-Wajiz*, 89–148; Watt, *Islamic Political Thought*, 90–93; and Amin, *Fajr al-Islam*, 234–35.

59. al-Maqdisi, *Al-Murshid al-Wajiz*, 149–83. See also Ju'ayt, *Al-Fitna al-Kubra*, 34–60.

60. al-Maqdisi, *Al-Murshid al-Wajiz*, 148–51.

61. Ibid., 161–75.

62. 'Amara, *Al-Islam wa-Falsafat al-Hukm*, 545–80.

63. H. I. Hasan, *Tarikh al-Islam*, 3:305–18.

64. al-Jabiri, *Al-'Aql al-Siyasi al-'Arabi*, 329–51.

65. Ibn 'Abd Rabbih, *al-'Aqd al-Farid*, 3:144, 116.

66. Ibid., 356–62.

67. 'Ishmawi, *Al-Khilafa al-Islamiyya*, 200–209.

68. al-Sayyid, "Mas'alat al-Shura," 37–47.

69. al-Bishri, "'An Mu'asasat al-Dawla," 74–79, 89; al-Sayyid, *Mafahim*, 35–40; al-Sayyid, *Al-Umma*, 164–66; and Kamali, "Varieties of Ra'y."

70. 'Ishmawi, *Al-Khilafa al-Islamiyya*, 181–92.

71. Watt, *Islamic Political Thought*, 73–77.

72. Murwwa, *Al-Naza'at al-Madiyya fi al-Falsafa*; Tizini, *Mashru' Ru'ya*

Jadid, vols. 1 and 2; Hanafi, *Al-Turath wa al-Tajdid*; and al-Jabiri, *Nahnu wa al-Turath*.

73. 'Id, *Azmat al-Tanwir*, 35, 37.

74. 'Abd al-Malik, *Al-Fikr al-'Arabi*, 86.

75. Khoury, *Al-Fikr al-'Arabi al-Hadith*.

76. On this topic and trends within liberalism, see 'Abd al-Malik, *Al-Fikr al-'Arabi*, 91–99.

77. See, for instance, Hourani, *Al-Fikr al-'Arabi*.

78. S. Musa, *Al-Haraka al-'Arabiyya*, chapters 2 and 3. See also Hourani, *Al-Fikr al-'Arabi*.

79. Jad'an, *Usus al-Taqaddum 'inda Mufakiri al-Islam*.

80. Muhafaza, *Al-Itijahat al-Fikriyya*, 23–43.

81. On this topic, see Fakhry, *Al-Harakat al-Fikriyya*.

82. See al-Najjar, "Mafhum al-Taqaddum," and Murad, "Hawla Tajdid Mafhum 'al-Nahda," 9–10.

83. Zahr al-Din, "Nahdawiyyat al-Amir Shakib Arsalan," 170–72.

84. Ibid., 172–76.

85. 'Id, *Azmat al-Tanwir*, p. 15.

86. Arkoun, *Tarikhiyyat al-Fikr al-'Arabi al-Islami*, 136–38.

87. Ibid., 16–22.

88. Ghalyun, *Ightiyal al-'Aql*, 298.

89. 'Id, *Azmat al-Tanwir*, p. 24.

90. al-Tabataba'i, *Nizariyyat al-Siyasa wa al-Hukm fi al-Islam*, 45–54.

91. Constitution of the Islamic Republic in Iran, article 2, p. 15.

92. Ibid., articles 5, 6, 7, 18, 76, 107.

93. Bil Haj, *Fasl al-Kalam fi Muwajahat Zulm al-Hukkam*, 31–46.

94. Ibid., 186–94, 99–136.

95. Moussalli, *Radical Islamic Fundamentalism*, 19–30.

96. Qutb, *Al-Islam wa Mushkilat al-Hadara*, 77–78, 83–87, and *Nahwa Mujtama' Islami*, 71–90.

97. Mitchell, *Muslim Brothers*, 103, 187–89; Moussalli, *Radical Islamic Fundamentalism*, 32–37; Hussain, *Islamic Movements*, 7–11, 91; and B. al-Hassan, *Milestones*, 7–31.

98. Qutb, *Hadha al-Din*, 32, 123, and *Ma'rakat*, 49, 60.

99. Qutb, *Al-'Adala*, 73, 107–8, 206-7, *Ma'alim fi al-Tariq*, 50, 71–77, *Ma'rakat*, 67, 85, 75, and *Fiqh al-Da'wa*, 61.

100. Qutb, *Fiqh al-Da'wa*, 84, *Ma'rakat*, 60, and *Al-'Adala*, 102–5.

101. Qutb, *Ma'rakat*, 66–70, *Al-'Adala*, 37, 107–8, 111, 157–69, *Fi Zilal*, 1:3:329, *Nahwa Mujtama' Islami*, 46–69, *Ma'alim fi al-Tariq*, 58–94, 132, and *Tafsir Ayat al-Riba*, 84.

102. Qutb, *Nahwa Mujtama' Islami*, 46–52.

103. Qutb, *Al-Salam*, 102–18, and *Al-'Adala*, 66–68, 111.

104. *Minbar al-Sharq*, no. 1, March 1993. On similar issues, see "Bahth 'an

Mujtama' Madani Manshud," *Mustaqbal al-'Alam al-Islami* 1, no. 4 (1991): 225–37, and Esposito and Piscatori, "Democratization and Islam," 437–38.

105. On al-Banna and the Muslim Brotherhood, see al-Sa'id, *Hasan al-Banna,* 93–94, 99–124, 132–39, 169–79; see also Mitchell, *Muslim Brothers;* Adams, *Islam and Modernism in Egypt;* and al-Husaini, *Moslem Brethren.* See also the views of 'Umar al-Tilmisani in Ahmad, *Al-Rafidun,* 199–200; Moussalli, "Hasan al-Banna's Islamist Discourse," 161–74; and Yanun, *Al-Hayat al-Hizbiyya fir Misr,* 20–23.

106. al-Banna, *Majmu'at Rasa'il al-Shahid Hasan al-Banna* (hereafter cited as *Majmu'at Rasa'il al-Shahid*), 165, *Majmu'at Rasa'il al-Imam al-Shahid Hasan al-Banna* (hereafter cited as *Majmu'at Rasa'il al-Imam*), 304, 343–47, and *Din wa-Siyasa,* 57–59.

107. al-Banna, *Din wa-Siyasa,* 40–45, and *Majmu'at Rasa'il al-Shahid,* 161–65. See also his *Memoirs* and al-Sa'id, *Hasan al-Banna.*

108. al-Banna, *Al-Imam Yatahadath,* 99, *Majmu'at Rasa'il al-Imam,* 99, 332–37, and *Majmu'at Rasa'il al-Shahid,* 160–61, 317.

109. *Al-Da'wa* 7 (1979): 9; al-Banna, *Minbar al-Jum'a,* 78–79, 136, and *Majmu'at Rasa'il al-Shahid,* 96, 165–67, 317, 320–23, 325. See also Lawrence, *Defenders of God,* 187–224.

110. al-Banna, *Rasa'il al-Imam,* 53, and *Majmu'at Rasa'il al-Shahid,* 96–97, 161–68.

111. al-Banna, *Al-Imam al-Shahid Yatahadath,* 15–16, *Nazarat,* 194, *Minbar al-Jum'a,* 24–25, 63, 72, 347, *Rasa'il al-Imam,* 53–55, *Majmu'at Rasa'il al-Shahid,* 317, and *Majmu'at Rasa'il al-Imam,* 63, 72, 101, 104.

112. al-Banna, *Kalimat Khalida,* 45.

113. Ibid., 45–46.

114. al-Banna, *Rasa'il al-Imam,* 56–58, and *Majmu'at Rasa'il al-Imam,* 355–56.

115. al-Banna, *Majmu'at Rasa'il al-Imam,* 318–19.

116. al-Banna, *Majmu'at Rasa'il al-Shahid,* 160–61, and *Al-Imam Yatahadath,* 99.

117. al-Banna, *Majmu'at Rasa'il al-Shahid,* 317–18, and *Majmu'at Rasa'il al-Imam,* 332–37, 63.

118. al-Banna, *Majmu'at Rasa'il al-Shahid,* 318–19.

119. Ibid., 320–23.

120. al-Banna, *Minbar al-Jum'a,* 78–79. See also *Al-Da'wa* 7 (1979): 9.

121. al-Banna, *Minbar al-Jum'a,* 79, 136; *Al-Da'wa* 7 (1979): 9.

122. al-Shawi, *Fiqh al-Hukuma al-Islamiyya,* 155–69.

123. *Qira'at Siyasiyya* 3, no. 2 (1993): 197–98; *Qadaya Dawliyya,* March 1993.

124. al-Nabahani, *Nizam al-Hukm,* 56–59.

125. Barghouty, "Al-Islam bayna al-Sulta," 237–38; "Tanzimat al-Harakat al-Islamiyya: Harakat al-Ikhwan al-Muslim fi al-Urdun," *Al-Hayat,* 14 August

1993, p. 3; and "Itijahat al-Haraka al-Islamiyya fi al-Urdun," *Al-Safir*, 20 August 1993, p. 13. See also Butterworth, "Political Islam."

126. Shafiq, "Awlawiyyat," 64–65.

127. al-Turabi, "Islam, Democracy, the State and the West," prepared by Louis Cantori and Arthur Lowrie, *Middle East Policy* 1, no. 3 (1992): 52–54.

128. al-Turabi, *Tajdid Usul al-Fiqh*, 10–16, and *Qadaya*, 17–18.

129. al-Turabi, *Qadaya*, 46–47.

130. al-Turabi, *Qadaya*, 47–48.

131. al-Turabi, *Qadaya*, 48–49, and *Tajdid Usul al-Fiqh*, 174.

132. al-Turabi, *Qadaya*, 49–51.

133. al-Turabi, *Qadaya*, 51–53.

134. al-Turabi, *Qadaya*, 53–54.

135. al-Turabi, "Utruhat," 89–90.

136. al-Turabi, "Utruhat," 90–91.

137. al-Turabi, *Qadaya*, 56–57.

138. al-Turabi, "Awlawiyyat," 21–26, 69–72, 81–82, 136–38, 167–96, and *Tajdid al-Fikr al-Islami*, 20, 73, 132–33.

139. al-Turabi, *Tajdid al-Fikr al-Islami*, 68–80, *Qadaya*, 25–27, 31–33, and "Awlawiyyat," 16. On this issue, see Sami', *Azmat*, 47–59.

140. al-Turabi, *Tajdid al-Fikr al-Islami*, 88–91, 100, 153–55, 162–78, and *Qadaya*, 21–23.

141. al-Turabi, *Qadaya*, 23–25.

142. al-Turabi, *Qadaya*, 25–26, and *Tajdid al-Fikr al-Islami*, 79–80.

143. al-Turabi, *Qadaya*, 26–27.

144. al-Turabi, *Qadaya*, 26–29; and *Tajdid al-Fikr al-Islami*, 68–70.

145. al-Turabi, *Tajdid al-Fikr al-Islami*, 70–72, "Awlawiyyat," 16, and *Qadaya*, 31–33.

146. al-Turabi, *Qadaya*, 34–35, 37–38.

147. al-Turabi, *Qadaya*, 41–3, and *Tajdid al-Fikr al-Islami*, 59–60, 65, 146, 174–75, 192.

148. al-Turabi, *Qadaya*, 44–46.

Chapter 2. The Classical and Medieval Interpretations of *Ikhtilaf* and Its Modern Islamist Expressions As Pluralism

1. See the Qur'anic verses al-Baqara 256, Yunus 99, al-An'am 107, and Hud 118.

2. See verses al-Nisa' 3:20 and al-Shura 48.

3. See verses al-Tawba 6, al-Hajj 40, and al-'Ankabut 46.

4. See verses al-Baqara 213, Yunus 19, al-Ma'ida 48, and al-Sajda 25. See also Harb, "Fi al-Ikhtilaf," 18–26.

5. al-Zarkashi, *Al-Burhan 'ala 'Ulum al-Qur'an*, 1:5–9.

6. al-Shahristani, *Al-Milal wa al-Nihal*, 201.

7. al-Ghazali, *Fada'ih al-Batiniyya*, 96–98.

8. Ibid., 2–4.

9. Ibn Taymiyya, *Fatawa*, 21:304–10. See also al-Jassas, *Al-Ijma'*, 30–44; Rahman, *Islam*, 85–99.

10. Subhi, *Fi 'Ilm al-Kalam*, 7–18.

11. Ibid., 19–34.

12. Ibid., 35–42.

13. Ibn Rushd, *Fasl al-Maqal*, 34–62.

14. al-Farabi, *Al-Madina al-Fadila*, chapter 36.

15. See, for instance, Ibn 'Arabi, *Nusus al-Hikam*, 79–107, 111.

16. See, for instance, the views of Jalal al-Din al-Rumi in Ghalib, *Jalal al-Din al-Rumi*, 654.

17. On this topic, see Harb, "Fi al-Ikhtilaf," 8–17.

18. Ibn 'Arabi, *Ahkam al-Qur'an*, 4:156–57.

19. 'Ishmawi, *Al-Khilafa al-Islamiyya*, 105–8.

20. Abu Yusuf, *Kitab al-Kharaj*, 14–15, 81–82. See al-Khalidi, *Ma'alim al-Khilafa*, 348–436.

21. al-Jassas, *Al-Ijma'*, 9–10.

22. Ibid., 11–12; Ibn Khaldun, *Muqaddima*, 1:453.

23. Ibid., 15–16.

24. On the development of legislation in Islam, see al-Bishri, "'An Mu'assasat al-Dawla," 79–82; al-Sayyid, *Mafahim*, 41–42; *Al-Ijtihad* 5, no. 19 (1993): 23–55. For an earlier version, see al-Mawardi, *Al-Ahkam al-Sultaniyya*, 3.

25. M. Isma'il, *Sociolojia*, 154–56; Kawtharani, *Al-Sulta wa al-Mujtama'*, 35–38, 43; and al-Bishri, "'An Mu'assasat al-Dawla," 83–90.

26. al-Bishri, "'An Mu'assasat al-Dawla," 86–90, and al-Sayyid, *Mafahim*, 41–42.

27. For more details, see Kawtharani, *Al-Sulta wa al-Mujtama'*, 46; M. Isma'il, *Sociolojia*, 140–43; and al-Sayyid, *Mafahim*, 77–91, 94–96.

28. Kawtharani, *Al-Sulta wa al-Mujtama'*, 47–49, and al-Sayyid, *Mafahim*, 100–101. See also, on the limitations on political rule as developed historically, Kamali, "Siyasah Shar'iyah or the Policies of Islamic Government."

29. al-Sayyid, *Mafahim*, 110–11.

30. Kawtharani, *Al-Sulta wa al-Mujtama'*, 35–38, 67–72; and al-Sayyid, *Mafahim*, 119–26.

31. On political differences, see al-Shahristani, *Al-Milal wa al-Nihal*, 17–24.

32. *Sunan al-Tirmizi*, 4:322, 469–70.

33. See verses al-Mujadala 19–20, al-Ahzab 20 and 22, Ghafir 5 and 30, Sad 13, al-Ra'd 36, Hud 17, and al-Mu'minun 51–53.

34. For instance, al-Tabari, *Jami' al-Bayan*.

35. al-Shahristani, *Al-Milal wa al-Nihal*, 3, 16.

36. Subhi, *Fi 'Ilm al-Kalam*, 166–72.

37. Verses al-'Imran 104 and 110.

38. al-Alusi, *Al-Ra'y al-'Am*, 22–26.

39. Ibid., 54–73.

40. Ibid., 131–64.

41. Ibid., 204–23.

42. Ibid., 225–34. See also al-Sammak, "Al-Ra'y al-'Am."

43. Verses al-'Alaq 9–12. See al-Bidawi, *Anwar al-Tanzil*, 746. On the issue of public opinion in Islam, see al-Najjar, *Dawr Hurriyyat*, 27–66.

44. al-Baghdadi, *Usul al-Din*, 254.

45. Verses al-Nisa' 97 and al-'Imran 104–5.

46. Verses al-Hujurat 6, al-Nisa' 83, Taha 43–44, and al-Nur 23.

47. al-Ghazali, *Tahafut al-Falasifa*, 82–83.

48. al-Shatibi, *Al-Muwafaqat*, 2:4–8. See also al-Durayni, *Al-Ijtihad wa al-Tajdid*, 9–45.

49. al-Durayni, *Al-Ijtihad wa al-Tajdid*, 12–14.

50. Ibid., 15–18.

51. See the articles by al-Bishri and Shafiq in al-Durayni, *Al-Ijtihad wa al-Tajdid*, 47–67.

52. al-Ghazali, *Ihya' 'Ulum al-Din*, 2:391–424.

53. al-Rayyis, *Al-Nazariyyat al-Siyasiyya al-Islamiyya*, 386.

54. Verse al-Nisa' 59.

55. See *Mu'jam Alfath al-Qur'an*, 97, 419, 325, 603.

56. Verses al-Nisa' 59–60.

57. al-Khudari, *Usul al-Fiqh*, 20.

58. Ibn Taymiyya, *Al-Sarim al-Maslul 'ala Shata'im al-Rasul*, 191–92. On incidents where the Prophet was opposed by his Companions, see Ibn Kathir, *Al-Bidaya wa al-Nihaya*, 3:4:105.

59. al-Asfahani, *Al-Mufradat fi Gharib al-Qur'an*, and al-Shawkani, *Irshad al-Fuhul*, 74.

60. Verse al-Hajj 41. See also Ibn Taymiyya, *Al-Hisba fi al-Islam*, 6.

61. Ibn Hazm, *Al-Fasl fi al-Milal wa al-Nihal*, 4:170–76.

62. Ibid., 171–75. See also 'Amara, *Al-Islam wa Falsafat al-Thawra*, 233–34, and 'Abd al-Khaliq, *Al-Mu'arada*, 54–139.

63. Abu Zahra, *Al-Madhahib al-Islamiyya*, 30.

64. See, for instance, Subhi, *Nazariyyat al-Imama*, 63–72.

65. al-Mawardi, *Al-Ahkam al-Sultaniyya*, 242–24, and Ibn Taymiyya, *Al-Hisba fi al-Islam*, 7–10.

66. al-Baqillani, *Al-Tamhid*, 184; and Ibn Taymiyya, *Al-Hisba fi al-Islam*, 54.

67. Hanafi, *Min al-'Aqida ila al-Thawra*, 5:315–21.

68. Ziyada, *Katib al-Sultan*, 56–60.

69. Ibid., 62–70.

70. Mitri, "Minorities in the Middle East," 60–64.

71. 'Ishmawi, *Al-Khilafa al-Islamiyya*, 219–23.

72. Bani al-Marja, *Sahwat al-Rajul al-Marid*, 39–43.

73. al-Diqa, *Ahl al-'Irfan wa Shawkat al-Sultan*, 35–75.

74. Kayali, "Elections and the Electoral Process in the Ottoman Empire, 1876–1919."

75. Ibid., 275.

76. Constitution of the Islamic Republic in Iran, articles 8, 9, 18, 19.

77. al-Zumar, "Minhaj Jama'at al-Jihad al-Islami," 113–21, and Mahfuz, *Alladhina Zulimu*, 226, 254, 267–68, 271, 273.

78. al-Zumar, "Minhaj Jama'at al-Jihad al-Islami," 122–23.

79. Faraj, "Al-Farida al-Gha'iba," 127–31.

80. Ibid., 132–41.

81. Sirriyya, "Risalat al-Iman," 31–32.

82. Ibid., 42–48, and Mahfuz, *Alladhina Zulimu*, 83, 120–23, 222, 233, 242.

83. Sirriyya, "Risalat al-Iman," 44–45.

84. Qutb, *Fi Zilal*, 2:689; 1:1:235, 1:2:234, 1:4:587; *Fi al-Tarikh*, 23–36, 76; and *Al-'Adala*, 35, 59–65, 73–80, 86, 113, 119.

85. Qutb, *Al-Islam wa Mushkilat al-Hadara*, 7–9, 96–107; *Nahwa Mujtama' Islami*, 150–52; *Hadha al-Din*, 84–87; *Ma'rakat*, 58; and *Ma'alim fi al-Tariq*, 59, 89.

86. Qutb, *Fiqh al-Da'wa*, 15–32, 88–89; *Al-'Adala*, 197; *Hadha al-Din*, 11, 29–30, 65–57; *Ma'alim fi al-Tariq*, 11–15, 22; *Al-Salam*, 118–43; *Al-Islam wa Mushkilat al-Hadara*, 189–93; and *Nahwa Mujtama' Islami*, 137–43.

87. Qutb, *Nahwa Mujtama' Islami*, 62, 92–99, 102–20, 123, 134; *Al-Salam*, 161–65; *Hadha al-Din*, 11, 91; *Ma'alim fi al-Tariq*, 64–67, 162–63; and *Al-'Adala*, 107, 198.

88. al-Sa'id, *Qadaya Fikriyya*, 15; Moussalli, *Radical Islamic Fundamentalism*, 34–36; Mahfuz, *Alladhina Zulimu*, 7–141; and Sirriyya, "Risalat al-Iman," 53–57.

89. 'Abd al-Rahman, "Mawqif al-Haraka al-Islamiyya," 150, 160–64; 'Ata, "Qadiyyat al-Ta'addudiyya," 118–20. See also al-Sa'id, *Qadaya Fikriyya*, 30–31; 'Abd al-Rahman, "Safahat min Mithaq," 165, 169, 173–74; and Ahmad, *Al-Tha'irun*, 185–86.

90. Ibid., 187–89, 193–97.

91. Ibid., 273–75, 290–91, 199–229. See also Mahfuz, *Alladhina Zulimu*, 213–83.

92. al-Turabi, *Qadaya*, 51–57, and *Tajdid al-Fikr al-Islami*, 45, 66–68, 75, 93–97, 162–63.

93. al-Turabi, *Tajdid al-Fikr al-Islami*, 200–203, 106–19, and *Al-Iman wa Atharuhu fi Hayat*, 112–21, 181–301, 325–29.

94. al-Turabi, *Tajdid Usul al-Fiqh*, 27–29.

95. al-Turabi, *Al-Itijah al-Islami*, 6–13, 42–49.

96. al-Turabi, *Tajdid al-Fikr al-Islami*, 108–9, 133–35, 160–65.

97. al-Turabi, *Tajdid Usul al-Fiqh*, 18–25, 32–35.

98. Ibid., 36–37, 42–45, and *Tajdid al-Fikr al-Islami,* 26–31, 36–49, 54–63, 76–77, 148–49, 172–73.

99. al-Turabi, *Tajdid al-Fikr al-Islami,* 68–71, and *Qadaya,* 72–77, 80–81.

100. al-Turabi, *Qadaya,* 10–19, 22–28.

101. Ibid., 20–21, 29–30.

102. Ibid., 34–37, 44–47.

103. al-Turabi, *Al-Salat ʿImad al-Din,* 124–33, 138–47, 156–58.

104. al-Turabi, *Tajdid al-Fikr al-Islami,* 29.

105. Ibid., 45, 66–68, 75, 93, 94, 97, 162–63.

106. al-Turabi, "Utruhat," 75–76.

107. Ibid., 77–80.

108. Ibid., 91–98.

109. al-Ghannushi, "Mustaqbal al-Tayyar al-Islami," 3–32, and *Bayrut al-Masaʾ,* 15 May 1993, p. 15; see also ʿAta, "Qadiyyat al-Taʿaddudiyya," 116–17.

110. al-Ghannushi and al-Turabi, *Al-Haraka al-Islamiyya wa al-Tahdith,* 34–35; see also al-Hirmasi, "Al-Islam al-Ihtijaji fi Tunis," 273–86.

111. al-Ghannushi, "Al-Islam wa al-Gharb," 36–37, and "Hiwar," 14–15, 35–37. See also Esposito and Piscatori, "Democratization and Islam," 426–38; G. Kramer, "Liberalization and Democracy," 22–25; and al-Zugul, "Al-Istratijiyya," 346–48.

112. al-Banna, *Al-Salam fi al-Islam,* 27–37. See also ʿAta, "Qadiyyat al-Taʿaddudiyya," 115–16. For similar views in Jordan, see al-Nabahani, *Al-Takatul al-Hizbi,* 23–57, and *Nizam al-Hukm,* 56–59.

113. al-Banna, *Al-Salam fi al-Islam,* 49–56.

114. al-Banna, *Majmuʿat Rasaʾil al-Shahid,* 308–10.

115. al-Nabahani, *Al-Takatul al-Hizbi,* 23–25.

116. Ibid., 24–57.

117. al-ʿAwwa, "Al-Taʿaddudiyya," 129–32.

118. Ibid., 133–34. For a summary of the historical acceptance of pluralism by scholars such as Ibn Taymiyya and authoritative exegesis of the Qurʾan such as *Tafsir al-Jilalayin,* see 136–52. For an independent source on the views of the scholars who accepted the people's choice as the legitimate means to govern, see al-Jassas, *Al-Ijmaʿ,* 29–41; on those who rejected it, such as the generality of Shiʿites, see 75–86. On the relationship between actual politics and the development of religion and *ijtihad,* see M. Ismaʿil, *Sociolojia,* 138–39.

119. al-ʿAwwa, *Fi al-Nizam al-Siyasi,* 77, and "Al-Taʿaddudiyya," 136–37, 152–53.

120. al-ʿAwwa, *Al-Hayat,* 3 August 1993, p. 19. See also his "Al-Taʿaddudiyya," 134–36.

121. al-ʿAwwa, *Al-Hayat,* 3 August 1993, p. 19. See also Khalafallah, *Al-Haraka al-Islamiyya,* 37, and Sharaf al-Din, "Al-Din wa al-Ahzab," 180.

Chapter 3. The Classical and Medieval Roots of *al-Huquq al-Shar'iyya* and Its Modern Islamist Conceptions As Human Rights

1. al-Shatibi, *Al-Muwafaqat*, 2:222 and passim, and al-Durayni, *Dirasat*, 81–95. See also these Qur'anic verses that support the idea of the sanctity of human life: Muhammad 4, al-Nisa' 104, al-Tawba 9, and al-Mulk 1–2.

2. al-Ghazali, *Ihya' 'Ulum al-Din*, 2:218–40, 279.

3. al-Shatibi, *Al-Muwafaqat*, 4:196 and passim.

4. Ibid., 4:258, 3:257. See also Durayni, *Dirasat*, 111–15.

5. al-Shatibi, *Al-Muwafaqat*, 2:231, 331; Ibn Taymiyya, *Fatawa*, 2:14–49.

6. For a general and traditional view of women's rights and role, see Khayrat, *Al-Mar'a fi al-Islam*.

7. Mufti and al-Waqil, *Al-Nazariyya al-Siyasiyya*, 35–42.

8. On justice, see verses al-Nisa' 58, al-Shura 15, al-Ma'ida 8 and 42, and al-Nahl 90.

9. See verses al-Hashr 7, al-Tawba 60, and Saba' 28.

10. Ibn Taymiyya, *Al-Siyasa al-Shar'iyya*, 6–11.

11. al-Mawardi, *Al-Ahkam al-Sultaniyya*, 314.

12. Ibn Taymiyya, *Fatawa*, 15:380. See verses al-Nur 27–28; also Mufti and al-Waqil, *Al-Nazariyya al-Siyasiyya*, 56–63.

13. See verses al-Nisa' 92, al-Ahzab 58, and al-Isra' 70.

14. For instance, see Ibn Taymiyya, *Fatawa*, 15:308. See also Mufti and al-Waqil, *Al-Nazariyya al-Siyasiyya*, 63–70.

15. Ibn Khaldun, *Al-Muqaddima*, 1:390.

16. Verses al-Baqara 256 and Yunus 99.

17. Verses al-Nahl 90, al-Nisa' 58, al-Shura 15, al-An'am 152, and al-Ma'ida 8.

18. *Al-Qamus al-Muhit*, 4:115, and *Al-Mabsut*, 10:111.

19. al-Baladhi, *Futuh al-Buldan*, 158–60.

20. Laurent, *L'Arménie entre Byzance et l'Islam*, 56; see also Yamut, *Ahl al-Dhimma*, 54–56, and al-Baladhi, *Futuh al-Buldan*, 21.

21. al-Baladhi, *Futuh al-Buldan*, 162.

22. Ibn Khaldun, *Al-Muqaddima*, 1:282, and al-Mawardi, *Al-Ahkam al-Sultaniyya*, 138.

23. Yamut, *Ahl al-Dhimma*, 126–29.

24. Watt, *Islamic Political Thought*, 49–50.

25. Ibid., 50–51.

26. al-Qaddumi, "Al-Siyasa," 380–83.

27. al-Tabari, *Tafsir*, 4:86, and Ibn Hisham, *Al-Sira*, 5:526–27, 555–59.

28. Watt, *Muhammad at Mecca*, 152–53.

29. Ibn Hisham, *Al-Sira*, 5:564–69; al-Tabari, *Tafsir*, 1:47–48; and Ahdab, *Arbitration*, 142, 14–18.

30. Coulson, *History of Islamic Law*, 27.

31. For more details, see Watt, *Muhammad at the Medina*, 193–220.

32. Watt, *Muhammad at the Medina,* 143–46.

33. Baydun, *Al-Ansar wa al-Rasul,* 91–94.

34. See Amin, *Fajr al-Islam,* 230–33, and Ibn Hisham, *Al-Sira,* 5:548–59.

35. For more information, see Ibn Kathir, *Tafsir al-Qur'an,* 1:250–51. See also verses al-Nur 48 and 251 and Sad 22 and 38.

36. Verse al-Baqara 213.

37. Verses al-Ma'ida 42–44. On this issue, see Ibn Kathir, *Tafsir al-Qur'an,* 2:58–59.

38. Ibid., 2:61–67.

39. Verses al-Ma'ida 45–50.

40. Verse al-Nisa' 105. For more information, see Ibn Kathir, *Tafsir al-Qur'an,* 1:355–56, 518–19.

41. Verse al-'Imran 23.

42. al-Tabari, *Tarikh,* 3:609.

43. On these and other rights, see al-Tabari, *Tarikh,* 4:109; Abu Yusuf, *Kitab al-Kharaj,* 70. See also S. Abu Khalil, *Tasamuh al-Islam,* 5–25.

44. al-Mawardi, *Al-Ahkam al-Sultaniyya,* 428.

45. Ibn Qutayba, *'Uyun al-Akhbar,* 99.

46. al-Tabari, *Tarikh,* 3:1389–90, 1438.

47. al-Ghazali, *Mishkat,* 6:310, 511.

48. al-Tabari, *Tafsir,* 4:63–64, and al-Mawardi, *Al-Ahkam al-Sultaniyya,* 126.

49. al-Jahshiari, *Kitab al-Wuzara',* 15–20.

50. Rida, *Tafsir al-Manar,* 4:84.

51. al-Qaddumi, "Al-Siyasa," 379–88.

52. See al-Qaddumi, "Al-Siyasa," 396–400.

53. 'Ishmawi, *Al-Khilafa al-Islamiyya,* 150.

54. al-Qaddumi, "Al-Siyasa," 389–90.

55. Amin, *Thuhr al-Islam,* 1:81–91.

56. Ibid., 1:210–11.

57. al-Baladhi, *Futuh al-Buldan,* 79.

58. Abu Yusuf, *Kitab al-Kharaj,* 144, and al-Baladhi, *Futuh al-Buldan,* 177.

59. al-Jahshiari, *Kitab al-Wuzara',* 38–43.

60. Abu 'Ubayd, *Al-Amwal,* 153.

61. Ibn Sa'd, *Tabaqat,* 5:276.

62. *Al-Ijtihad* 7, no. 28 (1995): 275–76.

63. Ibid., 285–86.

64. Van Koningsveld, "Muslim Slaves and Captives," 17.

65. Lewis, *The Jews of Islam,* 8–9. For more details, see Amin, *Duha al-Islam,* 323–72.

66. Lewis, *The Jews of Islam,* 28.

67. Qasim, *Al-Yahud fi Misr.*

68. Mitri, "Minorities in the Middle East," 60–64.

69. al-Kharbutli, *Adwa' Jadida 'ala Tarikh*, and Bani al-Marja, *Sahwat al-Rajul al-Marid*, 45–47.

70. Ibid., 165–70.

71. R. Haddad, *Syrian Minorities*, 49.

72. Bani al-Marja, *Sahwat al-Rajul al-Marid*, 174–80.

73. R. Haddad, *Syrian Minorities*, 32.

74. Qutb, *Ma'alim fi al-Tariq*, 65.

75. Qutb, *Al-Islam wa Mushkilat al-Hadara*, 54.

76. Ibid., 58–59.

77. Ibid., 60–64, 54–57, 80–88, and Qutb, *Khasa'is al-Tasawwur*, 68–69.

78. Qutb, *Mushkilat al-Hadara*, 178–81. See also Qutb, *Khasa'is al-Tasawwur*, 34–39.

79. Qutb, *Khasa'is al-Tasawwur*, 70–71.

80. Ibid., 28–33.

81. Ibid., 214–20.

82. Qutb, *Hadha al-Din*, 17–23.

83. Ibid., 84–92.

84. Qutb, *Fi al-Tarikh*, 7–10.

85. Ibid., 51–61.

86. Ibid., 62–68.

87. Qutb, *Nahwa Mujtama' Islami*, 94–96.

88. Qutb, *Al-Salam*, 167–75.

89. Ibid., 173–77.

90. al-Mawdudi, *Huquq Ahl al-Dhimma fi al-Islam*, 3–6.

91. Ibid., 6–37.

92. Constitution of the Islamic Republic in Iran, articles 12, 20.

93. Ibid., articles 13–14, 20–21.

94. Ibid., articles 19–22, 29–34. Compare with Mallat, *Renewal of Islamic Thought,* part 1.

95. Shukri, "Al-Nas al-Kamil," 85–86.

96. Ibid., 86–87, 97–100.

97. al-Rahhal, "Amrica wa Misr wa al-Haraka al-Islamiyya," 179–84.

98. Sirriyya, "Risalat al-Iman," 63–74.

99. al-Rahhal, "Amrica wa Misr wa al-Haraka al-Islamiyya," 184–86.

100. al-Banna, *Al-Salam fi al-Islam*, 21–29.

101. al-Banna, *Majmu'at Rasa'il al-Imam*, 168–69, 342–43.

102. al-Tilmisani, "An Interview," 199–202.

103. al-Qaradawi, *Ghayr al-Muslimin*, 5–7.

104. Ibid., 8–25.

105. Ibid., 31–41.

106. Ibid., 43–50.

107. Ibid., 69–78. See also al-Qaradawi, *Bayinat al-Hal al-Islami*, 233–40.

108. al-Qaradawi, *Khasa'is al-'Amal fi al-Islam*.

109. Hawwa, *Al-Madkhal*, 13–18. On the Muslim Brotherhood's participation in elections in Syria, see al-Janhani, "Al-Sahwa al-Islamiyya fi Bilad al-Sham," 105–20.

110. Hawwa, *Al-Madkhal*, 282.

111. Mawlawi, "Al-Mar'a wa Tahadiyyat al-Mujtama' al-Mu'asir."

112. Ibid., 58–61.

113. 'Izzat, *Al-Mar'a wa al-'Amal al-Siyasi*, 39–41, 247–49. On women's issues see also Mernissi, *Beyond the Veil* and *Islam and Democracy*.

114. "Statement of the Muslim Brotherhood."

115. al-Hamidi, "Awlawiyyat Muhimma," 14–21.

116. al-Ghannushi, *Al-Hurriyyat al-'Amma*, 25–28. See his book *Huquq al-Muwatana*.

117. al-Ghannushi, "Al-Islam wa al-Gharb," 37.

Selected Bibliography

Abaza, Mona. "The Discourse of Islamic Fundamentalism in the Middle East and Southeast Asia: A Critical Perspective." *Institute of Southeast Asian Studies* (Singapore) 6 (1991): 203–39.

'Abbas, Ahmad. *Al-Ikhwan al-Muslimin fi Rif Misr.* Cairo: Dar al-Tawzi' wa al-Nashr, 1987.

'Abbud, Salih ibn 'Abd Allah. *'Aqidat al-Shaykh Muhammad Ibn 'Abd al-Wahhab: Al-Salafiyya wa-Atharuha fi al-'Alam al-Islami.* Medina, Saudi Arabia: Al-Jami'a al-Islamiyya bi al-Madina al-Munawwara, al-Majlis al-'Ilmi, 1987–88.

'Abd al-Halim, Mahmud. *Al-Ikhwan al-Muslimin, Ahdath Sana'at al-Tarikh: Ra'y min al-Dakhil.* Alexandria: Dar al-Da'wa, 1979.

'Abd al-Khaliq, Nivin. *Al-Mu'arada fi al-Fikr al-Siyasi al-Islami.* Cairo: Maktabat al-Malik Faysal, 1985.

'Abd Allah, Isma'il Sabri, et al., eds. *Al-Harakat al-Islamiyya al-Mu'asira fi al-'Alam al-'Arabi.* Beirut: Markaz Dirasat al-Wahda al-'Arabiyya, 1987.

'Abd al-Malik. *Al-Fikr al-'Arabi.* Beirut: Dar al-Adab, 1978.

'Abd al-Rahman, 'Umar. "Mawqif al-Haraka al-Islamiyya min al-'Hizbi fi Misr." In *Al-Nabiy al-Musallah: al-Rafidun,* edited by Rif'at Sayyid Ahmad, 150–64.

———. "Safahat min Mithaq al-'Amal al-Islami." In *Al-Nabiy al-Musallah: al-Rafidun,* edited by Rif'at Sayyid Ahmad, 165–78.

'Abd al-Raziq, Ahmad Muhammad Jad. *Falsafat al-Mashru' al-Hadari: Bayna al-Ihya' al-Islami wa al-Tahdith al-Gharbi.* 2 vols. Herndon, Va.: International Institute of Islamic Thought, 1995.

'Abd al-Sami', 'Umr. *Al-Islamiyyun: Hiwarat Hawla al-Mustaqbal.* Cairo: Maktabat al-Turath al-Islami, 1992.

'Abdu, Muhammad. *Risalat al-Tawhid.* Beirut: Al-Mu'assasa al-'Arabiyya li al-Dirasat wa al-Nashr, c. 1981.

Abdullah, Ahsan. *Pan-Islamism.* Leicester: Islamic Foundation, 1992.

Abedin, Syed Z. "Islamic Fundamentalism, Islamic Ummah and the World Conference on Muslim Minorities." *Journal of the Institute of Muslim Minority Affairs* 12 (1991): 1–21.

Abu Ghunaymah, Zayid. *Al-Haraka al-Islamiyya wa Qadiyyat Filistin.* Amman: Dar al-Furqan, 1985.

Abu Khalil, As'ad. "The Incoherence of Islamic Fundamentalism: Arab Islamic

Thought at the End of the Twentieth Century." *Middle East Journal* 48, no. 4 (1994): 677–94.

———. "A Viable Partnership: Islam, Democracy, and the Arab World." *Harvard International Review* 15, no. 2 (1992–93): 22–23, 65.

Abu Khalil, Shawqi. *Tasamuh al-Islam wa Ta'asub Khusumih*. Beirut: Manshurat Ma'asasat May, 1990.

Abul-Fadl, Mona. *Introducing Islam from Within*. Leicester: Islamic Foundation, 1991.

Abu-Lughod, I. "Retreat from the Secular Path? Islamic Dilemmas of Arab Politics." *Review of Politics* 28, no. 4 (1966): 447–76.

Abu Rabi', Ibrahim. *Intellectual Origins of Islamic Resurgence in the Modern Arab World*. Albany: State University of New York Press, 1996.

———. "Islamic Resurgence and the 'Problematic of Tradition' in the Modern Arab World: The Contemporary Academic Debate." *Islamic Studies* (Islamabad) 34, no. 1 (1995): 43–66.

———. "A Note on Some Recent Western Writing on Islamic Resurgence." *Al-Tawhid* 11, nos. 3–4 (1994): 233–46.

———, ed. *Islamic Resurgence: Challenges, Directions and Future Perspectives. A Round Table with Ahmad Kurshad*. Tampa, Fla.: World and Islam Studies Enterprise, 1994.

AbuSulayman, AbdulHamid. *Towards an Islamic Theory of International Relations: New Directions for Methodology and Thought*. 2d ed. Herndon, Va.: International Institute of Islamic Thought, 1993.

Abu 'Ubayd. *Al-Amwal*. Cairo: Maktabat al-Azhariyya, c. 1968.

Abu Yusuf. *Kitab al-Kharaj*. Cairo: Bulaq, n.d.

Abu Zahra, Mahmud. *Al-Madhahib al-Islamiyya*. Cairo: Dar al-Fikr, n.d.

Adams, Charles. *Islam and Modernism in Egypt*. New York: Russell and Russell, 1986.

Addi, Lahouari. "Islamist Utopia and Democracy." *Annals* (American Academy of Political and Social Science) 542, no. 2 (1992): 120–30.

Adelowo, Dada. "The Concept of Tauhid in Islam: A Theological Review." *Islamic Quarterly* 35, no. 1 (1991): 23–36.

al-Afghani, Jamal al-Din. "Political Writings." Pt. 2 of *Al-A'mal al-Kamila*. Edited and introduced by Muhammad 'Amara. Beirut: Al-Mu'assasa al-'Arabiyya li al-Dirasat wa al-Nashr, 1980.

———. *Al-'Urwa al-Wuthqa*. Cairo: Dar al-'Arab, 1957.

Afshary, Reza. "An Essay on Islamic Cultural Relativism in the Discourse of Human Rights." *Human Rights Quarterly* 16 (1994): 235–76.

Ahady, Anwar-ul-Haq. "The Decline of Islamic Fundamentalism." *Journal of Asian and African Studies* 27, nos. 3–4 (1992): 229–43.

Ahdab, A. H., ed. *Arbitration with the Arab Countries*. Boston: Kluwer Law and Taxation Publishers, 1990.

Ahmad, Rif'at Sayyid. *Al-Bawwaba al-Sawda*: *Al-Tarikh al-Sirri li Mu'taqal.* Cairo: Al-Zahra' li al-I'lam al-'Arabi, 1986.

———. *Al-Din wa al-Dawla wa al-Thawra.* Cairo: Dar al-Hilal, 1985.

———. *Al-Nabiy al-Musallah: Al-Rafidun.* London: Riad el-Rayyes Books, 1991.

———. *Al-Nabiy al-Musallah: Al-Tha'irun.* London: Riad el-Rayyes Books, 1991.

———. *Tanzimat al-Ghadab al-Islami fi al-Sab'inat.* Cairo: Maktabat Madbuli, 1989.

Ahmad Khalafallah, Muhammad. *Al-Qur'an wa al-Dawla.* Cairo: Maktabat al-Anglo al-Misriyya, 1973.

al-Ahmadi, 'Ali. *Makatib al-Rasul.* Beirut: Dar al-Muhajir, n.d.

Ahmed, Akbar S. *Postmodernism and Islam: Predicament and Promise.* New York: Routledge, 1992.

Ahrari, M. E. "Islam as a Source of Conflict and Change in the Middle East." *Security Dialogue* 25, no. 2 (1994): 177–92.

Ajami, Fouad. *The Arab Predicament: Arab Political Thought and Practice since 1967.* Cambridge: Cambridge University Press, 1981.

Akhtar, Karm B., and Ahmad H. Sakr. *Islamic Fundamentalism.* Cedar Rapids, Iowa: Ingram Press, 1982.

'Ali [ibn Abi Talib]. *Nahj al-Balagha.* Edited by Muhammad 'Abdu. Beirut: Dar al-Huda al-Wataniyya, n.d.

'Ali, Haydar Ibrahim. *Al-Tayyarat al-Islamiyya wa Qadiyyat al-Ta'addudiyya.* Beirut: Center for Arab Unity Studies, 1996.

'Ali, Mustapha. *Al-Mufassal fi Tarikh al-'Arab qabla al-Islam.* Beirut: Dar al-'Ilm li al-Malayin; Baghdad: Maktabat al-Nahda, 1970.

Allen, Richard. *Imperialism and Nationalism in the Fertile Crescent: Sources and Prospects of the Arab-Israeli Conflict.* Oxford: Oxford University Press, 1975.

al-Alusi, 'Adil. *Al-Ra'y al-'Am fi al-Qarn al-Thalith 'Ashar.* Baghdad: Dar al-Shu'un al-Thaqafiyya al-'Amma, 1987.

'Amara, Muhammad. *Abu al-A'la al-Mawdudi wa al-Sahwa al-Islamiyya.* Beirut: Dar al-Wahda, 1986.

———. *Al-A'mal al-Kamilah: Jamal al-Din al-Afghani.* Beirut: Al-Mu'assasa al-'Arabiyya li al-Dirasat wa al-Nashr, c. 1980.

———. *Al-Din wa al-Dawla.* Cairo: Ahay'a al-'Amma li al-Kitab, 1986.

———. *Al-Islam wa Falsafat al-Hukm.* Beirut: Dar al-Shuruq, c. 1981.

———. *Al-Islam wa Falsafat al-Thawra.* Beirut: Al-Mu'assaa al-'Arabiyya li al-Dirasat wa al-Nashr, 1980.

———. *Al-Islam wa al-Hurub al-Diniyya.* Cairo: Dar al-Thaqafa al-Jadida, 1996.

———. *Al-Khilafa wa Nash'at al-Ahzab al-Siyasiyya.* Beirut: Al-Mu'assasa al-'Arabiyya li al-Dirasat wa al-Nashr, 1977.

———. *Muslimun Thuwwar.* Beirut: Al-Mu'assasa al-'Arabiyya li al-Dirasat wa al-Nashr, 1981.

Amin, Ahmad. *Duha al-Islam.* Cairo: Maktabat al-Nahda, 1961.

———. *Fajr al-Islam.* 4th ed. Beirut: Dar al-Kitab al-Lubnani, 1975.

———. *Thuhr al-Islam.* 3d ed. Beirut: Dar al-Kitab al-'Arabi, 1953.

Amuzegar, Jahangir. "The Truth and Illusion of Islamic Fundamentalism." *SAIS Review* 13 (1993): 127–39.

Anderson, Gerald. "Challenge of Islam for Christian Missions." *International Bulletin of Missionary Research* 17 (1993): 160–73.

Anderson, Lisa. "Liberalism in Northern Africa." *Current History* 89 (1990): 145–48.

———. "Liberalism, Islam, and the Arab State." *Dissent* 41 (1994): 439–44.

———. "Obligation and Accountability: Islamic Politics in North Africa." *Daedalus* 120 (1991): 93–112.

———. "Remaking the Middle East: The Prospects for Democracy and Stability." *Ithacas and International Affairs* 6 (1992): 163–78.

———. "The State in the Middle East and North Africa." *Comparative Politics* 20, no. 1 (1987): 1–18.

Anderson, Sean, and Stephen Sloan. *Historical Dictionary of Terrorism.* Metuchen, N.J.: Scarecrow Press, 1995.

Antoun, Richard, and Mary Elaine Hegland, eds. *Religious Resurgence: Contemporary Cases in Islam, Christianity, and Judaism.* Syracuse: Syracuse University Press, 1987.

Appleby, R. Scott. *Spokesmen for the Despised: Fundamentalist Leaders of the Middle East.* Chicago: University of Chicago Press, 1996.

"The Arab World Where Troubles for the U.S. Never End." *U.S. News and World Report,* 6 February 1984, 24.

Arjomand, Said Amir. *The Shadow of God and the Hidden Imam.* Chicago: University of Chicago Press, 1984.

———, ed. *Authority and Political Culture in Shi'ism.* Albany: State University of New York Press, 1988.

Arkoun, Muhammad. *Tarikhiyyat al-Fikr al-'Arabi al-Islami.* Beirut: Markaz al-Inma' al-Qawmi, 1986.

Armajani, Yahya. *Middle East: Past and Present.* Englewood Cliffs, N.J.: Prentice Hall, 1970.

al-Asfahani, al-Raghib. *Al-Mufradat fi Gharib al-Qur'an.* Beirut: Dar al-Ma'arif, n.d.

al-Asha'ri. *Maqalat al-Islamiyyin.* Cairo: Maktabat al-Nahda, 1954.

'Ata, 'Abd al-Khabir Mahmud. "Al-Haraka al-Islamiyya wa Qadiyyat al-Ta'ad-dudiyya." *Al-Majalla al-'Arabiyya li al-'Ulum al-Siyasiyya* 5 and 6 (1992): 103–28.

'Atwan, Hussein. *Al-Fuqaha' wa al-Khilafa.* Beirut: Dar al-Jil, 1991.

Avinery, Shlomo. "The Return to Islam." *Dissent* 40 (1993): 410–12.

al-'Awwa, Muhammad Salim. *Fi al-Nizam al-Siyasi al-Islami li al-Dawla al-Islamiyya.* Cairo: Dar al-Shuruq, 1989.

———. "Al-Taʿaddudiyya al-Siyasiyya min Manzur Islami." *Minbar al-Hiwar* 6, no. 20 (1991): 129–38.

Ayalon, Ami, ed. *Middle East Contemporary Survey.* Boulder, Colo.: Westview Press, 1989.

Ayoob, Mohammad. *The Politics of Islamic Reassertion.* New York: St. Martin's Press, 1981.

Ayubi, Nazih. *Over-Stating the Arab State: Politics and Society in the Middle East.* London: I. B. Tauris, 1995.

———. *Political Islam: Religion and Politics in the Arab World.* New York: Routledge, 1991.

al-Azm, Sadik. "Islamic Fundamentalism Reconsidered: A Critical Outline of Problems, Ideas and Approaches." Parts 1 and 2. *South Asia Bulletin* 13, nos. 1 and 2 (1993): 93–131; 14, no. 1 (1994): 73–98.

———. *Naqd al-Fikr al-Dini.* 6th ed. Beirut: Dar al-Taliʿa, 1988.

al-Azmeh, Aziz. *Islam and Modernities.* London: Verso, 1993.

al-Azmi, Tarik Hamid. "Religion, Identity, and State in Modern Islam." *Muslim World* 84, nos. 3–4 (1994): 334–41.

Azzam, Maha. "The Gulf Crisis: Perceptions in the Muslim World." *International Affairs* 67 (1991): 473–85.

Babeair, Abdulwahab Saleh. "Contemporary Islamic Revivalism: A Movement or a Moment?" *Islamic Quarterly* 37, no. 1 (1993): 5–23.

Badawi, M. A. Zaki. *The Reformers of Egypt.* London: Croom Helm, 1967.

al-Baghdadi. *Al-Farq bayna al-Firaq.* Cairo: Maktabat Nashr al-Thaqafa al-Islamiyya, 1948.

———. *Usul al-Din.* Beirut: Dar al-Kutub al-ʿIlmiyya, 1981.

al-Baladhi. *Futuh al-Buldan.* Beirut: Dar al-Nashr li al-Jamiʿiyyin, 1958.

al-Balihi, Ibrahim ibn ʿAbd al-Rahman. *Sayyid Qutb wa-Turathuhu al-Adabi wa al-Fikri.* Riyadh: n.p., 1972.

Bangura, Yusuf. *The Search for Identity: Ethnicity, Religion and Political Violence.* Geneva: United Nations Research Institute for Social Development, 1994.

Bani al-Marja, Muwaffaq. *Sahwat al-Rajul al-Marid.* Kuwait: Muʾassasat Saqr al-Khalij li al-Tibaʿa wa al-Nashr, 1984.

al-Banna, Hasan. *Din wa-Siyasa.* Beirut: Maktabat Huttin, 1970.

———. *Al-Imam al-Shahid Yatahadath ila Shabab al-ʿAlam al-Islami.* Beirut: Dar al-Qalam, 1974.

———. *Kalimat Khalida.* Beirut: n.p., 1972.

———. *Majmuʿat Rasaʾil al-Imam al-Shahid Hasan al-Banna.* Cairo: Dar al-Qalam, n.d.

———. *Majmuʿat Rasaʾil al-Shahid Hasan al-Banna.* Beirut: Dar al-Qalam, c. 1984.

———. *Memoirs of Hasan al-Banna Shaheed.* Translated by M. N. Shaikh. Karachi: International Islamic Publishers, 1981.

————. *Minbar al-Jum'a*. Alexandria: Dar al-Da'wa, 1978.

————. *Nazarat fi Islah al-Nafs wa al-Mujtama'*. Cairo: Maktabat al-I'tisam, 1969.

————. *Rasa'il al-Imam al-Shahid Hasan al-Banna*. Beirut: Dar al-Qur'an al-Karim, 1984.

————. *Al-Salam fi al-Islam*. 2d ed. Beirut: Manshurat al-'Asr al-Hadith, 1971.

al-Baqillani. *Al-Tamhid*. Beirut: Al-Maktaba al-Sharqiyya, 1957.

Barakat, Halim. *Al-Mujtama' al-'Arabi al-Ma'asir*. Beirut: Center for Arab Unity Studies, c. 1986.

Barakat, Muhammad T. *Sayyid Qutb: Khulasat Hayatih, Minhajuhuh fi al-Haraka wa al-Naqd al-Muwajjah ilayh*. Beirut: Dar al-Da'wa, n.d.

Barghouty, Iyad. "Al-Islam bayna al-Sulta wa al-Mu'arada." In *Qadaya Fikriyya: Al-Islam al-Siyasi, al-Usus al-Fikriyya wa al-Ahdaf al-'Amalliyya,* edited by Rif'at al-Sa'id. 234–41. Cairo: Dar al-Thaqafa al-Jadida, 1989.

"Al-Barnamaj al-Siyasi li Jabhat al-Inqadh." *Minbar al-Hiwar* 1, no. 1 (1993): 206–13.

"Bayan min al-Ikhawan al-Muslimin hawla Muwjat al-'Unf wa al-Irhab." *Qira'at Siyasiyya* 3, no. 2 (1993): 197–98.

Baydun, Ibrahim. *Al-Ansar wa al-Rasul*. Beirut: Ma'had al-Inma' al-'Arabi, 1989.

Beeley, B. "Global Options: Islamic Alternatives." In *A Global World? Re-Ordering Political Space,* edited by J. Anderson et al. Oxford: Oxford University Press, 1995.

al-Bidawi. *Anwar al-Tanzil*. Cairo: Dar al-Kutub al-'Arabiyya, n.d.

Bil Haj, Muhammad Abu 'Abd al-Fattah 'Ali. *Fasl al-Kalam fi Muwajahat Zulm al-Hukkam*. Beirut: n.p., 1994.

Binder, Leonard. *The Ideological Revolution in the Middle East*. New York: John Wiley and Sons, 1964.

————. *Islamic Liberalism: A Critique of Development Ideologies*. Chicago: University of Chicago Press, 1988.

al-Bishri, Tariq. "'An Mu'assasat al-Dawla fi al-Nuzum al-Islamiyya wa al-'Arabiyya." *Minbar al-Hiwar* 19 (Summer 1989): 74–89.

Bizri, Dalal. *Akhawat al-Zill wa al-Yaqin: Islamiyyat bayna al-Hadatha wa al-Taqlid*. Beirut: Dar al-Nahar li al-Nashr, 1996.

Brockelmann, Carl. *History of the Islamic Peoples*. 7th ed. Beirut: Dar al'Ilm li al-Malayin, 1972.

Brumberg, Daniel. "Islamic Fundamentalism, Democracy, and the Gulf War." In *Islamic Fundamentalisms and the Gulf Crisis,* edited by James Piscatori, 155–85. Chicago: University of Chicago Press, 1991.

Bulliet, Richard W. *Islam: The View from the Edge*. New York: Columbia University Press, 1994.

————. "The Israeli-PLO Accord: The Future of the Islamic Movement." *Foreign Affairs* 72 (1993): 38–44.

Burgat, François, and William Dowell. *The Islamic Movement in North Africa.* Austin: University of Texas Press, 1993.

Burke, Edmond. *Struggle for Survival in the Modern Middle East.* London: I. B. Tauris, 1994.

Burrows, Bernard. *Footnotes in the Sand: The Gulf in Transition.* London: Michael Russell, 1991.

Butterworth, Charles. "Political Islam." *Annals* (American Academy of Political and Social Sciences) 524 (1992): 26–37.

———. "State and Authority in Arabic Political Thought." In *The Foundations of the Arab State,* edited by Ghassan Salame, 91–111. London: Croom Helm, 1987.

Cantori, Louis J. "Democratization in the Middle East." *American-Arab Affairs* 36 (1991): 1–51.

Carré, Olivier. *Les Frères Musulmans: Égypte et Syrie: 1928–1982.* Paris: Callimard, c. 1983.

Charfi, Farida Faouzia. "When Galileo Meets Allah." *New Perspectives Quarterly* 11, no. 2 (1994): 30–32.

Charnayl, Jean Paul. *Islamic Culture and Socio-Economic Change.* Leiden: E. J. Brill, 1971.

Chelkowski, Peter, and Robert J. Pranger. *Ideology and Power in the Middle East: Studies in Honor of George Lenczowski.* Durham, N.C.: Duke University Press, 1988.

Choudhury, Golam W. *Islam and the Modern Muslim World.* London: Scorpion, 1993.

Choueiri, Youssef M. *Islamic Fundamentalism.* Boston: Twayne, 1990.

———. "Theoretical Paradigms of Islamic Movements." *Political Studies* 41, no. 1 (1993): 108–16.

Cleveland, W. L. *A History of the Middle East.* Boulder, Colo.: Westview Press, 1994.

Cole, Juan R. I., and Nikki R. Keddie, eds. *Shi'ism and Social Protest.* New Haven: Yale University Press, 1986.

Coulson, N. J. *A History of Islamic Law.* Edinburgh: Edinburgh University Press, 1971.

Cragg, Kenneth. *Contemporary Counsels in Islam.* Edinburgh: Edinburgh University Press, 1956.

Curtis, Michael, ed. *Religion and Politics in the Middle East.* Boulder, Colo.: Westview Press, 1981.

Dallal, Ahmad. "The Origins and Objectives of Islamic Revivalist Thought, 1750–1850." *Journal of the American Oriental Society* 113 (1993): 341–59.

al-Da'wa 7 (1979).

"The Deadly Party of Hizbullah: Hizbullah Threatens the West." *Maclean's* 102, no. 33 (1989): 28.

Deegan, H. "Democratization in the Middle East." In *The Middle East in the New World Order*, edited by Haifa A. Jawad. New York: St. Martin's Press, 1994.

Dekmejian, Hrair R. "The Arab Anatomy of Islamic Revival: Legitimacy Crisis, Ethnic Conflict and the Search for Islamic Alternatives." *Middle East Journal* 34 (1980): 1–12.

———. *Islam in Revolution: Fundamentalism in the Arab World*. 2nd ed. Syracuse: Syracuse University Press, 1995.

Dessouki, Ali E. Hillal. "The Impact of Islamism on the Arab System." In *The Islamist Dilemma: The Political Role of Islamist Movements in the Contemporary Arab World*, edited by Laura Guazzone, 247–64. Reading, England: Ithaca Press, 1995.

———, ed. *Islamic Resurgence in the Arab World*. New York: Praeger, 1982.

Al-Din fi al-Mujtama' al-'Arabi. Beirut: Center for Arab Unity Studies, 1990.

al-Diqa, Hasan. *Ahl al-'Irfan wa Shawkat al-Sultan*. Beirut: Islamic Shi'ite Supreme Council, 1994.

Djerejian, Edward. "One Man, One Vote, One Time." *New Perspectives Quarterly* 10, no. 3 (1993): 49.

Donohue, John, and John L. Esposito, eds. *Islam in Transition: Muslim Perspectives*. New York: Oxford University Press, 1982.

Dunn, Michael C. "Islamic Activists in the West: A New Issue Produces Backlashes." *Middle East Policy* 3, no. 1 (1994): 137–45.

al-Durayni, Muhammad Fathi. *Dirasat wa Buhuth fi al-Fikr al-Ma'asir*, Vol 1. Beirut: Dar Qutayba, 1988.

———, ed. *Al-Ijtihad wa al-Tajdid fi al-Fikr al-Islami*. Valletta, Malta: Islamic World Studies Center, 1991.

Durrani, K. S. *Impact of Islamic Fundamentalism*. Bangalore, India: ISPK, Bangalore, 1993.

East, Roger, and Tanya Joseph, eds. *Political Parties of Africa and the Middle East: A Reference Guide*. Harlow, England: Longman, 1993.

Ehteshami, Anoushiravan. *Islamic Fundamentalism*. Boulder, Colo.: Westview Press, 1996.

Eickelman, Dale F. "Changing Interpretations of Islamic Movements." In *Islam and the Political Economy of Meaning*, edited by William R. Roff, 13–30. Berkeley and Los Angeles: University of California Press, 1987.

———. "Islamic Liberalism Strikes Back." *Middle East Studies Association Bulletin* 27, no. 2 (1993): 163–68.

Enayat, Hamid. *Modern Islamic Political Thought*. Austin: University of Texas Press, 1982.

The Encyclopedia of Islam. Edited by Bernard Lewis, V. L. Menage, et al. Leiden, Netherlands: E. J. Brill, 1971.

Entelis, John P. *Comparative Politics of North Africa: Algeria, Morocco and Tunisia*. Syracuse: Syracuse University Press, 1980.

El-Erian, Mohamad A. *Jamjoom: A Profile of Islam, Past, Present, and Future: A*

Resource Book of Islam and the Muslim World. Melbourne: Islamic Publications, 1990.

Esack, Farid. *Qur'an, Liberation and Pluralism: An Islamic Perspective of Interreligious Solidarity against Oppression*. Oxford: Oneworld Publications, 1996.

Esposito, John L. *Islam and Development: Religion and Sociopolitical Change*. Syracuse: Syracuse University Press, 1980.

———. *Islam and Politics*. 3d ed. Syracuse: Syracuse University Press, 1991.

———. *Islam: The Straight Path*. Expanded ed. New York: Oxford University Press, 1994.

———. "Islamic Movements, Democratization and U.S. Foreign Policy." In *Riding the Tiger: The Middle East Challenge After the Cold War*, edited by Phebe Marr and William Lewis, 187–209. Boulder, Colo.: Westview Press, 1993.

———. *The Islamic Threat: Myth or Reality?* New York: Oxford University Press, 1992.

———. "The Persian Gulf War, Islamic Movements and the New World Order." *Iranian Journal of International Affairs* 5, no. 2 (1993): 340–65.

———. "Political Islam: Beyond the Green Menace." *Current History* 93 (1994): 19–24.

———, ed. *The Oxford Encyclopedia of the Modern Islamic World*. New York: Oxford University Press, 1995.

———, ed. *Voices of Resurgent Islam*. New York: Oxford University Press, 1983.

Esposito, John L., and James P. Piscatori. "Democratization and Islam." *Middle East Journal* 45, no. 3 (1991): 427–40.

Esposito, John, and John Voll. *Islam and Democracy*. Oxford: Oxford University Press, 1996.

Fakhry, Majid. *Al-Harakat al-Fikriyya wa Ruwwadiha al-Lubnaniyyun fi 'Asr al-Nahda, 1800–1922*. Beirut: Dar al-Nahar li al-Nashr, 1992.

Falk, Richard. "In Search of a New World Model." *Current History* 92 (1993): 145–49.

al-Farabi, Abu Nasr. *Al-Madina al-Fadila*. Beirut: Al-Maktaba al-Sharqiyya, 1980.

Farah, Caesar. "Political Dimensions of Islamic Fundamentalism." *Digest of Middle East Studies* 5 (1996): 1–14.

Faraj, 'Abd al-Salam. "Al-Farida al-Gha'iba." In *Al-Nabiy al-Musallah: al-Rafidun*, edited by Rif'at Sayyid Ahmad, 127–47. London: Riad El-Rayyes Books, 1990.

al-Fasi, Allal. *Durus fi al-Haraka al-Salafiyya*. Dayda, Morocco: Manshurat 'Uyun, 1986.

Filali-Ansari, A. "Islam and Liberal Democracy: The Challenge of Secularization." *Journal of Democracy* 7, no. 2 (1996): 76–80.

Flores, Alexander. "Secularism, Integralism and Political Islam." *Middle East Report* 183 (1993): 32–38.

Fuller, Graham E. *Islamic Fundamentalism in the Northern Tier Countries: An Integrative View.* Santa Monica, Calif.: Rand Corporation, 1991.

Fuller, Graham, and Iran Lesser. *A Sense of Siege: The Geopolitics of Islam and the West.* Boulder, Colo.: Westview Press, 1995.

Gause, F. Gregory. "Sovereignty, Statecraft and Stability in the Middle East." *Journal of International Affairs* 45, no. 2 (1992): 441–69.

Gellner, Ernest. *Culture, Identity, and Politics.* Cambridge: Cambridge University Press, 1987.

Gerami, Shahim. *Women and Fundamentalism.* Oxford: Garland, 1996.

Ghadbian, Najib. *Democratization and Islamist Challenge in the Arab World.* Boulder, Colo.: Westview Press, 1997.

Ghalib, Mustafa. *Jalal al-Din al-Rumi.* Beirut: Ma'asasat 'Iz al-Din li al-Tiba'a wa al-Nashr, 1982.

Ghalyun, Burhan. *Al-Dawla wa al-Din: Naqd al-Siyasa.* Beirut: Al-Mu'assasa al-'Arabiyya li al-Dirasat wa al-Nashr, 1991.

———. *Ightiyal al-'Aql: Mihnat al-Thaqafa al-'Arabiyya bayna al-Salafiyya wa al-Taba'iyya.* Beirut: Dar al-Tanwir, 1985.

al-Ghannushi, Rashid. "Hiwar." *Qira'at Siyasiyya* 1, no. 4 (1991): 14–37.

———. *Huquq al-Muwatana.* Herndon, Va.: International Institute of Islamic Thought, 1993.

———. *Al-Hurriyyat al-'Amma fi al-Dawla al-Islamiyya.* Beirut: Markaz Dirasat al-Wahda al-'Arabiyya, 1993.

———. "Al-Islam wa al-Gharb." *Al-Ghadir,* nos. 10–11 (1990).

———. "Ma'alim fi Istratijiyya al-Da'wa al-Islamiyya." *Al-Hiwar* 19 (1990).

———. *Mahawir Islamiyya.* Cairo: Matabi' al-Zahra', 1989.

———. "Mustaqbal al-Haraka al-Islamiyya." *Al-Huda* (Fez) 23 (1991).

———. "Mustaqbal al-Tayyar al-Islami." *Minbar al-Sharq* 1, no. 1 (1992): 3–32.

———. "Tahlil li al-'Anasir al-Mukawwina li al-Zahira al-Islamiyya fi Tunis." In *Al-Harakat al-Islamiyya fi al-Watan al-'Arabi,* edited by I. S. 'Abd Allah et al. Beirut: Markaz Dirasat al-Wahda al-'Arabiyya, 1987.

al-Ghannushi, Rashid, and Hasan al-Turabi. *Al-Haraka al-Islamiyya wa al-Tahdith.* Tunisia: Dar al-Raya, n.d.

al-Ghazali, Abu Hamid. *Fada'ih al-Batiniyya.* Cairo: Al-Dar al-Qawmiyya li al-Tiba'a wa al-Nashr, c. 1964.

———. *Ihya' 'Ulum al-Din.* Cairo: Ma'asasat al-Halabi, 1967.

———. *Al-Iqtisad fi al-I'tiqad.* Cairo: Al-Matba'a al-Mahmudiyya, n.d.

———. *Mishkat al-Anwar.* Aleppo: Al-Dar al-I'lmiyya, 6 vols., c. 1927.

———. *Al-Munqidh min al-Dalal.* Beirut: Dar al-Andalus, 1981.

———. *Al-Mustasfa min al-Usul.* Beirut: Dar al-Fikr, n.d.

———. *Al-Mustathhiri.* Cairo: Al-Matba'at al-Amiriyya, A.H. 1332.

———. *Tahafut al-Falasifa.* Cairo: Dar al-Ma'arif, n.d.

Gibb, Hamilton A. R. *Modern Trends in Islam.* Chicago: University of Chicago Press, 1947.

————. *Mohammedanism*. Oxford: Oxford University Press, c. 1976.

————. *Studies on the Civilization of Islam*. Boston: Beacon, 1962. Reprint, Princeton: Princeton University Press, 1982.

————, ed. *Whither Islam? A Survey of Modern Movements in the Moslem World*. London: Gollancz, 1932. Reprint, New York: AMS Press, 1973.

Gilsenan, Michael. *Recognizing Islam: Religion and Society in the Modern Middle East*. London: I. B. Tauris, 1994.

Glasse, Cyril. *The Concise Encyclopedia of Islam*. London: Stacey International, 1989.

Green, Jerrold D. "Islam, Religiopolitics, and Social Change." *Comparative Studies in Society and History* 27 (1985): 312–22.

Guazzone, Laura, ed. *The Islamist Dilemma: The Political Role of Islamist Movements in the Contemporary Arab World*. Reading, England: Ithaca Press, 1995.

Guolo, R. *Il partito di dio: l'Islam radicale contro l'Occidente*. Milan: Guerini e Associati, 1994.

Hadar, Leon T. "What Green Peril." *Foreign Affairs* 72, no. 3 (1993): 27–42.

Haddad, Robert M. *Syrian Minorities in the Muslim Society: An Interpretation*. Princeton: Princeton University Press, 1970.

Haddad, Yvonne. *Contemporary Islam and the Challenge of History*. Albany: State University of New York Press, 1982.

————. "Islamists and the 'Problem of Israel': The 1967 Awakening." *Middle East Journal* 46, no. 2 (1992): 266–85.

————. "The Qur'anic Justification for an Islamic Revolution: The View of Sayyid Qutb." *Middle East Journal* 37, no. 1 (1983): 14–29.

Haddad, Yvonne Y., Byron Haynes, and Ellison Finfly, eds. *The Contemporary Islamic Revival: A Critical Survey and Bibiliography*. Westport, Conn.: Greenwood Press, 1991.

————, eds. *The Islamic Impact*. Syracuse: Syracuse University Press, 1984.

Haider, Gulzar. "An 'Islamic Future' Without a Name." *Futures* 23 (1991): 311–16.

Halliday, Fred. *Islam and the Myth of Confrontation: Religion and Politics of the Middle East*. London: I. B. Tauris, 1995.

Halliday, Fred, and Hamza Alavi. *State and Ideology in the Middle East and Pakistan*. New York: Monthly Review Press, 1988.

Hamad, Wadood. "The Dialectics of Revolutionary Islamic Thought and Action." *Arab Review* 2, no. 3 (1994): 35–41.

Hamadah, Muhammad. *Bina' al-Umma bayna al-Islam wa al-Fikr al-Mu'asir*. Casablanca: Dar al-Thaqafa, 1986.

————. *Al-Watha'iq al-Siyasiyya wa al-Idariyya*. Beirut: Mu'assasat al-Risala, n.d.

Hamadani, Abbas. "Islamic Fundamentalism." *Mediterranean Quarterly* 4, no. 4 (1993): 38–47.

Hamdi, M. E. "Islam and Liberal Democracy: The Limits of the Western Model." *Journal of Democracy* 7, no. 2 (1996): 81–85.

al-Hamidi, Muhammad al-Hashimi. "Awlawiyyat Muhimma fi Daftar al-Harakat al-Islamiyya: Nahwa Mithaq Islami li al-'Adl wa al-Shura wa Huquq al-Insan." *Al-Mustaqbal al-Islami* 2 (1991): 13–21.

Hammuda, Husayn M. *Asrar Harakat al-Dubbat al-Ahrar wa al-Ikhwan al-Muslimin.* Cairo: Al-Zahra' li al-I'lam al-'Arabi, 1985.

Hanafi, Hasan. *Min al-'Aqida ila al-Thawra.* Cairo: Maktabat Madbuli, 1988.

———. *Al-Turath wa al-Tajdid: Mawqifuna min al-Thawra.* Cairo: Al-Markaz li al-Bahth wa al-Dirasat, 1980.

———. *Al-Yamin wa al-Yasar fi al-Fikr al-Dini.* Cairo: Dar al-Thaqafa al-Jadida, 1996.

Al-Harakat al-Islamiyya fi Muwajahat al-Taswiya. Beirut: Center for Strategic Studies, 1995.

Harb, 'Ali. "Fi al-Ikhtilaf." *Minbar al-Hiwar* 3, no. 12 (1988–89): 8–26.

Harik, Iliya. "Rethinking Civil Society: Pluralism in the Arab World." *Journal of Democracy* 5, no. 3 (1994): 43–56.

Harris, Christina P. *Nationalism and Revolution in Egypt: The Role of the Muslim Brotherhood.* Westport, Conn.: Hyperion Press, 1981.

al-Hasan, Badrul. *Milestones.* Karachi: International Islamic Publishers, 1981.

Hasan, Hasan 'Abbas. *Al-Fikr al-Shi'i.* Beirut: Al-Dar al-Alameda, 1988.

Hasan, Hasan Ibrahim. *Tarikh al-Islam.* Cairo: Maktabat al-Nahda al-Misriyya, c. 1964.

Hawwa, Sa'id. *Al-Madkhal ila Da'wat al-Ikhwan al-Muslimin bi-Munasabat Khamsin 'Aman 'ala Ta'sisiha.* Amman: Dar al-Arqam, c. 1979.

Hermassi, Mohamed Abdelbaki. "Islam, Democracy, and the Challenge of Political Change." In *Democracy in the Middle East: Defining the Challenge,* edited by Yehudah Mirsky and Matt Ahrens, 41–52. Washington, D.C.: Washington Institute for Near East Policy, 1993.

———. *Society and State in the Arab Maghreb.* Beirut: Center for Arab Unity Studies, 1987.

Heyworth-Dunne, James. *Religions and Political Trends in Modern Egypt.* Washington, D.C.: n.p., 1950.

al-Hibri, Azizah Y. *Islamic Constitutionalism and the Concept of Democracy.* New York: American Muslim Foundation, 1992.

Hilal, 'Ali al-Din Hilal. *Al-Siyasa wa al-Hukm fi Misr: 1923–52.* Cairo: Maktabat Nahdat al-Sharq, 1977.

Hinds, Martin. "The Siffin Judgment Agreement." *Journal of Semitic Studies* 17 (1972): 93–100.

al-Hirmasi, 'Abd al-Baqi. "Al-Islam al-Ihtijaji fi Tunis." In *Al-Harakat al-Islamiyya al-Mu'asira fi al-Watan al-'Arabi,* edited by Isma'il Sabri, 'Abd Allah, 247–99. 2d ed. Beirut: Center for Arab Unity Studies, 1989.

Hiro, Dilip. *Holy Wars: The Rise of Islamic Fundamentalism*. New York: Routledge, 1989.

———. *Inside the Middle East*. London: Routledge and Kegan Paul, 1981.

———. *Islamic Fundamentalism*. London: Grafton, 1988.

Hottinger, A. "How Dangerous Is Islamism?" *Swiss Review of World Affairs* 1 (1994): 10–12.

Hourani, Albert. *Al-Fikr al-ʿArabi fi ʿAsr al-Nahda*. Beirut: Dar al-Nahar li al-Nashr, 1977.

———. *History of the Arab Peoples*. Cambridge: Harvard University Press, 1990.

Hovsepian, Nubar. "Competing Identities in the Arab World." *Journal of International Affairs* 49 (1995): 1–24.

Hudson, Michael. "After the Gulf War: Prospects for Democratization in the Arab World." *Middle East Journal* 45, no. 3 (1991): 407–26.

———. *Arab Politics*. New Haven: Yale University Press, 1977.

———. "Arab Regimes and Democratization: Responses to the Challenge of Political Islam." In *The Islamist Dilemma*, edited by Laura Guazzone, 217–45. Reading, England: Ithaca Press, 1995.

Huergensmeyer, M. *The New Cold War? Religious Nationalism Confronts the Secular State*. Berkeley and Los Angeles: University of California Press, 1994.

Hunter, Shireen T. "The Rise of Islamist Movements and the Western Response: Clash of Civilizations or Clash of Interests?" In *The Islamist Dilemma*, edited by Laura Guazzone, 317–50. Reading, England: Ithaca Press, 1995.

———, ed. *The Politics of Islamic Revivalism: Diversity and Unity*. Bloomington: Indiana University Press, 1988.

Huntington, Samuel. "The Clash of Civilizations." *Foreign Affairs* 72, no. 3 (1993): 22–49.

Husain, Mir Zohair. *Global Islamic Politics*. New York: HarperCollins College Publishers, 1994.

al-Husaini, Ishaq Musa. *Moslem Brethren*. Beirut: Khayat's, 1956.

Hussain, Asaf. *Islamic Movements in Egypt, Pakistan, and Iran: An Annotated Bibliography*. New York: Mansell, 1983.

al-Huwaidi, Fahmi. "Al-Islam wa al-Dimuqratiyya." *Al-Mustaqbal al-ʿArabi* 166 (1992): 5–37.

———. *Al-Islam wa al-Dimuqratiyya*. Cairo: Markaz al-Ahram li al-Tarjama wa al-Nashr, 1993.

———. "Al-Sahwa al-Islamiyya wa al-Muwatana wa al-Musawat." *Al-Hiwar* 7 (1987): 53–70.

———. *Al-Qurʾan wa al-Sultan: Humum Islamiyya Muʿasira*. Cairo: Dar al-Shuruq, 1982.

Hyman, Anthony. "Islamic Bogeymen." *World Today* 46 (1990): 160–61.

———. "The Muslim Fundamentalism." *Conflict Studies* 174 (1985): 1–27.

Ibn ʿAbd Rabbih. *Al-ʿAqd al-Farid*. Beirut: Dar al-Andalus, 1988.

Ibn Abi Haddid. *Sharh Nahj al-Balagha*. Cairo edition, 1959.

Ibn Abi Talib. *See* ʿAli.

Ibn ʿArabi. *Nusus al-Hikam*. Beirut: Dar al-Kitab al-ʿArabi, 1980.

———. *Ahkam al-Qurʾan*. Cairo: al-Halabi, n.d.

Ibn Hazm. *Al-Faslfi al-Milal wa al-Nihal*. Cairo: Matbaʿat al-Tamaddun, A.H. 1321.

Ibn Hisham. *Al-Sira*. Beirut: Dar al-Jil, n.d.

Ibn Kathir. *Al-Bidaya wa al-Nihaya*. Cairo: Matbaʿat al-Saʿada, A.H. 1358.

———. *Tafsir al-Qurʾan*. Beirut: Dar Lubnan, 1992.

Ibn Khaldun. *Al-Muqaddima*. Beirut: Dar al-Qalam, 1978.

Ibn Qutayba. *Al-Imama wa al-Siyasa*. Cairo: Maktabat Mustafa al-Halabi, 1963.

———. *ʿUyun al-Akhbar*. Cairo: Al-Muʾassa al-Misriyya, 1963.

Ibn Rushd. *Fasl al-Maqal*. Edited by Muhammad ʿAmara. Beirut: Al-Muʾassasa al-ʿArabiyya li al-Dirasat wa al-Nashr, 1981.

Ibn Saʿd. *Tabaqat*. Beirut: Dar Sadr, 1960.

Ibn Taymiyya. *Fatawa*. Morocco: Maktabat al-Maʿarif, n.d.

———. *Al-Hisba fi al-Islam*. Kuwait: Dar al-Arqam, 1983.

———. *Minhaj al-Sunna al-Nabawiyya*. Cairo: Al-Matbaʿa al-Amiriyya, A.H. 1322.

———. *Al-Sarim al-Maslul ʿala Shataʾim al-Rasul*. Edited by Muhammad ʿAbd al-Hamid. Cairo: Matbaʿat al-Rasul, 1960.

———. *Al-Siyasa al-Sharʿiyya fi Isla al-Raʿiyya*. 4th ed. Cairo: Dar al-Kitab al-ʿArabi, 1969.

Ibrahim, Anwar. "The Ummah and Tomorrow's World." *Futures* 23 (1991): 302–10.

Ibrahim, Saad Eddin. "Islamic Activism: A Rejoinder." *Security Dialogue* 25, no 2 (1994): 193–98.

ʿId, ʿAbd al-Razzaq. *Azmat al-Tanwir*. Damascus: Al-Ahli li al-Tibaʿa, 1997.

ʿIlwani, Taha. *Islah al-Fikr al-Islami*. Herndon, Va.: International Institute of Islamic Thought, 1991.

al-Iji. *al-ʿAqida al-ʿAdawiyya*. Cairo: n.p., A.H. 1332.

ʿImad, ʿAbd al-Ghani. *Hakimiyyat Allah wa Sultan al-Faqih*. Beirut: Dar al-Taliʿa, 1997.

Iqbal, Muhammad. *The Reconstruction of Religious Thought in Islam*. Lahore: Ashraf, 1960.

ʿIshmawi, Muhammad Saʿid. *Al-Khilafa al-Islamiyya*. Cairo: Sina li al-Nashr, 1992.

———. "Shariʿa in the Discussion on Secularism and Democracy." In *Law and the Islamic World: Past and Present*, edited by Christopher Toll and Jakob Skovgaard-Petersen. Copenhagen: Royal Danish Academy of Sciences and Letters, 1995.

Ismaʿil, Mahmud. *Sociolojia al-Fikr al-Islami*. Cairo: Maktabat Madbuli, 1988.

Israeli, Raphael. *Fundamentalist Islam and Israel: Essays in Interpretation*. Lanham, Md.: University Press of America, 1993.

ʿIssa, Riyad. *Al-Hizbiyya al-Siyasiyya hata Suqut al-Dawla al-Umawiyya*. Damascus: n.p.: 1992.

ʿIzzat, Hiba Raʾuf. *Al-Marʾa wa al-ʿAmal al-Siyasi: Ruʾya Islamiyya.* Herndon, Va.: International Institute of Islamic Thought, 1995.

Jabir, Husayn. *Al-Tariq ila Jamaʿat al-Muslimin.* al-Mansura, Egypt: Dar al-Wafa, 1987.

al-Jabiri, Muhammad ʿAbid. *al-ʿAql al-Siyasi al-ʿArabi.* Beirut: Markaz Dirasat al-Wahda al-ʿArabiyya, 1991.

———. *Al-Fikr al-Siyasi al-ʿArabi.* Beirut: Markaz Dirasat al-Wahda al-ʿArabiyya, 1990.

———. *Al-Khitab al-ʿArabi al-Muʿasir.* Beirut: Dar al-Taliʿa, 1982.

———. *Nahnu wa al-Turath.* Beirut: Dar al-Taliʿa, 1980.

Jadʿan, Fahmi. *Usus al-Taqaddum ʿinda Mufakiri al-Islam fi al-ʿAsr al-Hadith.* Beirut: Al-Muʾassasa al-ʿArabiyya li al-Dirasat wa al-Nashr, 1981.

Jaʿfar, Hashim Ahmad ʿAwad. *Al-Abʿad al-Siyasiyya li Mafhum al-Hakimiyya: Ruʾya Maʿrifiyya.* Herndon, Va.: International Institute of Islamic Thought, 1996.

al-Jahshiari. *Kitab al-Wuzaraʾ wa al-Kuttab.* Cairo: n.p., 1938.

Jalabi, Khalis. *Fi al-Naqd al-Dhati: Darura al-Naqd al-Dhati li al-Haraka al-Islamiyya.* Beirut: Muʾassasat al-Risala, 1985.

al-Janhani, al-Habib. "Al-Sahwa al-Islamiyya fi Bilad al-Sham: Mithal Surya." In *Al-Harakat al-Islamiyya al-Muʿasira fi al-Watan al-ʿArabi,* edited by Ismaʿil Sabri ʿAbd Allah. 2d ed. Beirut: Center for Arab Unity Studies, 1989.

Jansen, Johannes J. G. *The Dual Nature of Islamic Fundamentalism.* Ithaca, N.Y.: Cornell University Press, 1997.

———. *The Neglected Duty: The Creed of Sadat's Assassins and Islamic Resurgence in the Middle East.* New York: Macmillan, 1986.

al-Jassas, Abu Bakr. *Al-Ijmaʿ: Dirasa fi Fikratihi: Bab al-Ijtihad.* Edited and introduced by Zuhayr Kibi. Beirut: Dar al-Muntakhab, 1993.

Jawad, Haifaa. "Pan-Islamism in the Middle East: Prospects and Future." *Islamic Quarterly* 37, no. 3 (1993): 207–22.

al-Jawjari, Adil. *Al-Hizb al-Islami.* Cairo: Arabic Center for Journalism and Publications, 1993.

Jerichow, Anders, and J. B. Simonsen, eds. *Islam in a Changing World: Europe and the Middle East.* Richmond/Surrey: Curzon Press, 1997.

Juʿayt, Hisham. *Al-Fitna al-Kubra.* Beirut: Dar al-Taliʿa, 1991.

Kabuli, Niaz Faizi. *Democracy According to Islam.* Pittsburgh: Dorrance, 1994.

Kamali, Mohammad H. "The Approved and Disapproved Varieties of Raʾy (Personal Opinion) in Islam." *American Journal of Islamic Social Sciences* 7, no. 1 (1990): 39–65.

———. "Siyasah Sharʾiyah or the Policies of Islamic Government." *American Journal of Islamic Social Sciences* 6, no. 4 (1991): 225–37.

Kaplan, Lawrence, ed. *Fundamentalism in Comparative Perspective.* Amherst: University of Massachusetts Press, 1992.

Karabell, Zachary. "The Wrong Threat: The United States and Islamic Fundamentalism." *World Policy Journal* 12 (1995): 37–48.

Kawtharani, Wajih. *Al-Sulta wa al-Mujtama ʿwa al-ʿAmal al-Siyasi.* Beirut: Center for Arab Unity Studies, 1988.

———. *Mashruʿ al-Nuhud al-ʿArabi.* Beirut: Dar al-Taliʿa, 1995.

Kayali, Hasan. "Elections and the Electoral Process in the Ottoman Empire, 1876–1919." *International Journal of Middle Eastern Studies* 27 (1995): 265–86.

Keddie, Nikki R. *An Islamic Response to Imperialism: Political and Religious Writings of Sayyid Jamal ad-Din "al-Afghani."* Berkeley and Los Angeles: University of California Press, 1968.

———. "Pan-Islam as Protonationalism." *Journal of Modern History* 41, no. 1 (1969): 17–28.

Kedourie, Elie. *Afghani and Abduh.* London: Frank Cass, 1966.

Kelidar, Abbas. "States without Foundations: The Political Evolution of State and Society in the Arab East." *Journal of Contemporary History* 28, no. 2 (1993): 315–38.

Kepel, Gilles. *Muslim Extremism in Egypt: The Prophet and the Pharaoh.* Berkeley and Los Angeles: University of California Press, 1984.

Kerr, David A. "The Challenge of Islamic Fundamentalism for Christians." *International Bulletin of Missionary Research* 17 (1993): 169–73.

Kerr, Malcolm. *Islamic Reform: The Political and Legal Theories of Muhammad ʿAbduh and Rashid Rida.* Berkeley and Los Angeles: University of California Press, 1966.

Khadduri, Majid. *Political Trends in the Arab World: The Role of Ideas and Ideals in Politics.* Baltimore: Johns Hopkins University Press, 1970.

Khalafallah, Ahmad. *Al-Fikr al-Tarbawi lada Jamaʿat al-Ikhwan al-Muslimin.* Cairo: Maktabat Wahba, 1984.

———. *Al-Haraka al-Islamiyya fi al-Watan al-ʿArabi.* Beirut: Markaz Dirasat al-Wahda al-ʿArabiyya, 1989.

al-Khalidi, Mahmud. *Al-Dimuqratiyya al-Gharbiyya fi Dawʾ al-Shariʿa al-Islamiyya.* Amman: Maktabat al-Risala al-Haditha, 1986.

———. *Maʿalim al-Khilafa fi al-Fikr al-Siyasi al-Islami.* Beirut: Dar al-Jil, 1984.

Khalidi, Salah ʿAbd al-Fattah. *Nazariyyat al-Taswir al-Fanni ʿinda Sayyid Qutb.* Amman: Dar al-Furqan, 1983.

al-Kharbutli, ʿAli Husni. *Adwaʾ Jadida ʿala Tarikh al-ʿAlam al-Islami.* Cairo: Maʿhad al-Dirasat al-Islamiyya, 1976.

Khayrat, Muhammad. *Al-Marʾa fi al-Islam.* Cairo: Daʾirat al-Maʿarif al-Islamiyya, 1975.

Khoury, Raʾif. *Al-Fikr al-ʿArabi al-Hadith.* Beirut: Dar al-Makshuf, 1943.

al-Khudari, Muhammad. *Usul al-Fiqh.* Cairo: Al-Maktaba al-Tijariyya, 1969.

al-Khumayni, Ayatollah. *Al-Hukuma al Islamiyya.* Kuwait: n.p., n.d.

Khuri, Fuad. *Imams and Emirs: State, Religion and Sects in Islam.* London: Saqi Books, 1990.

Korbani, A. G. *The Political Dictionary of Modern Middle East.* Lanham, Md.: University Press of America, 1995.

Kramer, Gudrun. "Cross-Links and Double Talk? Islamist Movements in the Political Process." In *The Islamist Dilemma,* edited by Laura Guazzone, 39–67. Reading, England: Ithaca Press, 1995.

———. "Islamist Notions of Democracy." *Middle East Report* 23, no. 183 (1993): 2–8.

———. "Liberalization and Democracy in the Arab World." *Middle East Report* 22, no. 172 (1992): 22–25, 35.

Kramer, Martin. *Arab Awakening and Islamic Revival.* New Brunswick, N.J.: Rutgers University Press, 1996.

———. *Islam Assembled: The Advent of the Muslim Congresses.* New York: Columbia University Press, 1986.

———. "Islam in the New World Order." *Middle East Contemporary Survey 1991* 15 (1993): 172–205.

———. "Islam versus Democracy." *Commentary* 95 (1993): 35–42.

———. *Political Islam.* Beverly Hills, Calif.: Sage Publications, 1980.

———, ed. *Shi'ism, Resistance, and Revolution.* Boulder, Colo.: Westview Press, 1987.

Kucukcan, Talip. "The Nature of Islamic Resurgence in Near and Middle Eastern Muslim Societies." *Hamdard Islamicus* 14 (1991): 65–104.

Kurdi, Rajih 'Abd al-Hamid. *Al-Ittijah al-Salafi: Bayna al-Asala wa al-Ma'asara.* Amman: Dar 'Ammar, 1989.

Laffin, John. *Holy War, Islam Fights.* London: Grafton, 1988.

Lambton, Ann. *State and Government in Medieval Islam.* Oxford: Oxford University Press, 1981.

Landau, Jacob M. *The Politics of Pan-Islamism: Ideology and Organization.* Oxford: Oxford University Press, 1992.

Lapidus, Ira. *Contemporary Islamic Movements in Historical Perspective.* Berkeley and Los Angeles: University of California Press, 1983.

Laurent, Vitalien. *L'Arménie entre Byzance et l'Islam.* Paris: Centre nationale de la recherche scientifique, 1981.

Lawrence, Bruce. *Defenders of God: The Fundamentalist Revolt Against the Modern Age.* San Francisco: Harper and Row, 1989.

———. *Religious Fundamentalism.* Durham, N.C.: Duke University Press, 1993.

———. *Shattering the Myth: Islam beyond Violence.* Princeton: Princeton University Press, 1997.

Leach, Hugh. "Observing Islam from Within and Without." *Asian Affairs* 21 (1991).

Lee, Robert D. *Overcoming Tradition and Modernity: The Search for Islamic Authenticity.* Boulder, Colo.: Westview Press, 1997.

Leiden, Karl, ed. *The Conflict of Traditionalism and Modernism in the Muslim Middle East.* Austin: University of Texas Press, 1969.

Lemu, Aisha B. *Laxity, Moderation and Extremism in Islam.* Herndon, Va.: International Institute of Islamic Thought, 1993.

Lewis, Bernard. *Islam and the West.* New York: Oxford University Press, 1993.

———. "Islam and Liberal Democracy." *Atlantic Monthly,* February 1993, 89–94.

———. *The Jews of Islam.* Princeton: Princeton University Press, 1984.

———. *The Political Language of Islam.* Chicago: University of Chicago Press, 1988.

———. "The Roots of Muslim Rage: Why So Many Muslims Deeply Resent the West, and Why Bitterness Will Not Be Easily Mollified." *Atlantic Monthly,* September 1990, 47–57.

———. *The Shaping of the Modern Middle East.* New York: Oxford University Press, 1994.

Lowrie, Arthur L. "The Campaign Against Islam and American Foreign Policy." *Middle East Policy* 4, nos. 1 and 2 (1995): 210–19.

Al-Mabsut Li al-Sarkhasi. Cairo: Matba'at al-Sa'ada, n.d.

MacEain, Denis. *Islam in the Modern World.* London: Croom Helm, 1983.

Maddy-Weitzman, Bruce, and Efraim Inbar, eds. *Religious Radicalism in the Greater Middle East.* London: Frank Cass, 1977.

Mahfuz, Muhammad. *Alladhina Zulimu.* London: Riad el-Rayyes Books, 1988.

Mallat, Chibli. "On Islam and the Democracy." In *Islam and Public Law: Classical and Contemporary Studies.* London: Graham and Trotman, 1993.

———. *The Renewal of Islamic Thought.* Cambridge: Cambridge University Press, 1993.

al-Maqdisi, Abi Shama. *Al-Murshid al-Wajiz ila 'Ulum tata'allaq bi al-Kitab al-Aziz.* Beirut: Dar Sadir, 1975.

Maqsood, Ruqaiyyah Waris. *Islam: A Dictionary.* Cheltenham, England: Stanley Thornes, 1996.

Mardini, Zuhayr. *Al-Ladudan: Al-Wafd wa al-Ikhwan.* Beirut: Dar Iqra', 1984.

Marr, Phebe. "The Islamic Revival: Security Issues." *Mediterranean Quarterly* 3 (1992).

Marr, Phebe, and William Lewis, eds. *Riding the Tiger: The Middle East Challenge for the Cold War.* Boulder, Colo.: Westview Press, 1993.

Marshall, P. "Bookwatch: Islamic Activism in the Middle East." *International Socialism* 60 (1993): 157–71.

Marty, Martin E., and R. Scott Appleby, eds. *Accounting for Fundamentalisms: The Dynamic Character of Movements.* Chicago: University of Chicago Press, 1994.

———. *Fundamentalisms Comprehended.* Chicago: University of Chicago Press, 1995.

———. *Fundamentalisms and Society: Reclaiming the Sciences, the Family, and Education.* Chicago: University of Chicago Press, 1993.

———. *Fundamentalisms and the State: Remaking Polities, Economies, and Militance.* Chicago: University of Chicago Press, 1993.

———. *Fundamentalisms Observed.* Chicago: University of Chicago Press, 1991.

al-Mas'udi. *Muruj al-Dhahab.* Beirut: Dar al-Andalus, n.d.

al-Mawardi. *Adab al-Din wa al-Dunya.* Cairo: Al-Babi, 1955.

———. *Al-Ahkam al-Sultaniyya.* Cairo: Al-Watan, n.d.

al-Mawdudi, Abu al-A'la. *Huquq Ahl al-Dhimma fi al-Islam.* Beirut: Holy Koran Publishing House, c. 1984.

———. *The Islamic Way of Life.* Lahore: Markazi Maktaba Jama'at-i-Islami, n.d.

———. *Al-Jihad fi-Sabilillah.* Beirut: Mu'assasat al-Risala, 1983.

———. *Jihad in Islam.* Beirut: Holy Koran Publishing House, 1980.

———. *Mafahim Islamiyya.* Kuwait: Dar al-Qalam, 1977.

———. *Minhaj al-Inqilab al-Islami.* 3d ed. Beirut: Mu'assasat al-Risala, 1981.

———. *Nahnu wa al-Hadara al-Gharbiyya.* Beirut: Mu'assasat al-Risala, 1983.

———. *The Process of Islamic Revolution.* Lahore: Islamic Publications, 1977.

———. *A Short History of Revivalist Movements in Islam.* Lahore: Islamic Publications, 1963.

———. *Towards Understanding Islam.* 8th ed. Lahore: Islamic Publications, 1960.

al-Mawlawi, Faysal. "Al-Mar'a wa Tahadiyyat al-Mujtama' al-Mu'asir." *Al-Insan al-Ma'asir* 3 (1996): 45–52.

Mayer, Ann Elizabeth. *Islam and Human Rights: Traditions and Politics.* 2d ed. Boulder, Colo.: Westview Press, 1995.

Mazrui, Ali A. "Islam at War and Communism in Retreat: What Is the Connection?" In *The Gulf War and the New World Order: International Relations of the Middle East,* edited by Tareq Y. Ismael and Jacqueline S. Ismael, 502–20. Gainesville: University Press of Florida, 1994.

Menashri, David, ed. *The Iranian Revolution and the Muslim World.* Boulder, Colo.: Westview Press, 1990.

Mernissi, Fatima. *Beyond the Veil: Male-Female Dynamics in a Modern Muslim Society.* New York: John Wiley and Sons, 1975.

———. *Islam and Democracy: Fear of the Modern World.* New York: Addison-Wesley, 1992.

Miller, Judith. "The Challenge of Radical Islam." *Foreign Affairs* 72, no. 2 (1993): 43–55.

Mitchell, Richard. *The Society of the Muslim Brothers.* Oxford: Oxford University Press, 1964.

Mitri, Tariq. "Minorities in the Middle East." In *Religion and Citizenship in Europe and the Arab World,* edited by Jorgen S. Neilsen, 60–68. London: Grey Seal, 1992.

Mohamed, Yasin. "Islamization: A Revivalist Response to Modernity." *Muslim Education Quarterly* 10, no. 2 (1993): 12–23.

Monshipour, Mahmood, and C. G. Kukla. "Islam, Democracy and Human Rights: The Continuing Debate in the West." *Middle East Policy* 2, no. 2 (1994): 22–39.

Moore, Clement Henry. "Political Parties." In *Polity and Society in Contemporary North Africa*, edited by I. William Zartman and William Mark Habeeb, 42–67. Boulder, Colo.: Westview Press, 1993.

———. *Politics in North Africa: Algeria, Morocco, and Tunisia*. Boston: Little, Brown, 1970.

Mortimer, Edward. *Faith and Power: The Politics of Islam*. London: Faber and Faber, 1982.

Moten, Abdul Rashid. *Political Science: An Islamic Perspective*. New York: St. Martin's Press, 1996.

Mottahedeh, Roy. *The Mantle of the Prophet: Religion and Politics in Iran*. New York: Pantheon, 1988.

Moussalli, Ahmad S. "Discourses on Human Rights and Pluralistic Democracy." In *Islam in a Changing World*, edited by Anders Jerichow and J. B. Simonsen, 45–90. London: Curzon Press, 1997.

———. "Hasan al-Banna's Islamist Discourse on Constitutional Rule and Islamic State." *Journal of Islamic Study* 4, no. 2 (1993): 161–74.

———. "Hasan al-Turabi's Islamist Discourse on Democracy and *Shura*." *Middle Eastern Studies* 30, no. 1 (1994): 52–63.

———. *Historical Dictionary of Islamic Fundamentalist Movements in the Arab World, Iran, and Turkey*. Metuchen, N.J: Scarecrow Press, 1999.

———. "Islamism and Modernity or Modernization of Islam." In *The Future of Cosmopolitanism in the Middle East*, edited by R. Meijer, 1–18. Amsterdam: Cultural Foundation, University of Amsterdam, 1997.

———. "Islamist Perspectives of Regime Political Response: The Case of Lebanon and Palestine." *Arab Studies Quarterly* (Summer 1996): 55–65.

———. "Modern Islamic Fundamentalist Discourses on Civil Society, Pluralism and Democracy." In *Civil Society in the Middle East*, edited by Augustus Richard Norton, 79–119. Leiden: E. J. Brill, 1995.

———. "Modern Islamic Fundamentalist Discourses on Civil Society, Pluralism and Democracy." In *Toward Civil Society in the Middle East?: A Primer*, edited by Jillian Schwedler, 35–36. Boulder, Colo.: Lynne Rienner, 1995.

———. *Radical Islamic Fundamentalism: The Ideological and Political Discourse of Sayyid Qutb*. Beirut: American University of Beirut, 1992; Syracuse: Syracuse University Press, 1993.

———. "Sayyid Qutb's View of Knowledge." *American Journal of Islamic Social Sciences* 7, no. 3 (1990): 315–34.

———. *Al-Usuliyya al-Islamiyya wa al-Nizam al-'Alami*. Beirut: Center for Strategic Studies, 1992.

————, ed. *Islamic Fundamentalism: Myths and Realities*. Reading, England: Ithaca Press, 1998.

al-Mudarrisi, Hadi. *Al-Islam wa al-Idiolojiyyat al-Munawi'a ila Ayn*. Beirut: Mu'assasat al-Balagh, 1987.

Mufti, Muhammad, and Sami al-Waqil. *Al-Nazariyya al-Siyasiyya al-Islamiyya fi Huquq al-Insan al-Shar'iyya*. Qatar: Al-Mahakim al-Shar'iyya, 1990.

Muhafaza, 'Ali. *Al-Itijahat al-Fikriyya 'inda al-Arab fi 'Asr al-Nahda, 1798–1914*. Beirut: Al-Ahliyya li al-Nashr, 1978.

Muhammad, Muhsin. *Man Qatala Hasan al-Banna*. Cairo: Dar al-Shuruq, 1987.

al-Muhasibi, al-Harith Ibn Asad. *Al-'Aql wa Fahm al-Qur'an*. 2d ed. Beirut: n.p., 1978.

Munson, Henry, Jr. *Islam and Revolution in the Middle East*. New Haven: Yale University Press, 1988.

Murad, Ibrahim. "Hawla Tajdid Mafhum al-Nahda fi al-Fikr al-'Arabi." *Al-Fikr al-'Arabi* 6, nos. 39–40 (1985).

Murwwa, Husayn. *Al-Naza'at al-Madiyya fi al-Falsafa al-'Arabiyya al-Islamiyya*. Beirut: Dar al-Farabi, 1991.

Musa, Kaval. "Politique et théologie: L'Impact sur les mouvements islamistes." *Cahiers de l'Orient* 34 (1994): 9–32.

Musa, Sulayman. *Al-Haraka al-'Arabiyya*. Beirut: Dar al-Nahar li al-Nashr, 1977.

al-Musawi, Muhsin. *Dawlat al-Rasul*. Beirut: Dar al-Bayan al-'Arabi, 1990.

Mustapha, Shukri. "Al-Nas al-Kamil." In *Al-Nabiy al-Musallah: Al-Rafidun*, edited by Rif'at Sayyid Ahmad, 53–110. London: Riad el-Rayyes Books, 1991.

Mutahhari, Mohammad S. *Jihad: The Holy War of Islam and Its Legitimacy in the Qur'an*. Tehran: Islamic Propagation Organization, 1985.

Mutalib, H. "Islamic Resurgence and the Twenty-First Century: Redefining the Old Agendas in a New Age." *American Journal of Islamic Social Sciences* 13, no. 1 (1996): 88–99.

al-Mutalib, Hussein, and Taj ul-Islam Hashmi. *Islam, Muslims, and the Modern State: Case Studies of Muslims in Thirteen Countries*. New York: St. Martin's Press, 1994.

al-Nabahani, Taqiy al-Din. *Nizam al-Hukm*. Jerusalem: Matba'at al-Thiryan, 1952.

————. *Al-Takatul al-Hizbi*. 2d ed. Jerusalem: n.p., 1953.

Nacos, B. L. *Terrorism and the Media: From the Iran Hostage Crisis to the World Trade Center Bombing*. New York: Columbia University Press, 1994.

al-Nadawi, Abu al-Hasan. *Madha Khasira al-'Alam bi-Inhitat al-Muslimin*. 8th ed. Beirut: Dar al-Kitab al-Lubnani, 1984.

Nadvi, Syed Habib ul Huque. *Islamic Fundamentalism: A Theology of Liberation and Renaissance*. Durban: Academia, 1995.

Nafi, Basheer. "Contemporary Islamic Political Forces: Traditional or Modern." *Arab Review* 3, no. 1 (1994): 29–33.

an-Na'im, Abullahi Ahmad. *Toward an Islamic Reformation: Civil Liberties,*

Human Rights, and International Law. Syracuse: Syracuse University Press, 1990.

al-Najjar, ʿAbd al-Majid. *Dawr Hurriyyat al-Raʾy fi al-Wahda al-Fikriyya bayna al-Muslimin.* Herndon, Va.: International Institute of Islamic Thought, 1992.

———. "Mafhum al-Taqaddum ʿinda al-Mufakkirin al-ʿArab fi ʿAsr al-Nahda." *Al-Fikr al-ʿArabi,* 6, nos. 39–40 (1985).

al-Najjar, Shukri. "Mafhum al-Taqaddum ʿinda al-Mufakkirin al-ʿArab fi ʿAsr al-Nahda." *Al-Fikr al-ʿArabi* 6, nos. 39–40 (1985).

Nasr, Seyyed Hossein. *Ideals and Realities of Islam.* London: Unwin Hyman, 1988.

———. *Traditional Islam in the Modern World.* London: KPI, 1987.

Nasr, Seyyed Hossein, Hamid Dabashi, and Seyyed Vali Reza Nasr, eds. *Expectation of the Millennium: Shiʿism in History.* Albany: State University of New York Press, 1989.

———, eds. *Shiʿism: Doctrines, Thought, and Spirituality.* Albany: State University of New York Press, 1988.

Nasr, Seyyed Vali Reza. *Mawdudi and the Making of Islamic Revivalism.* Oxford: Oxford University Press, 1996.

———. "Religious Modernism in the Arab World, India and Iran: The Perils and Prospects of a Discourse." *Muslim World* 83, no. 1 (1993): 20–47.

Nettler, Ronald, and Suha Taji-Farouki, eds. *Muslim-Jewish Encounters: Intellectual Traditions and Modern Politics.* Reading, England: Harwood, 1997.

Niblock, Tim, and Emma Murphy. *Economic and Political Liberalism in the Middle East.* London: British Academic Press, 1993.

Nielsen, J. S. "Will Religious Fundamentalism Become Increasingly Violent?" *International Journal on Group Rights* 2 (1994): 197–209.

Nielsen, Niels C. *Fundamentalism, Mythos, and World Religions.* Albany: State University of New York Press, 1993.

Nisrin, Taslima. "On Islamic Fundamentalism." *Humanist* 56 (1996): 24–27.

Norton, Augustus Richard. "The Challenge of Inclusion in the Middle East." *Current History* 94 (1995): 1–6.

———. *Civil Society in the Middle East.* Leiden: E. J. Brill, 1995.

———. "The Future of Civil Society in the Middle East." *Middle East Journal* 47, no. 2 (1993): 205–16.

O'Ballance, Edgar. *Islamic Fundamentalist Terrorism, 1979–95: The Iranian Connection.* New York: New York University Press, 1996.

Ogutco, Mehmet. "Islam and the West: Can Turkey Bridge the Gap?" *Futures* 26 (1994): 811–29.

Paris, Jonathan S. "When to Worry in the Middle East." *Orbis* 37 (Fall 1993): 545–53.

Peretz, Don. *Islam: Legacy of the Past, Challenge of the Future.* New York: New Horizon Press, 1984.

Peters, F. E. *Allah's Commonwealth.* New York: Simon and Schuster, 1973.

Peters, Rudolph. *Jihad in Classical and Modern Islam*. Princeton: Princeton University Press, 1995.

Pickthall, Mohammed Marmaduke. *The Meaning of the Glorious Koran*. New York: Knopf, 1930. Reprint, New York: Penguin, 1997.

Pieterse, J. N. "Fundamentalism Discourses: Enemy Images." *Women Against Fundamentalism Journal* 1, no. 5 (1994): 2–6.

Pipes, Daniel. "Islam's Intramural Struggle." *National Interest* 35 (1994): 84–86.

———. *In the Path of God: Islam and Political Power*. New York: Basic Books, 1983.

Piscatori, James. "Accounting for Islamic Fundamentalisms." In *Accounting for Fundamentalisms*, edited by Martin E. Marty and R. Scott Appleby, 361–73. Chicago: University of Chicago Press, 1994.

———. *Islam in a World of Nation-States*. Cambridge: Cambridge University Press, 1986.

———. *Islam in the Political Process*. New York: Cambridge University Press, 1983.

———, ed. *Islamic Fundamentalisms and the Gulf Crisis*. Chicago: University of Chicago Press, 1991.

Porteous, Tom. "The Islamisation of Modernity." *Middle East* 220 (February 1993): 19–22.

al-Qaddumi, Marwan. "Al-Siyasa al-Umawiyya tuja Ahl al-Dhimma." *Majallat al-Daʿwa al-Islamiyya* 5 (1988): 379–88.

Al-Qamus al-Muhit.

al-Qaradawi, Yusuf. *Awlawiyyat al-Haraka al-Islamiyya*. 13th ed. Beirut: Muʾassasat al-Risala, 1992.

———. *Bayinat al-Hal al-Islami*. Beirut: Muʾassasat al-Risala, n.d.

———. *Ghayr al-Muslimin*. 2d ed. Beirut: Muʾassasat al-Risala, 1983.

———. *Al-Hal al-Islami Farida wa Darura*. Cairo: Maktabat Wahba, 1977.

———. *Khasaʾis al-ʿAmal fi al-Islam*. 2d ed. Beirut: Muʾassasat al-Risala, 1983.

———. *Al-Sahwa al-Islamiyya bayna al-Juhud wa al-Tatarruf*. Qatar: Matbaʿat al-Dawha al-Haditha, 1982.

Qarqar, Muhammad. *Dawr al-Haraka al-Islamiyya fi Tasfiyyat al-Iqtaʿ*. Kuwait: Dar al-Buhuth al-ʿIlmiyya, 1980.

Qasim, Qasim ʿAbdu. *Al-Yahud fi Misr min al-Fatʾh al-ʿArabi hata al-Ghazu al-ʿUthmani*. Cairo: Dar al-Fikr li al-Dirasat wa al-Tawziʿ, 1987.

Qutb, Sayyid. *Al-ʿAdala al-Ijtimaʿiyya fi al-Islam*. Cairo: Dar al-Shuruq, c. 1980.

———. *Fi al-Tarikh: Fikra wa-Minhaj*. Cairo: Dar al-Shuruq, 1974.

———. *Fiqh al-Daʿwa*. Beirut: Muʾassasat al-Risala, 1970.

———. *Fi Zilal al-Qurʾan*. Beirut: Dar al-Shuruq, n.d.

———. *Hadha al-Din*. Cairo: Maktabat Wahba, n.d.

———. *In the Shades of the Qurʾan*. London: MWH, 1979.

———. *Al-Islam wa-Mushkilat al-Hadara*. Beirut: Dar al-Shuruq, c. 1983.

———. *Khasa'is al-Tasawwur al-Islami wa Muqawwimatih*. Vol. 1. Cairo: Issa al-Halabi, n.d.

———. "Limadha A'damuni." In *Al-Muslimin*, 34–35. Saudi Arabia, 1985.

———. *Ma'alim fi al-Tariq*. Beirut: Dar al-Shuruq, 1980.

———. *Ma'rakat al-Islam wa al-Ra'simaliyya*. Beirut: Dar al-Shuruq, 1975.

———. *Al-Mustaqbal li Hadha al-Din*. Cairo: Maktabat Wahba, 1965.

———. *Nahwa Mujtama' Islami*. Beirut: Dar al-Shuruq, 1983.

———. *Al-Salam al-'Alami wa al-Islam*. Beirut: Dar al-Shuruq, 1983.

———. *Tafsir Ayat al-Riba*. Beirut: Dar al-Shuruq, 1970.

———. *Tafsir Surat al-Shura*. Beirut: Dar al-Shuruq, n.d.

al-Rahhal, Salim. "Amrica wa Misr wa al-Haraka al-Islamiyya." In *Al-Nabiy al-Musallah: Al-Rafidun*, edited by Rif'at Sayyid Ahmad, 179–92. London: Riad el-Rayyes Books, 1990.

Rahman, Fazlur. *Islam*. New York: Holt, Rinehart and Winston, 1966.

———. *Islam and Modernity: The Transformation of an Intellectual Tradition*. Chicago: University of Chicago Press, 1982.

Ramadan, 'Abd al-Aziz. *Al-Ikhwan al-Muslimin wa al-Tanzim al-Sirri*. Cairo: Maktabat Roz al-Yusuf, 1982.

Ramazani, R. K. "Shi'ism in the Persian Gulf." In *Shi'ism and Social Protest*, edited by Juan R. I. Cole and Nikki R. Keddie, 30–53. New Haven: Yale University Press, 1986.

Rapoport, David C. "Comparing Militant Fundamentalist Movements and Groups." In *Fundamentalisms and the State*, edited by Martin E. Marty and R. Scott Appleby, 429–61. Chicago: University of Chicago Press, 1993.

al-Rayyis, Muhammad Diya' al-Din. *Al-Nazariyyat al-Siyasiyya al-Islamiyya*. Cairo: Maktabat al-Anglo al-Misriyya, 1957.

Regan, D. "Islamic Resurgence: Characteristics, Causes, Consequences and Implications." *Journal of Political and Military Sociology* 21, no. 2 (1993): 259–66.

Richards, Alan, and John Waterbury. *A Political Economy of the Middle East*. Boulder, Colo.: Westview Press, 1990.

Rida, Muhammad Rashid. *Tafsir al-Manar*. Cairo: Matba'at al-Manar, A.H. 1330.

Rizq, Jabir. *Al-Dawla wa al-Siyasa fi Fikr Hasan al-Banna*. Mansûra, Egypt: Dar al-Wafa, 1985.

Roberson, B. A. "Islam and Europe: An Enigma of a Myth?" *Middle East Journal*, 48, no. 2 (1994): 288–308.

Roff, William R. "Islamic Movements: One or Many?" In *Islam and the Political Economy of Meaning*, 31–52. Berkeley and Los Angeles: University of California Press, 1987.

———, ed. *Islam and the Political Economy of Meaning: Comparative Studies of Muslim Discourse*. London: Croom Helm; Berkeley and Los Angeles: University of California Press, 1987.

Rondot, Pierre. *The Militant Radical Current in the Muslim Community*. Brussels: Pro Mundi Vita, 1982.

Rosenthal, Franz. *The Muslim Concept of Freedom Prior to the Nineteenth Century*. Leiden: E. J. Brill, 1960.

Roy, Olivier. *The Failure of Political Islam*. London: I. B. Tauris, 1994.

Rubin, Barry. *Islamic Fundamentalism in Egyptian Politics*. New York: St. Martin's Press, 1990.

Ruedy, John, ed. *Islamism and Secularism in North Africa*. New York: St. Martin's Press, 1994.

Sachedina, Abdulaziz A. *Islamic Messianism: The Idea of the Mahdi in Twelver Shi'ism*. Albany: State University of New York Press, 1981.

Sadiq, Hasan. *Al-Firaq al-Islamiyya*. Cairo: Maktabat Madbuli, 1991.

Sadowski, Yahya. "The New Orientalism and the Democracy Debate." *Middle East Report* 183 (1993): 14–21, 40.

Safi, Louay M. *The Challenge of Modernity: The Quest for Authenticity in the Arab World*. Lanham, Md.: University Press of America, 1994.

Said, Abdul Aziz. "Islamic Fundamentalism and the West." *Mediterranean Quarterly* 3 (1992): 21–36.

al-Sa'id, Rif'at. *Hasan al-Banna, Ma'assis Harakat al-Ikhwan al-Muslimin*. Beirut: Dar al-Tali'a, 1980.

al-Sa'id, Rif'at. Ed. *Qadaya Fikriyya: Al-Islam al-Siyasi*. Cairo: Al-Thaqafa al-Jadida, 1989.

Saif, Walid. "Human Rights and Islamic Revivalism." *Islam and Christian-Muslim Relations* 5, no. 1 (1994): 57–65.

Salame, Ghassan. "Islam and the West." *Foreign Policy* 90 (1993): 22–37.

———, ed. *Democracy without Democrats? The Renewal of Politics in the Muslim World*. London: I. B. Tauris, 1994.

Sami', Hasan. *Azmat al-Hurriyya al-Siyasiyya fi al-Watan al-'Arabi*. Cairo: Al-Zahra' li al-I'lam al-'Arabi, 1988.

al-Sammak, Muhammad. "Al-Ra'y al-'Am." *Al-Ijtihad* 2, no. 7 (1990): 317–29.

al-Sanhuri, 'Abd al-Razzaq. *Fiqh al-Khilafa wa Tatawwuriha*. Cairo: Al-Hay'a al-Misriyya al-'Ama, 1989.

Saqr, A. *Islamic Fundamentalism*. Chicago: Kazi Publications, 1987.

Sara, Fayiz. *Al-Haraka al-Islamiyya fi al-Magrib al-'Arabi*. Beirut: Markaz al-Dirasat al-Istratijiyya, 1995.

Satloff, R. B, ed. *The Politics of Change in Saudi Arabia*. Boulder, Colo.: Westview Press, 1993.

al-Sayyid, Ridwan. "Contemporary Muslim Thought and Human Rights." *Islamochristiana* (Rome: Pontificio Istituto di Studi Arabi e d'Islamistica) 21 (1995): 27–41.

———. *Mafahim al-Jama'a fi al-Islam*. Beirut: Dar al-Tanwir, 1984.

———. "Mas'alat al-Shura." *Al-Ijtihad* 6, no. 25 (1994): 29–47.

———. *Siyasat al-Islam al-Ma'asir*. Beirut: Dar al-Kitab al-'Arabi, 1997.

———. *Al-Umma wa al-Jama'a wa al-Sulta*. Beirut: Dar Iqra', 1984.

Schliefer, S. Abdullah. "Jihad: Modernist Apologies, Modern Apologetics." *Islamic Quarterly* 28, no. 1 (1984): 25–46.

Schmid, E. "Turkey: Rising Power of Islamic Fundamentalism." *Women Against Fundamentalism Journal* 1, no. 6 (1994): 57–67.

Schwedler, Jillian, ed. *Toward Civil Society in the Middle East? A Primer.* Boulder, Colo.: Lynne Rienner, 1996.

Seddon, David. "Riot and Rebellion in North Africa." In *Power and Stability in the Middle East,* edited by Berch Berberoglu. London: Zed Books, 1989.

Semaan, Wanis A. "The Double-Edged Challenge of Islamic Fundamentalism." *Mission Studies* 11, no. 2 (1994): 173–80.

al-Shabani, Muhammad 'Abd Allah. *Nizam al-Hukm wa al-Idara fi al-Dawla al-Islamiyya.* Cairo: 'Alam al-Kutub, n.d.

Shafiq, Munir. "Awlawiyyat Amam al-Ijtihad wa al-Tajdid." In *Al-Ijtihad wa Tajdid fi al-Fikr al-Islami al-Ma'asir.* Valletta/Malta: Center for the Studies of the Muslim World, 1991.

———. *Al-Fikr al-Islami al-Ma'asir wa al-Tahaddiyat.* Beirut: Al-Nashr, 1991.

———. *Al-Islam fi Ma'rakat al-Hadara.* Beirut: Al-Nashr, 1991.

———. *Al-Islam wa Muwajahat al-Dawla al-Haditha.* 3d ed. Beirut: Al-Nashr, 1992.

———. *Al-Nizam al-Dawli al-Jadid wa Khiyar al-Muwajaha.* Beirut: Al-Nashr, 1992.

Shahin, Emad. *Political Ascent: Contemporary Islamic Movements in North Africa.* Boulder, Colo.: Westview Press, 1997.

al-Shahristani. *Al-Milal wa al-Nihal.* Beirut: Dar al-Ma'rifa, 1961.

Shams al-Din, Muhammad Mahdi. *Fi al-Ijtima' al-Siyasi al-Islami.* Beirut: Al-Mu'assasa al-Dawliyya li al-Dirasat wa al-Nashr, 1992.

Sharaf, Muhammad Jalal. *Nash'at al-Fikr al-Siyasi wa-Tatawwurihi fi al-Islam.* 2d. ed. Beirut: Dar al-Nahda, 1986.

Sharaf al-Din, Rislan. "Al-Din wa al-Ahzab al-Siyasiyya al-Diniyya." In *Al-Din fi al-Mujtama' al-'Arabi,* 171–88. Beirut: Center for Arab Unity Studies, 1990.

al-Sharfi, 'Abd al-Majid. "Mushkilat al-Hukm fi al-Fikr al-Islami al-Hadith." *Al-Ijtihad* 4, no. 14 (1992): 69–93.

Shari'ati, Ali. *Marxism and Other Western Fallacies.* Berkeley: Mizan Press, 1980.

———. *On the Sociology of Islam.* Berkeley: Mizan Press, 1979.

al-Shatibi. *Al-Muwafaqat fi Usul al-Shari'a.* Beirut: Dar al-Ma'rifa, 1982.

al-Shawi, Muhammad Tawfiq. *Fiqh al-Hukuma al-Islamiyya bayna al-Shi'a wa al-Sunna.* Ann Arbor: New Era Publications, 1995.

al-Shawkani. *Irshad al-Fuhul.* Cairo: Matba'at al-Sa'ada, A.H. 1327.

Sidahmed, Abdel Salam, and Anoushiravan Ehteshami, eds. *Islamic Fundamentalism.* Boulder, Colo.: Westview Press, 1996.

Sid-Ahmed, Mohamed. "Cybernetic Colonialism and the Moral Search." *New Perspectives Quarterly* 11, no. 2 (1994): 15–19.

Siddiq, 'Ali. *Al-Ikhwan al-Muslimin bayna Irhab Faruq wa 'Abd al-Nasir.* Cairo: Dar al-I'tisam, 1987.

Sihbudi, Riza. "Islamic 'Fundamentalism' and Democratization in the Middle East." *Iranian Journal of International Affairs* 6 (1994): 119–28.

Silverburg, Sanford R. *Middle East Bibliography.* Metuchen, N.J.: Scarecrow Press, 1992.

Sirriyya, Salih. "Risalat al-Iman." In *Al-Nabiy al-Musallah: Al-Rafidun,* edited by Rif'at Sayyid Ahmad, 31–52. London: Riad el-Rayyes Books, 1990.

Sisi, Abbas. *Hasan al-Banna: Mawqif fi al-Da'wa wa al-Tarbiyya.* Alexandria: Dar al-Da'wa, 1981.

Sisk, Timothy. *Islam and Democracy.* Washington, D.C.: United States Peace Institute Press, 1992.

Sivan, Emmanuel. *Interpretations of Islam: Past and Present.* Princeton, N.J.: Darwin Press, 1985.

———. *Islamic Fundamentalism and Anti-Semitism.* Jerusalem: Hebrew University, 1985.

———. *Radical Islam: Medieval Theology and Modern Politics.* New Haven: Yale University Press, 1990.

Sivan, Emmanuel, and Menachem Friedman, eds. *Religious Radicalism and Politics in the Middle East.* Albany: State University of New York Press, 1990.

Smith, Wilfred C. *Islam in Modern History.* Princeton: Princeton University Press, 1957.

Solh, Ragid. "Islamist Attitudes towards Democracy: A Review of the Ideas of Al-Ghazali, Al-Turabi and 'Amara." *British Journal of Middle Eastern Studies* 20 (1993): 57–63.

Spencer, William. *Islamic Fundamentalism in the Modern World.* Brookfield, Conn.: Millbrook Press, 1995.

"Statement of the Muslim Brotherhood on the Role of Muslim Women in Islamic Society and Its Stand on the Women's Rights to Vote, Be Elected, and Occupy Public and Governmental Posts, and Work in General." *Encounter* 1, no. 3 (1995): 85–89.

Stowasser, Barbara. "Women's Issues in Modern Islamic Thought." In *Arab Women: Old Boundaries, New Frontiers,* edited by J. E. Tucker. Bloomington: Indiana University Press, 1993.

———, ed. *The Islamic Impulse.* Washington, D.C.: Georgetown University, Center for Contemporary Arab Studies, 1987.

Subhi, Ahmad M. *Fi 'Ilm al-Kalam.* Beirut: Dar al-Nahda al-'Arabiyya, 1985.

———. *Nazariyyat al-Imama lada al-Shi'a al-Ithnay 'Ashariyya.* Cairo: Dar al-Ma'rifa, 1969.

Sunan al-Tirmizi. Cairo: Dar al-Fikr, c. 1978.

al-Suyuti. *Tarikh al-Khulafa'.* Beirut: Dar al-Qalam, 1986.

al-Tabari. *Jami' al-Bayan.* 2d ed. Cairo: Sharikat Mustafa al-Halabi, 1954.

———. *Tafsir.* 4th ed. Beirut: Dar al-Ma'rifa, 1986.

————. *Tarikh*. Cairo: Al-Maktaba al-Husayniyy, n.d.

al-Tabataba'i, Muhammad Husayn. *Nizariyyat al-Siyasa wa al-Hukm fi al-Islam*. Beirut: Al-Dar al-Islamiyya, 1982.

Tachau, Frank, ed. *Political Parties of the Middle East and North Africa*. Westport, Conn.: Greenwood Press, 1994.

Taheri, Amir. *Holy Terror: The Inside Story of Islamic Terrorism*. London: Hutchinson, 1987.

Taji-Farouki, Suha. "A Case-Study in Contemporary Political Islam and the Palestine Question: The Perspective of Hizb al-Tahrir." *Studies in Muslim-Jewish Relations* 2 (1995): 35–58.

————. "From Madrid to Washington: Palestinian Islamist Response to Israeli-Palestinian Peace Settlement." *World Faiths Encounter* 9 (1994): 49–58.

————. *A Fundamental Quest: Hizb al-Tahrir and the Search for the Islamic Caliphate*. London: Grey Seal, 1996.

————. "Hizb al-Tahrir." In *The Oxford Encyclopedia of the Modern Islamic World*, edited by John L. Esposito, 125–27. New York: Oxford University Press, 1995.

————. "Islamic Discourse and Modern Political Methods: An Analysis of al-Nabahani's Reading of the Canonical Text Sources of Islam." *American Journal of Islamic Social Sciences* 11, no. 3 (1994): 365–93.

————. "Islamic State-Theories and Contemporary Realities." In *Islamic Fundamentalism*, edited by Abdel Salam Sidahmed and Anoushirivan Ehteshami, 35–50. Boulder, Colo.: Westview Press, 1995.

————. "Nazariyyat al-Dawla al-Islamiyya wa al-Waqiʿ al-Maʿasir: Hala Dirasiyya." *Qira'at Siyasiyya* 5 (1995): 83–99

Tamadonfar, Mehran. *The Islamic Polity and Political Leadership: Fundamentalism, Sectarianism and Pragmatism*. Boulder, Colo.: Westview Press, 1989.

Tamimi, Azzam, ed. *Power-Sharing Islam?* London: Liberty for Muslim World Publications, 1993.

Taylor, Alan R. *The Islamic Question in Middle East Politics*. Boulder, Colo.: Westview Press, 1988.

Taylor, P. *States of Terror: Democracy and Political Violence*. London: Penguin and BBC Books, 1993.

Tessler, Mark, and J. Jesse. "Gender and Support for Islamist Movements: Evidence from Egypt, Kuwait and Palestine." *Muslim World* 86, no. 2 (1996): 200–28.

Tetreault, Mary Ann. "Gulf Winds: Inclement Political Weather in the Arabian Peninsula." *Current History* 95 (1996): 23–27.

Tibi, Bassam. *The Challenge of Fundamentalism: Political Islam and the New World Disorder*. Berkeley and Los Angeles: University of California Press, 1998.

————. *The Crisis of Modern Islam in a Preindustrial Culture in the Scientific-*

Technological Age. Translated by Judith von Sivers. Salt Lake City: University of Utah Press, 1988.

———. *Religious Fundamentalism and Ethnicity in the Crisis of the Nation-State in the Middle East: Subordinate Islamic and Pan-Arab Identities and Subordinate Islamic and Sectarian Identities.* Berkeley: University of California Press, 1992.

———. "The Renewed Role of Islam in the Political and Social Development of the Middle East." *Middle East Journal* 37, no. 1 (1983): 3–13.

al-Tilmisani, ʿUmar. "An Interview." In *Al-Nabiy al-Musallah: Al-Rafidun,* edited by Rifʿat Sayyid Ahmad, 207–09. London: Riad el-Rayyes Books, 1990.

Tizini, Tayyib. *Mashruʿ Ruʾya Jadid li al-Fikr al-ʿArabi mundhu Bidayatihi hatta al-Marhala al-Muʿasira.* Vol. 1, *Min al-Turath ila al-Thawra,* and vol. 2, *Al-Fikr al-ʿArabi fi Bawakirih wa Afaqih.* Damascus: Dar Dimashq li al-Tabʿ wa al-Nashr, 1979–82.

al-Turabi, Hasan. "Awlawiyyat al-Tayyar al-Islamiyya." *Minbar al-Sharq* 1 (1992).

———. *Al-Haraka al-Islamiyya fi al-Sudan.* Kuwait: Dar al-Qalam, 1988.

———. *Al-Iman wa Atharuhu fi Hayat al-Insan.* Jidda: Al-Dar al-Suʿudiyya li al-Nashr wa al-Tawziʿ, 1984.

———. *Al-Islam, Hiwarat fi al-Dimuqratiyya, al-Dawla, al-Gharb.* Beirut: Dar al-Jadid, 1995.

———. "The Islamic Awakening's New Wave." *New Perspectives Quarterly* 10, no. 3 (1993): 42–45.

———. *Al-Itijah al-Islami Yuqadim al-Marʾa bayna Taʿalim al-Din wa Taqalid al-Mujtamaʿ.* Jidda: Al-Dar al-Suʿudiyya li al-Nashr wa al-Tawziʿ, 1984.

———. *Qadaya al-Hurriyya wa al-Wahda, al-Shura wa al-Dimuqratiyya, al-Din wa al-Fan.* Jidda: Al-Dar al-Suʿudiyya li al-Nashr wa al-Tawziʿ, 1987.

———. *Al-Salat ʿImad al-Din.* Beirut: Dar al-Qalam, 1971.

———. "Al-Shura wa al-Dimuqratiyya: Ishkalat al-Mustala wa al-Mafhum." *Al-Mustaqbal al-ʿArabi* 75 (1985), 4–22.

———. *Tajdid al-Fikr al-Islami.* 2nd ed. Jidda: Al-Dar al-Suʿudiyya li al-Nashr wa al-Tawziʿ, 1987.

———. *Tajdid Usul al-Fiqh.* Jidda: Al-Dar al-Suʿudiyya li al-Nashr wa al-Tawziʿ, 1984.

———. "Utruhat al-Haraka al-Islamiyya fi Majal al-Hiwar Maʿa al-Gharb." *Shuʾun al-Awsat* 36 (1994), 70–92.

Turner, Bryan. *Orientalism, Postmodernism, and Globalism.* London and New York: Routledge, 1994.

al-ʿUnf al-Usuli: Al-Ibdaʿ min Nawafiz Jahannam. London: Riad el-Rayyes Books, 1995.

al-ʿUnf al-Usuli: Muwajahat al-Sayf wa al-Qalam. London: Riad el-Rayyes Books, 1995.

al-'Unf al-Usuli: Nuwwab al-Ard wa al-Sama'. London: Riad el-Rayyes Books, 1995.

'Uthman, Fathi. *Al-Salafiyya fi al-Mujtama'at al-Mu'asira.* Cairo: Dar Afaq al-Ghad, 1982.

Van Koningsveld, P. S. "Muslim Slaves and Captives in Western Europe during the Late Middle Ages." *Islam and Christian-Muslim Relations* 6, no. 1 (1995): 5–23.

Voll, John. *The Contemporary Islamic Revival: A Critical Survey and Bibliography.* Westport, Conn.: Greenwood Press, 1991.

———. *Islam: Continuity and Change in the Modern World.* 2d ed. Syracuse: Syracuse University Press, 1994.

Von Grunebaum, Gustave E. *Modern Islam: The Search for Cultural Identity.* 1962. Westport, Conn.: Greenwood Press, 1983.

Waal, A. "Rethinking Ethiopia." In *Conflict and Peace in the Horn of Africa: Federalism and Its Alternatives,* edited by Peter Woodward and Murray Forsyth. Aldershot, England: Dartmouth, 1994.

Waterbury, John. "Democracy without Democrats? The Potential for Political Liberalization in the Middle East." In *Democracy without Democrats?,* edited by Ghassan Salame, 23–47. London: I. B. Tauris, 1994.

"Wathiqat Muhakamat al-Nizam al-Masri." In *Al-Nabiy al-Musallah: Al-Tha 'irun,* edited by Rif'at Sayyid Ahmad, 273–83. London: Riad el-Rayyes Books, 1991.

Watt, W[illiam] Montgomery. "Islamic Fundamentalism." *Studia Missionalia* 41 (1992): 241–52.

———. *Islamic Fundamentalism and Modernity.* London: Routledge, 1988.

———. *Islamic Political Thought.* Edinburgh: Edinburgh University Press, 1968.

———. *Muhammad at Mecca.* Oxford: Clarendon Press, 1965.

———. *Muhammad at the Medina.* Oxford: Clarendon Press, 1966.

Weiner, Myron, and Ali Banuazizi, eds. *The Politics of Social Transformation in Afghanistan, Iran and Pakistan.* Syracuse: Syracuse University Press, 1994.

"Will Democracy Survive in Egypt?" *Reader's Digest* 131, no. 788 (1987): 149.

Wright, Robin. "Islam's New Political Face." *Current History* 90 (1991): 25–30.

———. *Sacred Rage: The Crusade of Modern Islam.* New York: Simon and Schuster, 1985.

Yakan, Fathi. *Abjadiyyat al-Tasawwur al-Haraki li al-'Amal al-Islami.* 11th ed. Beirut: Mu'assasat al-Risala, 1993.

———. *Harakat wa Madhahib fi Mizan al-Islam.* 10th ed. Beirut: Mu'assasat al-Risala, 1992.

———. *Al-Mawsu'a al-Harakiyya.* Amman: Dar al-Bashir, 1983.

———. *Nahwa Haraka Islamiyya 'Alamiyya.* 10th ed. Beirut: Mu'assasat al-Risala, 1993.

Yamut, Shafiq. *Ahl al-Dhimma.* Beirut: Al-Sharika al-'Alamiyya li al-Kitab, 1991.

Yanun, Labib. *Al-Hayat al-Hizbiyya fir Misr.* Cairo: Maktabat al-Anglo al-Misriyya, 1970.

Yousef, Michael. *Revolt Against Modernity: Muslim Zealots and the West.* Leiden: E. J. Brill, 1985.

al-Zabidi. *Taj al-'Arus.* Beirut: Dar al-Ma'rifa, 1986.

Zafarul, Islam Khan. "Hukumat-e Islami: Imam Khumayni's Contribution to Islamic Political Thought." *Al-Tawhid* 10, nos. 2–3 (1992–93): 237–47.

Zahr al-Din, Salih. "Nahdawiyyat al-Amir Shakib Arsalan." *Al-Fikr al-'Arabi* 6, nos. 39–40 (1985): 170–76.

al-Zarkashi. *Al-Burhan 'ala 'Ulum al-Qur'an.* Beirut: Dar al-Ma'rifa, n.d.

Zartman, I. William. "Democracy and Islam: The Cultural Dialectic." *Annals* (American Academy of Political and Social Sciences) 524 (1992): 191.

Zartman, I. William, and William Mark Habeeb, eds. *Polity and Society in Contemporary North Africa.* Boulder, Colo.: Westview Press, 1993.

Zebiri, Kate. *Mahmud Shaltut and Islamic Modernism.* Oxford: Oxford University Press, 1995.

Ziyada, Khalid. *Katib al-Sultan.* London: Riad el-Rayyes Books, 1991.

Zubaida, Sami. *Islam, the People and the State: Essays on Political Ideas and Movements in the Middle East.* 2d ed. London: I. B. Tauris, 1993.

al-Zugul, 'Abd al-Qadir. "Al-Istratijiyya al-Jadida li Harakat al-Itija al-Islami." In *Al-Din fi al-Mujtama' al-'Arabi,* 3:339–50. Beirut: Center for Arab Unity Studies, 1990.

al-Zumar, 'Abbud. "Minhaj Jama'at al-Jihad al-Islami." In *Al-Nabiy al-Musallah: Al-Rafidun,* edited by Rif'at Sayyid Ahmad, 110–26. London: Riad el-Rayyes Books, 1990.

Index

Ahmad S. Moussalli is professor of political science at the American University of Beirut. He was a senior fellow for 1999–2000 at the United States Institute of Peace, has been a visiting scholar at the Center for Muslim-Christian Understanding at Georgetown University and at the University of Copenhagen.

Moussalli is the author of numerous articles and books, including *Moderate and Radical Islamic Fundamentalism: The Quest for Modernity, Legitimacy, and the Islamic State* (UPF, 1999), *Historical Dictionary of Islamic Fundamentalist Movements in the Arab World, Iran, and Turkey* (1999), *Radical Islamic Fundamentalism: The Ideological and Political Discourse of Sayyid Qutb* (1992), *A Theoretical Reading in Islamic Fundamentalist Discourse* (1993), *Islamic Fundamentalism: A Study in Sayyid Qutb's Ideological and Political Discourse* (1993), and *World Order and Islamic Fundamentalism* (1992), and is the editor of *Islamic Fundamentalism: Myths and Realities* (1998).